Grandma Hanna's Family of Heroes Lady In The Mist

Alone, but never alone!

I0540618

Author:
Fred Blom

Copyright © 2025 Fred Blom

All Rights Reserved

Dedication
Lady in the Mist

I met Ilene, when I was eight years old. I remember seeing her in passing when I was six. It was on a family walk down through a dense woody area and into a wide valley. The talking to Ilene was not advised, but how could my personality resist. The oldest house I have ever seen was resting near a beautiful creek. There was a small dark object bobbing around near the creek, cutting grass with a hand scythe.

The old woman I walked close to revealed eyes as blue as the water in the creek that trickled by her. She requested me to visit again sometime. So over the next four years, I made ever attempt to see her and to find out as much as I could about her. On your own since she was thirteen years old, was a bit unconceivable to me. She didn't seem to want to be left alone, as I had been advised of.

This book is actually a promise of sixty years in the making. I will never forget you as you have given me such a great deal for having nothing, I informed her several times. She was assured in her mind, that I would forget her very soon, as she was but an old woman. Time had passed her by and most all had avoided her. Not a day goes by, that I am not thankful for Ilene.

My adopted Grandma Hanna was my instruction of communication between Ilene and of course Grandma Hanna. I first met God on the road to running away from home. At the same time I met Grandma Hanna and also Ilene. A triangle was created for what reasons I didn't know at the time. This triangle built my life! Through all my years I have never met any other two people with more of the love of God. Love and dedication to you two!

Preface
Lady in the Mist

Alone, but never alone! Thank you my old friend Ilene. She was a heavenly soul. She may have been a prophet which I could not recognize. Her head was so full of bible passages. I have never known anyone to contain that much of the bible and believed it all. Can you give up everything you have and call it a glory to God? When everything looked like it was impossible, the hand of God would reach out to her. This was her belief! Ilene lived in a time that I thought was way more difficult than when I lived. She taught me so much. I promised that I would remember her always and I do. Let me share some of the great adventures of Ilene.

Ilene was living on her own since she was thirteen. Her beauty was held in the hands of a few, but what did it gain her? It was wilderness with few others even around. Scratching out a living from her goats, garden and whatever was around her. There was a short magical moment in getting married or not? There seemed to be someone or something coming across her path to assist her at just the right time. What was the magic in that? No matter how many people there are in the world, there is a different path for everyone! I want you to come with me! Please, it's important! Imagine if you will that it is possible for others to learn from you. Some paths may be similar, while other can be almost unexplainable. Let's just suppose that there is a greater good out there. Let's say that if you open your heart, your mind and perhaps your soul to the possibility that you find something that few have? Let's also say that just because something bad or maybe to your dislikes happens to you that you don't just throw it out, but learn and grow from it. Like an example of a parents discipline to a child? Compare this to that which is greater than you and to whom you could become?

For there is nothing covered that shall not be revealed; neither hid, that shall not be known.
(Luke 12:2)

The old times of when these events happen were as fun as the actual story. The word of God has ninety-nine bible passages that reflect that he would rise up the stones to praise him if the people would not. Can you learn from your surroundings and those that cross your path for just a moment? Ilene always watched and observed her surroundings all her life. Could you live in a one mile circle all your life? If Ilene didn't give glory to God, no on does.

There are so many different things that we just take for granted. We probably don't mean to, but life just happens. I have at many times taken the time to try a little harder to see things around me, to try to listen a little better, to have a calm temperament and the devotion to the circle I live in. She obviously didn't raise me, but I give her the credit for a lot of what I have become. Now, I personally believe she was placed by God in my life and that she was a glory to God. Be kind to the old people around you!

I feel that I was very lucky to have known Ilene for the short time that I did. My adopted Grandma Hanna from the previous book I wrote and Ilene a person who allowed me to call her a friend. I was a connection between the two ladies, which lived their whole life just ten miles apart. I was a strange communication connection between the two. I could flow God thru one and then onto the other. Unexplainable! Thank you my adopted Grandma Hanna for encouraging me to be a friend to Ilene.

Ilene had many goats that were very important to her. There was much learned from the close contributors to Ilene. I only knew Ilene for four years, but I would say that she taught me more than anyone else in my life. She believed that nothing moves or exists without the hand of God making it so. I feel honored to have known two women that were both born in 1879 after the Civil war. They were total opposites in every way, except they had a biblical foundation that is unsurpassed by anyone I have ever known. They only lived like ten miles apart, but never knew each other. One was blessed with every material wants and one lived with a small herd of goats and not a friend or family helper anywhere. I was blessed with everything non-material from these two. I would not want any other life!

Acknowledgement
Lady in the Mist

Thank you to all the Ilene's and the Grandma Hanna's of the worlds, who have lent a hand in the direction of moral, respect, guidance and humility teachings to those around them. To have so little and give so much!

To be alone, but never think you are alone. It's always someone crossing your path, just when you need that help. Thanks Ilene for sharing all your life memories. Thanks to all for the sharing of moments to this fulfillment of remembering a soul.

Thank you to all the preachers who have gone out of their way to help those follow the path, that God has for each of us, before the foundations of the earth were set in place. I have often thought I had a hard path, until I am reminded of Ilene's path.

Thanks to Grandma Hanna for completing the communication circle.

Thanks to the King James Bible.

Table of Contents

Good Times

The mist rolled in off the lake and down the small river past the one room cabin, which sat off to the edge of the woods. "Happy birthday Ilene, Papa and Mama offered simultaneously! It was the humorous Papa with his trimmed black beard and hearty laugh, at almost everything. Mama with her long braids of pearl white hair was the white to Papa's black. Mama handed Ilene a plain brown box that made Ilene squeal with delight. It was the unknown contents and the thought of love from her parents, which brought about the delight. "Thank you, thank you. Ilene gushed! The gratitude was well know, even if the contents were yet unknown.

When the box finally revealed its content, tears of joy rolled down Ilene's face. "What's this all about Papa requested? "Just so happy, Ilene replied! "Even so, why must there be tears today, Papa requested? You are the most beautiful creature God has placed on the face of this earth. "True, true, Mama added! "Oh Papa and Mama, Ilene questioned. "Look at your Mama, Papa insisted, as he put his arm around her. Mama gave a love tap of her elbow to John, her husband. "In this wilderness, Pat Rasmussen questioned? 'Very much so, Papa reiterated! "Then Ilene is twice what I am, Mama complimented!

Ilene began to open the box to reveal its contents. Two beautiful long dresses, a long heavy winter coat, several pair of socks, boots, under garments and a brassiere. Ilene held the brassiere out in front of her in amazement. "Its way past due, Mama declared! You are definitely becoming a woman. "We will have to watch out for boys, Papa chuckled! "What boys, Ilene questioned, with a puzzled frown? There

1

are no other people for miles. "There will be others soon, I am thinking, Mama offered with encouragement.

Soon Ilene was back to looking through the gift box. She pulled out the long white dress and held it up to her front. "I didn't know white could look so beautiful, Ilene remarked with a smile. "It's for summer, Mama stated! "I could never wear this for working, Ilene offered in reply! I will keep it for good, but I don't really even know what that might mean? The dress was quickly placed back in the box and the dark blue with flowers was retrieved. It too was held up for a view in front of her. This one is also wonderful, but I think I will wear it on days I don't think I will get quite so dirty. Just to make it last longer. Then it was the long blue coats turn. The coat was actually put on. "I think you will love your new coat in cold weather, Mama stated. "This will be delightful, Ilene suggested. She pulled the coat to snuggle around her neck, just to try its warmth. Just delightful! A pair of the mittens was tried on with the coat. Then the scarf was added. "It just looks like you need some colder weather, Papa laughed!

"I wouldn't be surprised if there wouldn't be a town up there on the ridge, Papa suggested, as he pointed to the ridge above the valley they lived in. We are homesteading this valley as a gift from the government, one hundred and sixty acres. Good thing I was an officer in the union army, I think it gave us a leg up, for serving as an officer in the war from hell. "It is a beautiful valley, Papa, Ilene offered as a showing of gratitude. Thank you for giving so much of your life to the Civil War.

"We have one more thing for you my dearest, Papa offered! Papa walked into the house and soon returned with a polished piece of Hickory about four feet long and having a large well shaped knot on the end of it. "It's beautiful

Papa, Mama, Ilene offered more excitement of appreciation! This will really help me herding the goats. It's beautifully polished! It must have taken hours and hours. Ilene walked a short bit and returned to where her parents were standing. It's just perfect, Ilene offered with a smile! Ilene felt the heft of the walking stick and examined it closely. She tapped it hard on the ground to see its strength. "Very nice, Ilene whispered! This is ever so generous! Thank you so much, Mama and

Papa! A very health hug and a kiss on the cheek were given to each parent.

"Well the mist of fog is quite thick today, Papa proclaimed. It is quite a trip to the outpost, so I had better get started on my way. We need to get supplies in before winter sneaks in on us. We can always use more firewood, so you two can work on that today. Papa left the two and began to harness up the wagon for the required trip. It is far better to make this trip before we get snow on the ground, Papa mumbled to himself as he walked away.

Mama and Ilene went to fetch four of the goats for Papa to tether in the wagon. These four would be used for trade. They always went into winter with fewer goats to care for. The goats would lay down in the wagon and travel faster. They would munch on the grass provided for them on their trip. Good-byes and I love you, was offered for good measure. Even a day or two of travel was worth it. There were always fears with the offering of every, good-bye or I love you.

The two finished their chores and headed out to the woods above where the cabin was positioned. The herd of goats followed them to the spot where they were going to work. It was very common for the goats to do so as a reactionary thing. As long as there was a place to graze, they wouldn't go far. Dry trees were always the first search. Once they were found, it would be cutting for some time. The wood would be stacked up and wait until the wagon returned to haul it back to the small one room house.

The fog began to push off the side of the hill above the house, but seemed as if it was glued to the valley below. "Mama, do you think I will get married and build a cabin right here beside yours, Ilene questioned?

"That would be a dream and a wish, Mama replied, to be able to have our family together always. Grandma and Grandpa are still in Ohio and that's a long way away. They are getting older and are very settled in Ohio for over twenty years now. There was just no land in Ohio to be given by the Union for settling.

Soon there was a screeching sound, which brought the attention of the two searching in the sky around them. They let go of the buck saw in

3

their hands. Ilene picked up her Hickory walking stick and moved towards the small herd of goats nearby. "It's just an eagle looking for a fish perhaps, Mama instructed. The baby goats are of fair size now, so I don't think an eagle will bother them. Once the lake starts to freeze, they will move south.

Ilene stood by the goats for a short bit and watched the eagle drift away into the distance. As she walked back to the wood cutting, the small herd instinctively followed her back, as she was more than just a Sheppard to them. Ilene propped her new prize walking stick against the tree. Several of the goats began to lie down under the tree. "It must be morning nap time, Ilene suggested! "Resting for their new crop of babies next spring, Mama laughed. The two continued to cut their log into fire size pieces. There was minimal talk and gazing around.

Soon the tree was completely cut up. Then it required a rest break, as a discussion was contemplated as to the nest tree to be cut down. There was a very tall Norway pine, not far away. "Well, it is a dead tree and good for firewood, Mama stated, as she pointed towards the great tree. "I don't disagree about the goodness of the tree, Ilene stated. It is a lot of fun to cut down a tree, but the bigger they are, makes it a little scarier. "Prepared, cautious and quick to action, Mama declared to Ilene. In all things in life use that statement. "Ok, let's take down the biggest tree I have ever been a part of, Ilene stated firmly.

The two carried the Bucksaw together a short distance to the great Norway pine. "This tree is bigger around than the two of us together, Mama declared. "It looks like such a good tree, Ilene offered in observation. I wonder what happen to it. "Well, it looks like it is about one hundred and fifty years old, so I will just guess it got old, Mama surmised.

All things have a life span. I will take one hundred and fifty years to live, Mama offered with a small laugh. "I agree with that, but it gives me a chill, Ilene offered in return.

"How so, Mama questioned? "The thought of each of us getting old and passing away, Ilene answered. "I have a lot of my one hundred fifty years left, so no worries here, Mama chimed back with a laugh.

4

Ilene offered a slight smile back as the two began cutting the great tree. "Prepared, cautious and quick to action, Ilene sounded out as the cutting became more aggressive. The two were soon done with the face cut on the giant tree. "Ok, now the back cut, Mama instructed. You just take a look to see that you can quickly move away from the tree as it falls. Not directly back, but off at a very slight angle away from the tree. Never move forward in front of the tree. It doesn't matter how big the tree is. Prepared, then cautious and then quick to action, Mama stated! The back cut is always two to four inches above the face cut.

After several minutes of placing the back cut in the great tree, there was a slight crack sound from the Norway tree. "Slide the Bucksaw straight back and leave it on the ground, Mama instructed. Just as the two started to move back at a slight angle away from the great tree, Ilene saw a young goat coming over to their location. Her instinct made her turn to run to the unaware animal. Mama saw her reaction towards the small animal. She would have to cross the face of the now slowly falling great tree. "No, no, Mama quickly yelled as she turned and rushed from the backside of the tree falling tree towards Ilene. She leaped towards Ilene, catching her by the arm and landing on her as they hit the ground.

The two lay on the ground as the great tree crashed down with an out thrust of air. "Oh, oh Ilene, Mama sounded with a tired whisper! Don't be a silly girl! Your life is more important than that goat. You forgot cautious, Mama offered, as she hugged her daughter on the ground! The two got up and brushed themselves off as they turned to look for the small goat. They found the small goat back with the herd and offered the unaware animal a hug of relief. "Never cross over in front of a falling tree, Mama instructed, the girl and the small animal.

The two went back to cutting up the huge tree. Few words were spoken about the great tree as they cut away at it. It would be a multi-day job for sure.

The daily chore requirements were soon upon them, so the wood cutting job was ended. "Sorry, Mama, Ilene offered as they walked back to the house with the small herd following them. "Just want you to get your one hundred fifty years, Mama replied with a laugh. "Oh,

Mama, you make life so wonderful, even when life is so scary, Ilene replied, with a laugh of her own.

It was starting to get dark, when they finally heard Papa coming with the wagon and team. The two quickly started putting on their coats to ward off the fall night air chill. They came out of the small one room house, just as Papa pulled up in front. It was exciting to just see Papa after a long day. With everything looking ok and being home, brought a huge sigh of relief. "Hello family, Papa shouted out at the team came to a halt. "Greetings Papa of our family, Ilene offered with a bit of bouncing up and down with excitement. Just as soon as Papa's foot hit the ground, there was the big family hug. "It's good to be missed Papa offered with a laugh.

There was a plow sitting on top of a wagon of lumber. "This is an unusual load, Ilene spouted out! "Yes it is, but we will leave it for tomorrow, Papa instructed. You two unload the supplies into the house, while I put the team up for the night. Papa led the team to the shadows of the creek for water. The rope and canvas cover was quickly removed from the load. Supplies of flour, corn meal, cured bacon sides, coffee, beans, a bit of sugar, a jug of maple syrup, garden seeds for next spring and even some sacks of seeds for Papa's new farming project.

"How, is Papa going to get that heavy plow off the top of the lumber on the wagon, Ilene questioned Mama? "I am sure he has a plan, Mama replied, with a puzzled look on her face. It has taken a long time to get this plow to start our farming of this valley. Look at these long boards with the steel spikes thru them. They all hook together to make what is called a harrow. "Look Mama, here are some new scythes, Ilene spouted out with her discovery.

"We have six new chickens, Mama instructed Ilene, as she peered into a small wooden crate.

Let's carry the crate around to the lean and put these chickens in with the other three. Papa led the team to the make shift coral, just as Mama and Ilene carried the crate to the lean.

The small chicken coup was in one side of the lean and the goats could have the other side. The horse team really only had a wind break. Papa wanted to expand the lean, so it would be large enough for the horses to get out of the weather. Everyone wanted to have a barn, but it would just have to wait until money was sufficient. Another good year of trapping and a good sale of goats and they should be there. Life was good!

The Slings

Supper was being prepared and supplies were put away. Papa pulled out two leather strap items from one of the wood boxes. "Sling shots Papa sounded out! I also have a gift of stones. We have two bags of stones, as a matter of fact, Winchester cartridges, cartridges for my pistol and two new knives. It just ended up being part of the trade for the plow. Ilene started to examine one of the sling shots. I use to be fairly good with one of these, but I haven't used one in several years. "This is for hunting right, Ilene asked? "Rabbits and grouse for us, Papa replied. "Is this what David used to fight Goliath with, Ilene questioned? "Yes, Papa offered. He also used it to defend his goats and sheep. If you practice with the sling, you can become a very good marksman. It is easy to carry in your pocket with a few stones. At the idea of that, Ilene quickly put one of the slings and a few stones into her pocket. "Here, strap this knife belt on too with a new knife, Papa requested proudly. It was like Christmas Ilene thought.

It was hard to concentrate on the bible reading around the table, Ilene pondered. It was too much excitement now and for tomorrow. Happiness ruled Ilene and her thoughts as she drifted off to sleep. It was thoughts of protecting her goats with the accuracy of her sling. The family had everything, what more could one want?

The chores moved by quickly the next morning. The Milking the goats and then they were given their handful of grain. Then they were off to the creek for a drink of water. Then they would just wander around and find whatever grass was close. Papa could sense Ilene and her anxiousness to throw the sling. Small blocks of wood were set up on wood rounds along the end of the house. "We will practice here, so we can find the stones easily for reuse, Papa offered with his typical laugh. Papa was hitting the small blocks fairly quickly, but Ilene had hits and misses. Mama was about the same in her accuracy. They all had their laughs when the target was found. "Just keep practicing whenever you have time, Papa encouraged.

"I don't know exactly when, but a young man by the name of Peter Rock, will come and get five more goats from us, Papa instructed out of the blue. He will be hauling us two more loads of lumber. That will be enough to complete our small barn. We dug in the poles two years ago, so I guess it is about time to get some boards up. "I am happy for you Papa, Ilene offered with a hug of excitement. It's like having a little dream come true. "Thanks, sweetie, Papa replied! Life gets a little better every year.

Papa tacked a ramp of sorts quickly from lumber in guided out from under the plow. It worked quite well to slide the plow down to the safety of the ground. An item Papa called a wheelbarrow was also unloaded. The three worked together in harnessing the horse and hooking up to the plow. Everyone needed to know how to do everything around the little farm. It was great fun to just walk behind in the furrow the plow made. It cut deep into the earth, turning it over and revealing the richness of the soil. A small half acre patch was done first for the garden. It was done by hand spading before. The job was so much better and faster now. The three were so excited about getting this plowing done before the ground froze, but only Papa really understood the importance.

Ilene quickly left to tend to the goats. The grass was always the shortest near the house, so they would have to be left to go further. Papa went to plowing the field to raise grain for next year. It was a misty morning, but not as much as yesterday. Ilene watched as Papa disappeared into the mist. The plowing was quiet, except for a very small rattle of chain where the team was attached to the plow.

Mama was excited about using the wheelbarrow to clean out the lean and the chicken coup. Dragging a sled on the ground or moving the manure with the use of the wheel.

The job became so much easier. Life became so much easier. Life was getting so good! Mama would also move in and out of sight threw the mist.

Ilene starred out into the mist. She had here sling in her pocket, her knife belted around her waist and her handy walking staff with the club end in hand, but she couldn't see into the mist. "What if there was a lion, a bear or a wolf coming through the mist, Ilene whispered into the mist? I would be helpless! She was far enough away from the house, Mama and Papa as to not even be able to see them. There was no sound from them to even hear them. It was so quiet. The only sound to be heard was Billy's small bell on his neck, when he moved so slightly. It was always staying close to Billy, because you couldn't see the other twenty-five goats. For whatever reasons the other goats would not stray too far from Billy. Even in the mist!

The mist finally started to rise, so you could look under it, as if it was a thick blanket. Ilene would squat down for a better look under the mist. Mama could now be heard splitting wood. She couldn't be seen yet, only heard. Ilene thought that it was like being blind, when you were in the mist. It made here listen so much more intently. The mist began drifting silently away from in front of her. It revealed a great stag standing on the top of the hill in front of her. It was a huge, remarkable animal. Ilene didn't have a clue to its presents. She stood there in awe, as she had never been so close to such a grand view of a huge stag.

Papa wouldn't ever hunt a deer or Elk until it was cold. Ice had to be gotten out of the creek or lake and put into the underground ice house. There was a root cellar for the vegetables and an ice house for the meat. Ice from last year was just about gone and new ice would have to replace it. It was mostly fish that was put into the ice house. A few goats were kept for eating or selling. More goat milk was used for drinking, than water. It was kept cold in the ice house. Ilene stood half day dreaming, staring at the stag.

It was Mama walking up behind her, which made the great beast go leaping away.

"What a sight, Mama proclaimed as she approached. I hope the stag is not thinking about our hat stacks.

10

"I have the stake, hammer and collar for Billy, Mama declared her plan. We will take the herd down to the other end of where Papa is plowing. There is better grass down there near the trees. We will stake Billy down there and the others will stay close. Papa wants us to get started on the new lean. He is calling it our barn, even though he knows it's not quite there. The two were soon nailing the boards up on the poles, as Papa had described to Mama. "This is so exciting Mama, to be building a barn, Ilene clamored, as the small shape began to reveal it dimensions.

"Mama, do you know anything about this Mr. Rock, Ilene questioned? "I really don't, but perhaps when he arrives he can stay for a bit, Mama tried to explain. Papa said he referred to his Papa as Captain Rock! They had received a track of land like we did, after the war from the government. Somewhere east of here, I believe. Captain Rock was wounded in the war and a few years after they had started to build a life there, he passed away. So I think it is just him and his mother. Papa thought they were going to sell the farm and do something with a trading post?

"I see, Ilene offered! Peter Rock, Ilene chuckled! "Why the humor, Mama requested? "It makes me smile, because of the name Peter in the bible and Rock is also a name referred to in bible, pertaining to Peter, Ilene offered her explanation of happiness. "Oh, nice, Mama added with a smile! "I wonder how old he is, Ilene questioned? "Papa just said he was a nice young man, Mama offered, as she stopped and turned towards Ilene with a smile on her face. "Oh Mama, I was just curious, Ilene offered in reaction. Let's get another board! Mama, I am only thirteen!

By supper time the load of boards were all nailed into place. Papa was very pleased at the huge success. There were praises of love and pride shed onto Mama and Ilene. Maybe a little boast of how the plowing had turned a piece of earth into a field.

The rich dark earth looked lovely. The aroma of fresh earth was so grand, that is found its way into the house. It didn't however stop Ilene from questioning Papa on who Peter Rock happened to be. There really wasn't much Papa offered. He was maybe a couple years older than Ilene. He seemed very capable for his age. He was somewhat excited

11

to start some kind of trading post or store, rather than farming the farm they had homesteaded. It was just his mother and him. It was a sorry sweetie, I don't know more. I need an early night of it, was all Papa wanted. It had been a hard day.

What Do We Do Now?

The next morning Papa just wanted to get to the plowing the rest of his field. The mist had moved into the valley off the lake again. It was the valley and creek off the lake, which seemed to act like a magnet for the mist. There were no more boards to put on the little barn, so it would be a wood cutting day. The goats were moved to the far end of the new field, like yesterday. No one wanted to use the haystacks, unless it was necessary. You just never knew what winter would bring?

Within the mist everything seemed to be quieter. The cutting with the Bucksaw was only heard by the two using it. Even Billy's small bell was now so far away at the end of the newly plowed field, it couldn't be heard by Mama and Ilene. The rounds cut off the huge pine were stacked up, just in case there was a snow storm. More than likely the wood would be hauled by wagon up the pile by the house. It was just always being able to think ahead. Be prepared! The mist began its traditional lifting, where you could begin to see under it. There was no conversation between Ilene and Mama, Just cut a piece and then stack a piece. They were however curious about how much plowing Papa was getting done, so a view under the mist was taken by both. The slow lifting of the mist left no anxiousness, as the work continued.

It was the stopping of Ilene and viewing into the distance under the mist, that brought a remark. The horses are just standing and not plowing, Ilene commented. They are not at the end of the field either. Papa may have walked up to the house for a break perhaps? Mama walked towards Ilene, but at a twenty foot separation.

Her angle of view down across the hill was quite different. "I think Papa is lying on the ground, Mama questioned? The two began to walk and peer under the mist towards the team of horses. They started to walk a little faster and then it was a full run towards the location. It was the unknown of Papa definitely lying on the ground.

It was a collapse to the ground and quickly looking Papa over for injuries. It was a gentle shake and a continuous calling of, "John, John, by Mama? What is it? What is it? John offered only a bit of moan. "It's cold out, but Papa is sweating a lot. He is feverish! We need to get him back to the house quickly. Let's try to get under each arm on either side of him or half carry or drag him to the house. The two made their attempt with great difficulty. Papa would cough every few steps. After stopping several times they were finally in the house. Papa had zero strength. A cooked noodle had more strength. John was dropped off on the bed. "Ilene, you run to the icehouse and get some ice in a bucket, Mama instructed. We will get some cold cloths on Papa, to bring this temperature down.

Ilene left to get the goats back home. Walking over to the team of horses and starring at them as what to do. She tipped the plow up and gave the command of, "Get up there! The team started to pull the plow and it turned the soil over. The steering of the plow was easy, as the horses knew how to pull straight. Soon the end of the field was reached, so Ilene gave the command of, "Whoa! Ilene unhooked the plow and then began to bring the horse team back to the lean. The harness equipment was removed from the team and stored in its typical place on the wall of the lean. The horses were led down to the creek for a drink. That was the beauty of the creek not yet being frozen.

There was a spot by the bank that was dug quite deep, so as to make the water deeper. It made it easier to chop through the ice in the winter for fetching water. It was quite a chore to go down during the night and the day of course to keep the ice off the water hole. Ilene did all of the chores as she knew Mama would be busy with Papa and trying to figure out what to do with him next. As Ilene entered the house her first question was, "Mama, is Papa getting better?

"I don't know, Mama replied in a whisper. Go to the icehouse and get some more ice before it gets dark.

It was a great project through the night to get Papa's temperature down. Taking the rarely used lantern to get a buck of water from the creek or off to the icehouse for more ice. On a return trip from the icehouse in the early morning hours, Mama was found crying on the side of the bed. "Mama, Ilene whispered? "Papa is gone, Mama cried! "Gone, Ilene whispered! She could feel a chill go down her back. "No, He can't be, Ilene offered! Ilene laid her head on Papa's chest to listen for a heartbeat. She moved her head around to several positions to listen. Nothing! She finally just stopped in the last position and cried. Mama laid her arm over Ilene and her head beside Ilene's and offered up her emotions.

It was early morning when Ilene just got up and went outside to do the chores. The chores had to be done no matter what. The mist was thick and could be tasted as soon as one parted their mouth. It was deathly quiet walking through the mist, in more ways than one. The goats were given their handful of grain, and then they were given some hay. It just didn't feel like a day to take the goats out to find grass.

Mama was found sitting at the table with her head down and praying, as Ilene brought the eggs into the house. She made some coffee and offered a cup to Mama without asking. She fried a couple of eggs and cut a piece of bread for each of them. It was just the instinct to do so. The food was placed, but just stared at for the longest of time. The silence was broken with a single question from Ilene, "What do we do now? There was no response from Mama.

"I am going to go to the top of the hill, where we like to picnic, Ilene offered. It's Papa's favorite place on the farm. I am going to dig a grave for Papa. Ilene walked to the other side of the table and placed her hands on Mama's shoulders and offered a kiss to the top of her head. She turned without a word and walked out the door. There were tools hanging on the side of the wall inside the small lean. A pick ax and a shovel were retrieved. Then it was a long walk to the top of the hill behind the house.

Ilene had never been a part of someone dying, so she wasn't sure what to think. She had a job to do, but she could only shake her head at what it really was. It didn't seem real.

15

The big Oak trees had all of the leaves turned to their brilliant colors. They were beautiful and the family would normally be very excited. Many times the family had packed a picnic basket and came to this spot, just for the shear happiness it brought. You could see the lake and the entire creek running through the small farm. You were high enough to actually see the top of the bluff on the other side of the creek. The grass was quite good on the other side of the creek. It was just that the goats didn't like to cross over thru the water. The family just cut the grass on the other side of the creek for hay. The hay stacks were put up and then in the winter with the creek frozen, you could haul the hay home.

Ilene soon found herself just sitting and remembering all the things that her, Mama and Papa could be seen doing. She forced herself up and began to dig what she thought the size of the grave should be. Every time she actually remembered what she was doing, it brought tears. "No, no, no, she would shout out! She had to clear her mind and think about this as just a job of digging a hole. The dirt was all piled on one side of the hole, as she thought it would be easier to place Papa in the hole. "Place Papa in the hole, Ilene whispered? The sound of the whisper made her dizzy. She fell forward on the edge of the hole in her dizziness. "I can't breathe, she whispered! It felt like her head was swimming from the dizziness. "Deep breaths she whispered to herself. Dig the best hole you can for Papa!

Soon she was back to digging in a mindless manner. "Don't think, just dig, she whispered! Don't think, just dig! The dirt was beginning to be harder to get thrown out of the hole. Ilene stopped and looked around. The edge of the hole was the depth of her eyes. How was she going to get out of the hole? It seemed a bit of a panic for a moment. She leaned the shovel to the side of the hole and stepped up onto the blade of the shovel, which pushed her up a few inches. The pick ax could just be reached. Ilene raised the pick ax up and slammed it into the ground. She pulled on the handle of the ax, while here feet seemed to wildly dig at the edge of the hole to climb out. The ax let go from the earth and she tumbled back into the hole.

A numb young lady found herself starring into the sky, lying on her back in the bottom of the hole. She started to shake with fear laying there. She forced herself up. "Think, think, Ilene commanded herself, in a shaky voice! She took the shovel and cut a spot for her foot to be placed. Then she cut another foot hole on the adjacent side of the hole. Then it was another foot hole cut a short way above the first two foot holes. The shovel was placed as before to get the first few inch advantage. The pick ax was raised up and plunged into the earth. Pulling on the ax handle and finding a place to place a foot, then another was just the thing. Ilene was soon lying on the ground, but out of the hole.

Ilene lay there starring into the sky. "How are we going to get Papa into the hole, she whispered to the sky? Ilene laid the shovel and the pickax to the side and began a slow walk back to the house. Mama was found with the team hitched up to the wagon and placed close to the front of the house. Papa was found lying on the bed with his best clothes on. "Help Papa like we did the other day, Mama requested quietly? One was under each arm as they hefted Papa up and to the back of the wagon. Papa was sat on the back of the wagon with his legs hanging down. Mama got up into the wagon and Papa was laid back on Mama's lap. "Grab a rope from that hook on the front of the house, so we can lower Papa into the grave, Mama requested soberly?

Ilene laid the rope in the back of the wagon and then quickly walked back into the house to retrieve a chair blanket from Papa's favorite chair. She placed it in the back of the wagon without a word spoken. She climbed up on the wagon seat and coaxed the horses onward. It was up the hill and pulling the wagon close to the end of the hole.

It was a totally silent moment as the two got under each arm and laid Papa on the ground beside the hole. "Go get the ladder from beside the house, Mama requested? I am going to sit with Papa for a minute. In silence Ilene got back into the seat of the wagon and went down the hill to fetch the ladder.

There was no rush, just silence. Ilene soon returned with the ladder for whatever reason. Mama was sitting, holding John Rasmussen's head in her lap, crying her heart out. Ilene sat down by Mama and offered her tears. Tears beget tears!

Pat Rasmussen stood up with a word and placed John's head down. She walked to the wagon and retrieved the ladder and placed it into the end of the grave. The rope was placed under John's arms and John was brought close to the end of the grave. Pat got onto the ladder. "I don't want Papa to fall into the hole, Ilene, Mama requested. You pull up on the rope and I will move down the ladder. The process was easier said than done. Soon Mama was straightening Papa out in the bottom of the grave. His arms were folded over his chest. The rope removed. Ilene ran to the wagon and retrieved the chair blanket. "Put this over Papa's face, because I don't want to put dirt on his face, Ilene requested soberly. Mama covered John with the blanket. She kissed her hand and touched it against the area where John's head lay under the blanket.

The ladder was removed and words of love were offered. Ilene picked up the shovel to start putting the dirt into the grave, while Mama knelt beside the grave. "I can't put the dirt on Papa, Ilene tearfully proclaimed! She dropped the shovel and took a couple of steps backwards. "Recite the 23rd Psalm, Mama requested? It is one of John's favorite passages. He had told me many times he recited it during the war, just to get him through it. Ilene began to recite the favorite passage.

> *Psalm 23: The Lord is my shepherd; I shall not want. He maketh me to lie down in green pastures: he leadeth me beside the still waters. He restoreth my soul: he leadeth me in the paths of righteousness for his name's sake. Yea, though I walk through the valley of the shadow of death, I will fear no evil: for thou art with me; thy rod and thy staff they comfort me. Thou preparest a table before me in the presence of mine enemies: thou anointest my head with oil; my cup runneth over. Surely goodness and mercy shall follow me all the days of my life: and I will dwell in the house of the LORD forever.*

Mama rose up off her knees and began to shovel the dirt into the grave. Ilene just stood there and watched Mama work. It seemed that Mama was getting quite out of breathe with an added cough. Ilene quickly went over and helped her sit down and continued on with the dirt into the grave. It was Papa's cough and perspiration the other day, which alarmed her. The word Influenza echoed through her head. Ilene shoveled away without word or thought. The soil was well mounded up and made to look the best it could look.

Ilene helped Mama into the back of the wagon, with her legs hanging over the end. Then the tools were added to the wagon. It was a slow ride back to the house. Ilene parked the wagon in front of the house, so Mama wouldn't have to walk far. "I will do the chores if you want to lie down for a while, Ilene offered. Mama moved slowly into the house, as Ilene unhitched the team. Ilene moved slowly about doing the chores, in a sober mine set. No gleeful petting of the goats, no thankful expression of thanking the chickens for their eggs and not even a hug to the horses for their strength of work. There was a thank you Heavenly Father that the creek is not frozen yet. It was easier to take the animals to the water, than the water to the animals.

There was Mama lying down on the bed, when Ilene returned to the house. Ilene said nothing, as she poured a pan of water to wash the eggs and place them in the wire basket on the table. Then she silently got more fire wood and water into the house. It was even a quiet walk over to Mama's bedside and a gentle hand lay on Mama's forehead. It was hot and wet!

"Oh, Mama, Ilene whispered! Ilene grabbed the bucket and ran to the Icehouse to fetch some ice to cool Mama down, just as she had done for Papa. Cold water from the creek was used for wiping on Mama and ice was placed on her. The cloths soaked in the cold creek water seemed to be better than the ice. The cloths were added up and down the body. When Ilene got to one end, she stated over at the head and replaced them all the way down in a continuous process. Mama had said it was the temperature that had to be gotten under control, when she worked on Papa.

It was early in the morning, when Ilene startled herself awake. She had fallen asleep, leaning on the edge of the bed. She quickly stood up and placed her hand on Mama's forehead. She felt cooler. "Mama, Mama, Ilene whispered? Ilene held her hand in front of her Mama's nose to feel for breath. Nothing! She pulled the cloths back and listened to her chest. She picked up her head several times and replaced it to a different position. She could not hear a heartbeat? Ilene placed her hand on the side of Mama's neck, for a pulse. "Mama, Mama, Ilene shouted! Nothing!

Ilene looked around the dark little house. The candle on the table had gone out. It was dark and quiet! There was no talking, no laughing and surely no plans for the day. "What do I do now, Ilene whispered? It was the same question she had asked yesterday. The answer was at the top of the hill. The very thought made her shiver with a chill and it wasn't from the cold in the room.

It was a slow walk by habit to the animals. There was a handful of grain to the goats, the chickens and the horses. Ilene stood there starring at the animals as they quickly gobbled up what was given to them or was she just starring at nothing? She shook herself into reality and led the horses out to the creek for water. She let the goats out of their gate to follow along. They had no cares about anything. Just food and water, Ilene thought. Ilene milked the two goats and placed the milk into the icehouse. Again she found herself just standing and starring at the ice. Did she not put enough ice on Mama, she questioned? There was always some ice on her as she put the cold cloths from the creek on her?

Ilene felt tired and weak, as she walked around to the front of the house. She placed her hand on her forehead. It felt fine she thought? She walked into the house and got a drink of water. It was a slow walk over to the bed, that Mama was lying in. She placed a hand on Mama's forehead. It seemed very cool. "Mama, Mama, Ilene spoke in a normal tone? There was no movement or answer. She wasn't expecting and answer, Mama was gone. Nothing seemed real. "God,

What have you done, Ilene whispered?

Ilene filled the canteen and walked out to the wagon. The pickax and shovel were retrieved from the wagon and then it was the slow long walk up the hill behind the house. The grave from yesterday could be seen, as soon as you walked behind the house. Just not in the mist. Today was different, only in the sense that Ilene had no emotions yet or maybe left? Just numbness! Today the numbness matched the mist. Probably the only day she had ever known that the mist seemed to have a purpose. She could feel herself walking up the hill, but didn't really have a clue, as to it she was going in the right direction. It didn't matter she told herself. The thought was so heavy in her head; it came out, "I don't matter, she whispered!

Papa's grave was finally reached, by accident she guessed. The numbness helped Ilene to start digging the next grave. She carefully eyed the starting distance, so that the two graves could be even. A rest break with a stare launched into the distance up the rest of the hill showed a glimpse of the great Stag. The mist would part and show the revelation and then mist would move and conceal the only magic in the moment. When she was as deep as her knees, she climbed out and walked back to the house. Without hesitation she walked into the house and straight over to Mama. She sat on the edge of the bed and pulled Mama into a sitting position and gave her a lasting hug. "Mama, do you want to wear your best dress today, Ilene requested? Ilene carefully laid Mama back down and walked over to a small open closet in the corner of the room. She found Mama's favorite dress and proceeded to dress her in it. Then she brushed her hair and put on her favorite scarf. Mama never like getting dirt into her hair, she thought.

Mama was carried out to the wagon and carefully placed. Then her chair blanket was retrieved from her rocking chair. Mama loved to sit in her rocker and cover up with the chair blanket, Ilene reminisced. The team was hitched up and the slow ride up the hill began, as it did yesterday. "How could someone get Influenza so quick, Ilene whispered to herself? Papa one day, then Mama the next day, so tomorrow will probably be her day?

Ilene tripped with the ladder she was attempting to slide into the grave. "Tomorrow is my day, Ilene shouted! A chill came over here. She began to shake all over. Her breathe became very rapid, as if she had just had to run away from some kind of devil. She jumped down into the hole and began to dig rapidly. If she was going to breathe, it had just as well been for the reason of getting the grave dug.

"Leave no room to think, Ilene instructed herself! Leave no room to think! Even the ladder was quickly moved from one end of the grave to the other. Dig one half and then the other half of the grave. The exhaustion was gradually catching up with her. Ilene stopped and couldn't see the top of the grave. It was deeper than Papa's, so she climbed out. It was a slow walk over to the back of the wagon. A slow wipe of her headscarf over here face to gain some calmness.

Mama was clasped in a hugging position, as Ilene walked with her to edge of the grave. She sat Mama down beside the ladder and balanced her with one hand as she started down the ladder. Then she hugged her as before. "Mama, I love you, Ilene spoke calmly! I don't know what I am doing or why? I am sure I will see you soon. Mama was laid out flat and Ilene folded her arms over here waist. Then it was back to the wagon to get the chair blanket. The blanket was taken down into the depth of the grave and carefully spread out over Mama. Every wrinkle was smoothed out. It was ever so careful to see that there head was covered, as to what Ilene thought was appropriate. Ilene placed a kiss upon the tips of her fingers and placed it on Mama's head.

Ilene crawled slowly out of the grave and pulled the ladder out. She was caught in the same dilemma as before with Papa's grave. She couldn't put the dirt in the grave. After a few deep breaths, she turned away and slowly started scraping the soil into the edge of the grave without looking. It continued the whole time, until she realized the dirt was almost gone. She stopped and stared at the freshly dug hole. After a long stare she began to heap the dirt into something that would look like Papa's. It looked like she was done, but her mind searched for something more.

Ilene thought carefully about Papa's favorite bible verse which came with him from the war. Mama's favorite bible verse came when she found Papa. Mama would say often, that life is all about love. Ilene stood before Mama's grave and spoke clearly the 1 Corinthians chapter thirteen bible scripture.

> *1 Corinthains 13: Though I speak with the tongues of men and of angels, and have not charity, I am become as sounding brass, or a tinkling cymbal. And though I have the gift of prophecy, and understand all mysteries, and all knowledge; and though I have all faith, so that I could remove mountains, and have not charity, I am nothing. And though I bestow all my goods to*

feed the poor, *and though I give my body to be burned, and have not charity, it profiteth me nothing. Charity suffereth long,* and *is kind; charity envieth not; charity vaunteth not itself, is not puffed up, Doth not behave itself unseemly, seeketh not her own, is not easily provoked, thinketh no evil; Rejoiceth not in iniquity, but rejoiceth in the truth; Beareth all things, believeth all things, hopeth all things, endureth all things. Charity never faileth: but whether* there be *prophecies, they shall fail; whether* there be *tongues, they shall cease; whether* there be *knowledge, it shall vanish away. For we know in part, and we prophesy in part. But when that which is perfect is come, then that which is in part shall be done away. When I was a child, I spake as a child, I understood as a child, I thought as a child: but when I became a man, I put away childish things. For now we see through a glass, darkly; but then face to face: now I know in part; but then shall I know even as also I am known. And now abideth faith, hope, charity, these three; but the greatest of these is charity.*

Just as soon as Ilene finished saying the scripture, she began to mark out and dig a third grave. She was numb and no great decision had to be resolved. After she was as deep as her knees, she retrieved the ladder, and then just continued digging. A quick drink of water and a short rest was all that was required. Oh, there was a quick glance up to the top of the hill, to see if the great Stag was still there, but nothing was seen.

It had been a long time, since she had seen the view. The mist had lifted some time ago and it had an easy view of the house at the bottom of the hill. The grave was as deep as to her chin, so it seemed sufficient. So it was time to climb out. She felt like she was ready for tomorrow.

The shovel was pressed into the dirt pile firmly. "Will someone come to finish burying me, Ilene spoke out loud? Jesus, I pray it to be so! For

23

whatever reason, Ilene began to cry into the crook of her arm, as she held onto the shovel. After several minutes, she took a deep breath and picked up the pickax and put it into the wagon. The ladder was left in the end of the grave. The horses had been very patient, she thought, as she drove slowly down the hill and came to a stop beside the house. The horses were unhitched and unharnessed. A walk to the creek and a good drink of water, then it was an added portion of hay. Extra hay was given to the goats. Extra grain was given to the chickens. The small door to their coup was left open. The coral gate was left open. The rest of the chores were completed, then a couple of eggs consumed with a glass of milk.

Ilene washed up, the canteen was filled, and then three blankets were rolled up and tied. Even the blankets seemed to be heft about half way up the hill. Darkness was falling, but it really didn't matter she thought. Soon the third grave was reached. The blankets were tossed down into the darkness of the hole. A slow climb down into the darkness, then the straightening of the blankets was preformed. One was laid down and two were used to cover up with. A drink was had and then the canteen was placed in the corner of the darkness.

As Ilene came to rest, she thought of Papa's favorite bible verse and then Mama's favorite bible verse. What was her favorite verse she contemplated? "Mathew chapter five, Ilene whispered and began to speak the words into the darkness of the night.

> *Mathew 5:1 And seeing the multitudes, he went up into a mountain: and when he was set, his disciples came unto him:*
>
> *2 And he opened his mouth, and taught them, saying,*
>
> *3 Blessed are the poor in spirit: for theirs is the kingdom of heaven.*
>
> *4 Blessed are they that mourn: for they shall be comforted.*

5 Blessed are *the meek: for they shall inherit the earth.*

6 Blessed are *they which do hunger and thirst after righteousness: for they shall be filled.*

7 Blessed are *the merciful: for they shall obtain mercy.*

8 Blessed are *the pure in heart: for they shall see God.*

9 Blessed are *the peacemakers: for they shall be called the children of God.*

10 Blessed are *they which are persecuted for righteousness' sake: for theirs is the kingdom of heaven.*

11 Blessed are ye, when men *shall revile you, and persecute* you, *and shall say all manner of evil against you falsely, for my sake.*

12 Rejoice, and be exceeding glad: for great is *your reward in heaven: for so persecuted they the prophets which were before you.*

13 Ye are the salt of the earth: but if the salt have lost his savour, wherewith shall it be salted? it is thenceforth good for nothing, but to be cast out, and to be trodden under foot of men.

14 Ye are the light of the world. A city that is set on an hill cannot be hid.

15 Neither do men light a candle, and put it under a bushel, but on a candlestick; and it giveth light unto all that are in the house.

16 Let your light so shine before men, that they may see your good works, and glorify your Father which is in heaven.

17 Think not that I am come to destroy the law, or the prophets: I am not come to destroy, but to fulfil.

18 For verily I say unto you, Till heaven and earth pass, one jot or one tittle shall in no wise pass from the law, till all be fulfilled.

19 Whosoever therefore shall break one of these least commandments, and shall teach men so, he shall be called the least in the kingdom of heaven: but whosoever shall do and teach them, *the same shall be called great in the kingdom of heaven.20For I say unto you, That except your righteousness shall exceed* the righteousness *of the scribes and Pharisees, ye shall in no case enter into the kingdom of heaven.*

21 Ye have heard that it was said by them of old time, Thou shalt not kill; and whosoever shall kill shall be in danger of the judgment:

22 But I say unto you, That whosoever is angry with his brother without a cause shall be in danger of the judgment: and whosoever shall say to his brother, Raca, shall be in danger of the council: but whosoever shall say, Thou fool, shall be in danger of hell fire.

23 Therefore if thou bring thy gift to the altar, and there rememberest that thy brother hath ought against thee;

24 Leave there thy gift before the altar, and go thy way; first be reconciled to thy brother, and then come and offer thy gift.

25 Agree with thine adversary quickly, whiles thou art in the way with him; lest at any time the adversary deliver thee to the judge, and the judge deliver thee to the officer, and thou be cast into prison.

26 Verily I say unto thee, Thou shalt by no means come out thence, till thou hast paid the uttermost farthing.

27 Ye have heard that it was said by them of old time, Thou shalt not commit adultery:

28 But I say unto you, That whosoever looketh on a woman to lust after her hath committed adultery with her already in his heart.

29 And if thy right eye offend thee, pluck it out, and cast it *from thee: for it is profitable for thee that one of thy members should perish, and* not *that thy whole body should be cast into hell.*

30 And if thy right hand offend thee, cut it off, and cast it *from thee: for it is profitable for thee that one of thy members should perish, and* not *that thy whole body should be cast into hell.*

31 It hath been said, Whosoever shall put away his wife, let him give her a writing of divorcement:

32 But I say unto you, That whosoever shall put away his wife, saving for the cause of fornication, causeth her to commit adultery: and whosoever shall marry her that is divorced committeth adultery.

33 Again, ye have heard that it hath been said by them of old time, Thou shalt not forswear thyself, but shalt perform unto the Lord thine oaths:

34 But I say unto you, Swear not at all; neither by heaven; for it is God's throne:

35 Nor by the earth; for it is his footstool: neither by Jerusalem; for it is the city of the great King.

36 Neither shalt thou swear by thy head, because thou canst not make one hair white or black.

37 But let your communication be, Yea, yea; Nay, nay: for whatsoever is more than these cometh of evil.

38 Ye have heard that it hath been said, An eye for an eye, and a tooth for a tooth:

39 But I say unto you, That ye resist not evil: but whosoever shall smite thee on thy right cheek, turn to him the other also.

40 And if any man will sue thee at the law, and take away thy coat, let him have thy cloke also.

41 And whosoever shall compel thee to go a mile, go with him twain.

42 Give to him that asketh thee, and from him that would borrow of thee turn not thou away.

43 Ye have heard that it hath been said, Thou shalt love thy neighbour, and hate thine enemy.

44 But I say unto you, Love your enemies, bless them that curse you, do good to them that hate you, and pray for them which despitefully use you, and persecute you;

45 That ye may be the children of your Father which is in heaven: for he maketh his sun to rise on the evil and on the good, and sendeth rain on the just and on the unjust.

46 For if ye love them which love you, what reward have ye? do not even the publicans the same?

47 And if ye salute your brethren only, what do ye more than others? do not even the publicans so?

48 Be ye therefore perfect, even as your Father which is in heaven is perfect.

The words were spoken into the night slowly and with deliberation and heart. "Good night, Papa! Good night, Mama! Jesus have mercy, Ilene spoke and headed off to sleep. The stars revealed themselves above in the crisp night. It would be washed away every now and again as the mist rolled in a little at a time. Soon it was a fight for the night sky. Sleepy eyes could no longer watch to see who would win the battle.

The Light Shown

 There was a great light of penetration into the grave in the middle of the night. It was enough to awaken Ilene. She rose up and stepped a couple of steps up the ladder. The moon seemed to be sitting on the earth. It was brighter and greater in size, than she had ever seen. A Great Stag stood on top of the ridge and starred at the moon in all of his majesty. The glory of God's creation had never been so revealing to Ilene before. She crawled up out of the grave and bowed very low to the ground. "I have never been so sad and yet so warmed by you Heavenly Father, Ilene spoke quietly. Is it in your mercy, to raise us up? After a long time of just being quiet, Ilene returned to her grave.

The mist of the night may be able to shut off the stars in the night sky, but the moon was of strength grander than the mist. The glowing light seemed to penetrate even into the darkest corner of her grave. There was a beckoning call in the light to rise up. God would take his own creation and glorify himself. It was the over whelming sadness that was within Ilene that wanted to be gone. Small whispers of glory to her Heavenly Father parted from her lips into the night.

It wasn't a restful night, with thoughts of life ending, light from the moon shining into the grave or what God's mercy might be? At some point Ilene dozed off. "Hello, hello, a voice called out?

Are you ill in the grave? Come forth from the grave and live, the voice commanded! Ilene came awake and starred up at a face starring down at her. "Are you ill or hurt, the voice requested?

"I thought I would be, Ilene replied, but I don't think that I am.

"Then I shall come down and assist you from this grave, the voice instructed! It was without time to contest anything and the tall stranger

30

was soon down the ladder and assisting Ilene up the ladder. Her blankets were quickly rolled, tied and thrust up out of the hole. A canteen was tossed up and a quick moving tall stranger was up the ladder.

The tall stranger was quick to hug her and kiss her on the forehead. "You are cool to the kiss, so be well and live, the tall stranger insisted! I see you have had great difficulties. The man had black curly hair to his shoulders. He had no beard, so his smile seemed to jump off his face with almost a laugh at his spoken words. My name is Peter Rock, the stranger offered! My friend down there is Jonathan Williams, Peter offered as he pointed down the hill. Just call him John if you like, I do! He is rounding up the goats and horses. What has happened here?

Ilene took a deep breath with the quiet reply of, "Mama and Papa have died from Influenza. Ilene just stood there starring down the hill. "I am so very sorry for your loss, Peter offered! I owed your Papa, Mama and you of course, two loads of lumber. This was part of a deal I made with your Papa. You don't have to go through with any of this of course. Especially with all that had transpired. It was two loads of lumber and we still were going to get five goats from you. The kids from the five nannies were to come back to you and I was supposed to get you a new Billy for the starting of a new herd or at least an expansion of your herd.

The young man seemed to be so sure of who he was. He seemed to reflect a tone of happiness off on Ilene. She had never seen him before. It was only Papa telling her that he would come for a delivery. She had forgotten, because of all that had happened. "Where, do you come from, Ilene asked? "From the hand of God, of course, Peter advised Ilene! Peter laughed and offered a one arm hug to Ilene. Soon, we will live on top of the ridge right by you.

We have been building a Trading store up there, Peter pointed to the ridge behind the trees. Alice my mother, Jonathan and I are going to be traders in the store.

It was a continuous stare into the distance. Ilene wasn't even sure she heard half of what Peter was saying. "Perhaps you should stay with us, Peter offered? "No, Ilene quickly offered! I guess I am going to have to live! "Of course you will, my friend, Peter enthusiastically

31

proclaimed! Peter grabbed Ilene in a hug and danced around in a small circle. Live, live, you beautiful creation of God! Ilene grabbed Peter in a hug, to stop from being rotated.

"Our trading building is nearly done and we are in business, Peter instructed! We have plenty of room for you to stay. It's just my mother and I. Johnny and his family live just a short distance away. There are too many trees on the ridge to see our trading post from here. There is a trail down the side of the ridge to walk down to your valley. It's a little steep for a horse, so you would have to go down the creek to travel by wagon and horse. "I will take the lumber and finish Papa's bigger lean, Ilene offered. You can take the five goats and bring back the kids, when they can wean. "Your Lamancha goats are very well liked, Peter enthusiastically offered. Johnny and I actually own the business together. He is going to keep the goats at his place for cleaning around the dooryard and the milk of course. So maybe we can have one that you are milking right now and the other four can be dry goats?

"Sure, if you like, Ilene offered unenthusiastically. We will start by unloading the lumber and we will help you with your little barn, Peter offered, as he took Ilene by the hand and began to walk down the hill. Johnny met them by the wagon of lumber, offering his usual happy comment of, "Oh Pete, you found a beautiful young lady in the woods. "Yes indeed I have, Peter replied! This is Ilene and she has had a bit of bad luck. Both of her parents have died from Influenza and she has buried them up on the hill. "So sorry, baby sister, Johnny offered with a hug. We are not far away, so we can help you with anything you need. "Thank you, Ilene offered with a bit of a whisper!

Jonathan was a few inches taller than Peter. Jonathan seemed a bit older, but was cleaned shaven. His light sandy hair was short. Jonathan wore cowboy style hat and blue Levi shirt with jeans. Peter had a homemade knit style hat on. They were two such different men, but obviously very good friends.

"We have a few tools in the wagon, so let's get some of this lumber put onto this building project, Peter suggested. "There are some hinges and latch for a door in the lean, inside the house, Ilene quietly offered. "Great, Peter responded! Just bring anything you have out here and we will use it up.

32

Ilene went to the house to retrieve any items that might be used for Papa's little barn. She never even noticed Peter following her with her blankets and canteen. Peter silently placed the items on the table. He then went over to the fireplace and started a fire. Ilene just stood there looking at Papa and Mama's bed. There was the big box of nails, which Mama and she had been using for the boards they had put on the little barn. She picked them up to bring out first. "I will take those Peter offered. "I will bring the window, hinges and latch, Ilene suggested.

Soon the trio was back to working on the little barn. The two young men were moving so fast, that Ilene felt like she should do something else. "I am sorry, but I am just not into this building today, Ilene offered. I haven't gathered the eggs, fed the chickens or milked the three goats. Ilene just turned to take care of the chores she thought she would never do again. She thought she would be dead sleeping in the grave at the top of the hill. The chores got finished in a long amount of time, from the normal time.

"I am going to make the three of us something to eat, Ilene offered as she came around the corner of the new structure. Johnny offered a, "I am fine! Peter's answer was, "Sounds great! Ilene went to the root cellar and grabbed a couple of potatoes. Then she fetched the bucket and went to the creek for water. The eggs were washed and put into the basket on the table. The eggs had accumulated, as no one had been eating them.

Thirty some eggs, just about ran the eggs out of their containment. The table was set and the milk poured. Nine eggs were scrambled up in a bowl and a second pan was prepared. The potatoes were about done, so Ilene left to call for Peter and Jonathan.

"Peter, Jonathan, come eat please? "Right away Peter replied! With Ilene's slow walk, the two young men almost beat her to the house.

"You will have to use the cold water in the bucket to wash up in the basin over there; Ilene commented and pointed towards the basin. The food was placed on the table with Ilene starring at it as if it was foreign to her. It was usually a prayer led by Papa, before eating the meal. Peter quickly broke the silence with a prayer. "Hear our prayer, most Holy and merciful Father in Heaven! We thank you for this beautiful meal.

33

Thank you for sending us to help our friend! Please strengthen our friend Ilene and help her through this time of great sorrow.

Ilene felt tears beginning to flow and had to clap a hand over her mouth to stop any sound from being released. Peter stopped the prayer and stood up. He walked over behind Ilene and placed his hands on each of her shoulders. "We love you Ilene, Peter offered! We will carry you as long as you need. "Amen and amen, Jonathan added! "Thank you, but please eat, Ilene suggested! It is the word friend. I have never heard anyone call me friend? "Well friend, we will call you friend, every time we see you, Peter offered with a jolly tone. The food was consumed rather quickly and the two young men were back out the door to do a bit more work before darkness crept in.

Ilene cleaned up the supper dishes, and then proceeded to get more firewood in. Then it was down to the creek to get some more water. Things were out of schedule, so she thought the team of horses should have another drink of water. They were led down for a drink and then returned to the coral. "Do you need a team of horses, Ilene asked the two young men as they were finishing up on the door? "We will buy and trade and sell just about everything, Peter replied. You will need your team to farm with though?

"No, Ilene offered with a big sigh! No horses, no wagon, no plow or harrow for me. "Perhaps a small horse or quarter horse, Peter questioned, like one to ride or pull a small wagon, perhaps? You know, firewood, ice for the icehouse or hay from the meadow? Maybe even to come see us at the outpost? Jonathan laughed and gave Peter a nudge with his elbow.

"Ok, we will work something out, Peter suggested. Right now we need to get the goats loaded up in the wagon and get home. Pick out the ones you want us to have. We will get the other load of lumber over here tomorrow and work on your little barn. The goats were loaded and Ilene's team of horse's was harnessed and hitched up to her wagon. The two stood in front of Ilene and questioned at the same time. "Are you going to be ok or should one of us stay with you? "I am fine, Ilene suggested. Thanks! "Ok then, Peter offered! We will see you tomorrow! Each of the young men climbed aboard a wagon and made their leave. The day seemed strange in so many ways. The big team of horses took up most of the small coral, almost more than the twenty goats left. Ilene often referred to the two big horses, as hay burners. The wagon was gone, five of the goats gone and the good stuff inside of me gone. Ilene felt so empty. Would she never feel like a real person, ever again? Her hand rested on the pouch in her right side. The pouch Mama helped her to make. It carried the sling and a handful of stones. The knife on the belt was on the left side. Why did she bother to carry these items with her all the time?

It was getting dark and time to go in she guessed. Something compelled her to walk to the side of the house and set up a couple of blocks of wood. The sling had not been used in a couple of days. It was usually the time after chores in the mornings, which she would do a short bit of practice. She walked back her usual twenty yards and starred at the blocks of wood. Is there a purpose she questioned herself? Is this my life now? Should I leave the valley?

The thought of that gave her a chill. "Mama, Papa, Ilene whispered towards the hill! A short stare at the hill top, still revealed the darker earth mounds. "One, two and three graves, she whispered! She was suddenly angered inside. The sling came out of its pouch, with a stone added. "Whir, whir and a slight snap of the leather. The stone gave a slight whine and a thud into a piece of wood. Then another stone found its way into the sling.

"Whir, whir, whir and the light snap. Whine, thud and another piece of wood feel quickly. A third followed suite with the same result. It had always been a single rotation of the sling and an aim. It was the third rotation and the uncontrolled anger, which brought about a, watch out, impacted. Ilene walked over to the pieces of wood by the house to pick up her stones. The aiming was almost secondary. She picked up the first piece of wood, to set it back up on the tree round. The stone was found tightly in bedded into the wood. This had not happened before. The second and third piece of wood revealed the same in bedded stone. Papa had said, "Keep practicing and you will become excellent! "Why be excellent, if you are not here Papa and Mama, whispered with tears streaming down her face? She had to remove two of the stones with the use of her knife. She couldn't throw any more stones. It was just into the house. The fire was stoked in the fireplace. No candle needed to be lit. Ilene sat in Mama's rocking chair and felt the heat of the fire. The only sound was the crackling fire, which was often wonderful. It seemed harsh somehow. "Don't think, don't think, she whispered! The shear tiredness with the heat of the fire, said" sleeps, sleep, sleep!

Ilene woke early and forced herself to eat some oats. It tasted better when there was someone talking. She hurried even if it was still dark. At least the goats would make some sounds. The chickens always offered their cackles and fussing. Eight more eggs, Ilene questioned? More eggs than she could eat. She hardly had gotten rid of that many eggs when Peter and Jonathan were here yesterday. They were coming back today, so she could send some with them.

There was a mist today, but not as great as the last few days. Ilene hard boiled some eggs as she washed the new ones to be added to the wire basket. She liked the idea of an easy quick snack of a hardboiled egg. Light started to break the horizon, as she stood beside the house to throw a couple of stones. What could she make for Peter and Jonathan for a meal today, she questioned in her head? Without thinking, three stones were thrown at their targets. There was no meat left in the ice house.

There were two wethers, among the goats, but she didn't feel like processing a goat. Papa had said, "Ilene use your sling and hunt in the forest. Sell the goats for things you need. It would be the smart thing to do.

Ilene began to walk up the hill behind the house. She was headed towards the graves, but redirected herself to another direction. She didn't want to hunt near Papa and Mama's graves. Once she reached the edge of the woods she walked about twenty yards off the edge slowly. The sling and stone were ready, but was she? Hitting a block of wood was far different than throwing a stone at a rabbit, grouse, turkey or a deer. "Not a deer, she whispered! Her heart was beating like she had run a mile. "Father in Heaven, help me, Ilene whispered! Suddenly there was a snowshoe hare. Half white and half brown rabbit starring back at her. No pausing or thinking, she did the three rotations with the sling. "Whir, whir, whir and a light snap it created. The silence offered a slight singing of the stone and a soft thud. The rabbit never moved where it had sat. As she picked up the rabbit, she found a sickening

36

feeling in her stomach. The excitement of such an accurate hit and getting the rabbit wasn't there. "Thank you for the food lord, Ilene whispered in gratitude. Ilene took a leather strap from her pouch and tied the rabbit up in a close tree. The rabbit was cleaned and skinned on the spot. She headed down the hill to the creek and washed it. The rabbit was cut up and vegetables were prepared for the cooking pot. She had a lot of potatoes, carrots, squash and onions. Now she had a rabbit! The pot could hang over the fire and cook slowly. There seemed to be a lot, but she had guests coming?

A couple of odd sounds from outside drew her attention. A quick pace brought her out of the house. "Good morning friend, Peter sounded out! "Good morning friend, Jonathan sounded right after. "Good morning Peter, Good morning Jonathan, Ilene replied! That felt good, Ilene thought to herself. Friend, what a nice feelings she thought. "What is this Pinto horse, Ilene questioned? "Well, Jonathan started to state. We call it a painted quarter horse! It is a gift for you. The gift is actually from my sister, Jonathan continued. "I don't even know your sister, Ilene questioned?

"Well, Ilene meet Sam, Jonathan introduced. My sister is Andy to her friends. Her name is really Andrea! I have always called her Andy. "I would like to meet her and thank her for such a wonderful gift, Ilene offered with as much enthusiasm as she could muster, which wasn't much. Jonathan turned away as if to hold back tears.

Peter stepped close to Ilene. "You see Ilene, Peter stated! Andy is no longer with us! She got smallpox when she was very young. She survived the small pox, put it had a crippling effect on her. She wanted to have her own horse, but she just couldn't ride it by herself. Jonathan would hold her and ride Sam. Sam was given to Andrea about four years ago, as a colt. It was her whole life. Andrea died about three months ago and the family just couldn't get rid of Sam. At least until now! For some reason when Jonathan called you little sister yesterday, he really felt it. Jonathan really wants you to have Sam, Peter offered sincerely! Here you go friend! Meet your new friend! Peter handed the reins of Sam to Ilene.

Ilene led the horse over to Jonathan, as he got his tools out of the wagon. "Thank you Jonathan for the most wonderful gift I have every received,

Ilene whispered, as she grabbed a hold on Jonathan for a great hug. The two stood there hugging for several minutes. You can call me friend or little sister anytime! Now, I have never ridden a horse before, so you will have to show me how. "Happy too, Jonathan offered with a smile! "Sam is so beautiful, Ilene offered with a smile! There is such an array of patches of browns over the white.

"Watch this, Jonathan suggested! Walk about twenty feet leading Sam and just let go of the reins, and then keep walking and stop. Ilene followed the instructions. Sam stopped, and then continued after a minute to stand near Ilene. Now just walk over by me and leave Sam, Jonathan suggested. Ilene had walked about twenty feet towards Jonathan and Sam turned and followed. Now when Sam gets here, give him a hug. Andy would hug him all the time. She did it because she loved him, but also because she needed to hold on to him to stand up. Sam continued to the two and Ilene offered the hug. Hug him always little sister!

"Just put your foot in the stirrup and swing yourself up, Jonathan instructed. A little rein this way or that will get him to turn. Just go riding for a bit and see how you do. We have some other stuff in the second wagon, we will show you later. You ride and we will get to work on the little barn. "You beautiful horse Sam, Ilene praised as she rode slowly up the hill.

It was a slow ride to the top of the hill and then along the edge of the woods. The slightest pull of the reins to the left or right got a movement this way or that. "This is fun Sam, Ilene offered, as she leaned forward and gave the horse a hug. Ilene rode all around the perimeter of the valley. She ended up back in front of the house at the creek. It was an offering of a drink to Sam. Ilene had seen Papa take the saddle and bridle off his horse many times, so she proceeded as she remembered. Papa had a saddle stand in the house, so that was where she would keep her saddle and bridle. She could remember him saying it would keep in better condition. A good rubbing of saddle oil was another instruction he gave himself. "Come on Sam, let's get you some hay, Ilene suggested. Sam followed after Ilene and waited for the coral to get open and just continued on into it. A good portion of hay was offered with a hug to Sam. Ilene looked around to spot where Peter and Jonathan were located. The roof was done, so she walked over to the entrance door and opened it for a look inside.

No one there! The little window let in a lot of light. There was another smaller door for the goats to go in or out. You could just lock them in if you choose to do so. There was a stall just inside the regular door for Sam. Nice Ilene thought! A new chicken coup built on the wall with a small ramp part way down the wall. There was a hay bunk along one wall for the goats to get their hay. Ilene noticed a small door along the top, so you could put the hay in from outside. Ilene went back to the horse stall to further investigate. There was a hole to put a water bucket and a door to open from the outside to put the hay in a small hay rack. The stall was big enough for Sam to turn around in. Even to have a small gate to keep the goats out of the stall too.

Peter was right about the talent that Jonathan had in building. The thought of Papa being so proud to have such a small barn, made Ilene run out of the building and quickly close the door. There were many deep breaths to get her composure back.

Where are Peter and Jonathan, Ilene's mind raced? Ilene searched the pasture for the sight of the two. Near the Aspen's on the far end of the pasture was the wagon with the two headed back this way. She walked back to the house to check on the stew. "Ooh, that sure smells good, she instructed herself! After a quick check she walked back out by the small whatever that had been pulled behind the wagon this morning. It was like a sled with wheels. It had side boards that could be removed. There was a harness for Sam to pull this wonder.

There was a new ax, some rope, some wonderful smelling soap in the tune of many bars. It smelled like Lilac's and was so heavenly. A wooden crate, that she felt she shouldn't open. She was quite distracted, until the team and wagon pulled up beside where she was investigating. "Did you have a nice ride, Jonathan asked, with a beaming smile? "Oh yes, Ilene beamed right back, with a rush of a few steps to give a great hug. "Well, praise the Father, Son and the Holy Spirit, Peter offered with great enthusiasm! Ilene turned and gave Peter a great hug too. "Oh nice, Peter jested! Not just hugs for the old man. "I am only twenty-two, Jonathan refuted! "I know, but I am only seventeen, so that makes you old, Peter teased, as he gave Jonathan a little elbow. "Jonathan may have given you his beloved Andy's horse, but look at the stuff mother and I have for you. "You two have built me a beautiful barn, Ilene proclaimed. Why anything more? "Wait, wait, Jonathan protested! First observe this beautiful sled wagon. First you take this pry and a block to lift just before this wheel. Jonathan quickly took a block of wood and a short thick piece of wood about six feet long and placed it just so in front of one of the wheels. He pulled a pin out of the axle and pulled off one of the wheels. He let the wooden lever come up and the let the runner of his sled down to the ground. I can do each wheel without the lever, but I made a lever to make it easier for you to lift. Jonathan picked up on the side of the wagon sled and put the wheel back on.

"So, Peter interrupted! The wonderful craftsman Jonathan has made you a wagon with its wheels. Then there is a wonderful sled for you to sit on, ride and haul. Then you can take these bows and place them on with this canvas and have a tent to live in. Not done yet, Peter offered with a laugh! You can use these side boards for hauling almost anything. Then there is this wonderful harness for Sam to do all the hard work. Noticed the barn with the nice storage box hanging on the side, Peter offered as he pointed back to the small barn. You can put your tack all in the box to store it until you need it?

While Peter did his boasting, Jonathan walked over to the coral and brought Sam out and placed Sam in front of the wagon sled. Jonathan began to demonstrate how to harness Sam to the wagon sled. Ilene offered more hugs and, "I just love you guys! "Then we have succeeded Peter shouted! We were sent to lift you up! Praise God for that! We love you right back, Jonathan offered!

Jonathan led Sam up to the side of the barn and placed the canvas in the tack box. "We can put the extra ax and post auger in this box too. "Post auger, Ilene questioned? "Not familiar, Peter indulged? We went up to the Aspens and cut some new posts to improve your coral. Come over here and I will show you. Peter walked over to the coral with the other two following.

We need a new post here, Peter pointed. The tool was placed in the given position and Peter began to rotate the post auger. It cut into the earth and then he pulled it out, when it looked filled up. He tapped the earth out beside the hole and proceeded to do some more in the same hole. You can go as deep as you like, up to this handle, Peter beamed. Well, as long as the ground is not frozen.

"Let's bring the rest of this stuff up to the house, Jonathan suggested. Ilene latched an arm onto each one of the two young men. "I have to remember this day, Ilene offered with a bit of joy! You two are so wonderful and I never want to forget you! I wish I had made some bread, but we have stew to eat and it's ready.

"Ok friend, I could eat, Peter offered with exuberance! "Ok little sister, I 'm in, Jonathan added!

Sam was led with the three around to the front of the house. The wagon sled came to a stop. "With one big step you can be in the wagon sled, Jonathan instructed. "I can reach my side of this crate from the ground, Peter demonstrated! The two brought the crate in behind Ilene. "Ok, take the cover off the crate, Peter requested? Ilene picked the cover up and placed it on its side, leaning it to the crate. "New blue speckled dishes, Ilene remarked, as she tapped one against her finger nails? Peter assisted by helping place the dishes on the table. "My mother, Alice, loves new dishes, Peter informed Ilene. Ilene turned to the crate to see the nest item. Levi's, Ilene questioned? "Levis shirts and jeans, Peter advised! Four sets and I do hope they fit? I can take them back for a different size if they don't? "I have always worn a dress, but Papa said that these wear like iron, Ilene confessed. I didn't think I was allowed to wear these? "Of course you are, Jonathan proclaimed! You are as good as us, Jonathan proclaimed, as he offered another hug. Ilene gave an extra hug back. She loved the hugs, but wasn't going to say so.

Ilene removed a very pointed nice looking knife from the crate. Jonathan started to explain that it was a fillet knife for easy cleaning of fish. Peter hurried out of the house to fetch the box with soap in it. His rushing back into the house was blurted with, "Mother loves this soap; Peter informed the reason for the box of bars of soap.

I thought you might me offended by this, but mother said nonsense! Ilene took one of the bars out and smelled it. I think you are wonderful and a friend. I didn't want you to think that I gave you this, because you're not clean or anything. "Nonsense, Ilene offered, as she came close to Peter and kissed him on the cheek. "Whoa, Jonathan quickly

41

added! Where's mine? Jonathan laughed and held his cheek out towards Ilene. Ilene obliged him with a kiss on the cheek.

"God has blessed me, Jonathan pronounced! I will never wash my cheek again! "No washing my cheek, Peter added! Ilene took a bar of soap in each hand and handed them to the two at the same time, with a laugh.

It was back to the crate for new discoveries. A total collection of soft towels, dish cloths, towels for dishes, silver ware, a small cook pot, a frying pan, new boots, socks, a new red, a Boss of the Plains hat, three very colorful scarves and red blue flowered dress.

The dress was hugged, but tears began to flow. "I told you to leave the dress out, Jonathan instructed to Peter! "No, no Ilene confessed! I love it! Just a tear because it is so wonderful! It was a dress and a three way hug. "Mother loves scarves, so she gave you three silk scarves, peter offered with a beam of excitement. She wears them around her neck, around her waist and around her head. She always has a scarf on! Let's eat, Ilene pronounced! Ilene began to place the new dishes around the table. "I have to run out to the ice house, Ilene instructed. "I will get the milk, Jonathan offered.

As Jonathan fetched the pitcher of milk with the cheese cloth over it, he noticed that there were only three blocks of ice left in the ice house. No meat, he whispered to himself. Was there meat in the stew? He hurried back to the house.

The stew was dished up on the new plates. "This sure smells good, Jonathan offered! "Fresh rabbit stew, Ilene offered with a smile! The three sat down, as Ilene offered, let me pray? She held a hand out to each of the young men. "Oh, Peter offered in surprise! Sorry, not use to the hand held part. "Father, in Heaven, holy is thy name, Ilene stated! Bless this food, bless Peter and bless Jonathan!

Help us always to receive the path you set before us, even if we don't understand it. Thank you for the generosity of Peter, Jonathan, Mother Alice and little sister Andrea! Keep Papa and Mama until I see them with you in heaven. Bless and keep us always! Amen!"How, did you get a rabbit, Peter asked, while they ate. "With my sling, Ilene confessed! "You mean like a sling shot, Jonathan asked? "No, just a sling, Ilene claimed, as she pulled it out of her pouch, placing it on the table. She also took out a single stone and placed it on the table. "Impressive, Peter claimed! "Yes, yes, Jonathan proclaimed! You will have to show us later.

"Yes, I can beside the house, Ilene offered. I take a few practice shots every day. This is my first rabbit, so I was a little nervous about it this morning. "This morning, Jonathan questioned? "Yes, before you two came over, Ilene replied. It was a prayer, as what I could feed you two and God provided this rabbit.

Peter and Jonathan were soon back, to working on the coral as promised. Ilene cleaned up quickly with the dishes, as she felt like she was going to miss out on something. The beautiful red and blue flowered dress begged for a hug and a try on. There was no mirror, so she tried to see herself the best she could. She felt wonderful! The dress was a little big, but ok. The bust was a little tight. She questioned in her mind, if that was the way it was suppose to be? Where was that bra thing, Papa and Mama had given her? She found it and proceeded to get it on. It seemed a bit tight? The dress was put on again. There seemed to be body parts showing where she thought they shouldn't show? "Nut's, Ilene proclaimed! Mama, where are you to ask about these things?

Ilene removed the dress and the bra and put on a pair of the Levi pants and shirt. This was comfortable and seemed to look ok. She hung the dress up and put the bra away. It had warmed up enough so that a poncho or coat was not needed. She would just wear these and go help Peter and Jonathan. Ilene tied a scarf on around her head like a bandana. "Now I am ready to work, Ilene whispered to herself.

"Look at you Ms Rancher, Peter sounded off at the sight of Ilene! Cooler than the creek and prettier than a sunset! "Very nice, Jonathan added! "How, did the dress fit, that mother picked out, Peter asked? "I had it on, but I didn't come out to show you, Ilene confessed. It looked real pretty, but? Ilene stopped talking and put her hands over here face. The two young men came over to Ilene. "But, what, Peter asked? "I was embarrassed, Ilene confessed! Peter looked at Jonathan and shrugged. "Ilene, were friends, Jonathan assured! Hey, if you are uncomfortable about what it looks like. You don't have to wear it. "It would be easier if I was asking your mother,

Peter, Ilene offered, as she removed her hands from her face. You two have done so much for me. No complaints! My, my body showed a lot in the neck area! Ilene placed her hands at the area where the reveal had showed. "No problem, Peter quickly replied! I will take the dress with me and have mother help with that. She will know right away as what to do. Let's get the dress and put it in the crates and load it into the wagon to take back home. Peter and John each took an arm of Ilene and marched here back to the house. The dress was gathered up and put into the crate. Peter grabbed up the Boss of the Plains hat and plopped it on Ilene's head. "Your hat my friend, Peter announced! Always need a hat. The crate was put into the wagon sled. The three stood in the wagon sled and Ilene was let drive Sam and the wagon sled back to where they had been working. "Very Nice, Jonathan complimented! Now with your Boss of the Plains hat, you are a beautiful! Official rancher! The hat makes the person. Peter tipped his hat to Ilene. "Miss, have a great life, Peter offered! "Miss Ilene, Jonathan added, with the tip of his hat!

"If you need anything, just go up to the trading post and mother can help you, Peter suggested. Johnny and I are taking the wagons to Minneapolis for supplies for the weather turns. It is about a two week trip. "You have a very good team of horses and wagon, so we really appreciate having them, Jonathan commented. We owe you trade for some time to come! The timing of having them couldn't be better. Two wagons make the trip twice as sweet.

"When it freezes up we will start to haul ice from the lake, Peter instructed. The best way to the lake is along your creek, so we would be happy if you let us cross your valley along the creek? We would happily fill your ice house for letting us do so? "You two are welcome here anytime, Ilene offered with a smile. I have been spoiled the last few days, being able to see you so much. I am going to miss you two! You two have helped me more than words can say! What did you tell me? You came to lift me up and carry me for awhile? Thank God and thank you two! "Praise the lord for guiding us to you, Peter confessed! "Amen, Jonathan added! See you soon, Jonathan added! "Good-Bye Ilene, Peter added! We love you!

Sam

Ilene walked over to Sam standing in the middle of the coral. She put her arm around Sam's neck and just stood there hugging the horse. "There is a lot of comfort in just standing here and giving you a hug, Sam, Ilene whispered to the horse! I can see how little sister Andrea must have enjoyed doing this very act. Sam, I will probably think of Andy, every time I give you a hug. It's strange and yet not so, Sam. The hand of God works in so many ways, even though you Sam.

The improvement to the coral wasn't even something that Ilene would have thought of. The extra boards were used to make the wind protective fence on the north and west. The sun shelter or rain shelter was a nice addition too. "Jonathan is a clever builder, Ilene whispered to the horse. Ilene started to walk over to the tackle box on the side of the small barn. Sam followed without a word of suggestion. Ilene opened the box and saw what she was looking for. A brush and a curry comb. Nice, she whispered! These two items went into the box so quick, Sam, I wasn't sure I heard what they were used for? Ilene began to curry and brush Sam. "I bet you like this, don't you Sam, Ilene whispered? I loved it when Mama brushed my hair. My hair has never been cut since I was a baby. I think about it every once in a while, but I talk myself out of it, just because Mama liked it long. Papa did too, because Mama's hair was long.

"Well Sam, we will leave you outside until the weather gets to be ugly, if that is ok? Let me see about the barn door, Ilene questioned herself? Jonathan showed me how to lock the door to the stall open. Oh, that's easy. Ilene remarked as she fasten the door to the barn and the stall just inside open. I guess you can go inside if you like. The goats have their little door and there all inside with the chickens in their coup. I can feel the mist coming in and it might be cold? "Good night Sam, Ilene offered, as she gave the horse a couple of pats.

Ilene added some water to the rabbit stew and poked the fire up a bit. When Mama made most foods and had something left, she just added water and left it hang over the low fire. Mama had especially enforced that if there was meat in the pot. She lit a candle and began to read the bible. The quietness tried to chase the bible away, but she wasn't going to let that happen. The quietness made her shiver, even if it wasn't cold.

The bible was read, a bowl of stew was eaten and the supper cleaning finished. Then the extra clothes she had been gifted were sought out for a new place to be stored. They all didn't seem like they wanted to fit in her small cupboard. Ilene walked over to Mama and Papa's cupboard. She couldn't remove their clothes for a little more space. Some sadness and rage came creeping up on her, so she grabbed her coat and ran out into the dark. The colored scarf floated in the air as she ran. It showed up as black and not color as she ran. She found herself stooped over and kneeling beside the creek. It was a quick wash of her hands and a couple of scoops of water to quench a thirst that had found her.

The cool mist found her face as she knelt by the creek. There were no summer crickets or frogs making their sounds. The night was black and quiet. The moon couldn't release it light as it had the other night. Where was God's hand created glory as the other night, when the moon sat on the edge of the earth? The time marched on as Ilene sought for anything that would give God the glory. Anything that would help her find some peace?

Ilene fell backwards on the ground and starred into the vastness of the night. There was still nothing, as the clouds had covered the stars. "It is so, so dark, Ilene whispered into the black! Let thy glory come forth, that I may have some peace Lord!

Suddenly there was a great bugle into the night. Ilene jumped to her feet in shock and almost terror. She turned from the creek and faced the hill behind her.

"Sweet Jesus, Ilene spoke loudly! The bugle sounded again. Give God the glory, so that I may have peace? Ask, and you shall receive? It was

46

a bit shocking, but I guess it has also brought me peace? Ilene walked away from the creek, through the dark misty night. She could see a sparse bit of light above the trees on the ridge to the top of the hill. The great stag Elk couldn't be seen however. Ilene couldn't see her hand in front of her face, as she stood waiting for the bugle to sound again. She smiled into the darkness of the night. Ilene reflected a smile of peace as a thank you. She followed an occasional bleat of one of the goats to find her way back to the house.

Morning came with its quietness. She had expected the cluck of the chickens or a small bleat from one of the goats to at least give her a greeting. They were not right beside the house anymore, so she guessed the small distance greater was just enough to keep that from happening. Opening the door reveal an inch of snow, which was a surprise, as she had thought the mist would be thicker, than it was last night. The new snow was always fun she thought, but when the cold came, fun lost out. When the creek would freeze over, fun lost out. But, that was not to happen today! The little door in front of the hay bunk, made it fun to give the goats their hay. Then the door to the stall for Sam was opened and hay added. "Good morning Sam, Ilene offered! A quiet low greeting was returned, which gave Ilene a bit of excitement. There were three milking straps on one wall of the small barn. Ilene tethered the two goats that had to be milked. This was nice, Ilene thought. They can't move all over while I milk them. "Jonathan is so clever, Ilene whispered! The milking was done, chickens fed and eggs gathered.

Breakfast was easy to decide, because it was milk, eggs and eggs. "So many eggs, Ilene whispered! What had to be done today was the question? Can't haul the hay stacks home yet, until the creek froze. There was the wood that Mama and she had cut on the top of the hill? Papa never had a chance to help with the wagon. Go hook up Sam to the wagon sled and haul the wood down to the house.

You never had too much wood. It would be best to get that done, before the hill got covered with snow or even ice. It could be risky for Sam.

Sam and Ilene were soon on their way up the hill towards the rounds of wood cut and stacked. The pile soon came into view. Ilene coaxed Sam nice and close to the pile for easy loading. It wasn't far from Papa and Mama's graves, so Ilene made a quiet walk over to the now snow covered mounds. There were huge prints of an animal on the top of the two mounds. She placed her hand next to one of the prints and found it larger than her mitten hand. Her heart began to beat quickly, for whatever reason. It was just something that wasn't supposed to be there. Ilene looked around for anything else that shouldn't be there. Nothing! It was over to Sam and the wagon sled. A load of rounds from the tree was quickly loaded. Ilene eyed the load and took a couple back off. She wasn't sure how many Sam could pull. She looped the reins up and decided to walk with Sam. "No extra weight on the load from me, Sam, Ilene whispered. Ilene walked ahead of Sam. "Come on Sam, let's go Ilene coaxed, in a quiet voice? Sam easily leaned into the load and followed Ilene. Ilene walked without another word all the way to the house's wood pile. She gave Sam a hug and a command of sorts. "Wait here Sam, while I unload. Ilene offered a bucket of water to Sam, while she unloaded the wood. An armful of hay was gathered up and placed on the wagon sled. There was nothing up on the hill for Sam to eat, so the hay would be a good touch, while Sam waited patiently for her to load the wood.

The fourth load of wood was a welcome sight. "I think I have had enough for today Sam, Ilene whispered, as she walked ahead of Sam down the hill to the wood pile beside the house. You never have enough wood in winter. Maybe I need a thick coat like you Sam, Ilene laughed! The wagon sled was parked near the tackle box, so there would be no great distance to put the harness away. Sam followed Ilene to the coral, without coaxing. Just open the gate and let him in. A hug was offered to Sam, but it really was more for her and Ilene knew it. I am not looking forward to hauling hay from the meadow, but then you are not complaining so why should I, Ilene offer of a laugh.

There was a bit of light to be had, Ilene thought and she didn't feel like supper or sitting in the quiet house. She plucked the ax from its position on a large tree round, which she used for splitting smaller rounds on.

A brisk march to the lake to check the thickness of the ice was in order. It had been four weeks since Pete and Jonathan had been here."I guess I was being a bit hopeful for you guys to come by here after your two week trip to get supplies; Ilene spoke her mind out loud. Maybe you think that the ice isn't thick enough yet. It's been cold for a month and the water from the lake is barely trickling anymore. Ilene stood starring at the water slowly running off the lake. I am going to be chopping a hole in the lake, filling a barrel and having Sam pulling the water back every day. "I really don't like that, Ilene offered loudly!

It was a swing of the ax ahead of her with each step. It was about twenty feet onto the lake, when she began to chop a hole in the ice in earnest. "I prefer six inches thick ice, Ilene pronounced, as if someone would hear and care in any way. Twelve by twelve and six inches think is my order! Any bigger and they are heavy to lift. I was looking forward to having Pete and Jonathan helping me with filling, my icehouse. The chopping soon revealed that the ice was a little more than her six inches. Well family, it looks like tomorrow we start cutting this ice. The word family hurt, as Ilene looked around to see what was not there. She took off running for the house and didn't stop until she had flung herself into Mama's chair.

After chores the next morning, there was a great temptation to saddle Sam and go up to the trading store and see if Pete and Jonathan were there, but she just couldn't go. Even the grabbing of herself by the front of her coat, with commanding instruction, "Get to the trading post young lady! "I just can't, she replied to herself! It brought tears, until she heard a small tingle of chain on a horse drawn wagon. Sam was quickly put back into the coral and with fleet of foot she climbed up the side of the coral to have a better look down the valley. It was a team of horses and wagon. It had to be Pete and Jonathan? Ilene jumped down from the position she had on the coral fence.

It was a run around to the front of the house, but a slow walk, as she rounded the corner. "Don't show too much excitement, she told herself!

The wagon slowly moved towards her and now she could identify, that it indeed was her two friends.

The wagon stopped and Jonathan gave a hearty, "Good morning! "Good morning Jonathan, Ilene replied happily! Good morning, Pete! Pete's joyful demeanor was totally diminished. "Hello, Pete finally offered! "I was just about to get Sam and start hauling ice from the lake, Ilene confessed. I checked the ice at twenty feet from shore and it was about eight inches thick. Are you intending to haul ice, Ilene asked?

"Yes, we are Jonathan reflected their intent. That is if I can get my friend Pete motivated.

"Peter, are you not well, Ilene inquired? "Pete is well and not well at the same time, Jonathan offered in a low tone. We just need to lift Pete up and carry him for a while. Like we helped you Ilene! How are you getting along? "It is a struggle a times, but I am just happy to see you two, Ilene replied with a smile. Do we need more tools? "No I think we have enough tools, Jonathan suggested, as he looked into the wagon box. Climb up if you like? "I will just walk down and meet you at the lake, Ilene suggested. Ilene ran back into the house and returned with a rope. "Going to lasso the ice blocks and pull them out, Jonathan laughed? "Safety, mind you, Ilene shouted after the two on the wagon.

Jonathan pulled onto the edge of the lake, with the horse just off the shore. Pete climbed down off the wagon and Ilene gave him a good long hug. It brought about very little emotion from Pete. Two wet noodles was the return hug. "I am very glad to see you two, Ilene offered! I have missed you! Jonathan, maybe Pete shouldn't be here to work, if he doesn't feel well, Ilene questioned? "He needs to stay busy, so he's not thinking about other things, Jonathan instructed. It's not a physical thing, it's mental. Ilene didn't ask another question, but took up the ax and reopened the hole she had chopped last night. "Ok, I will start sawing some blocks, Jonathan informed the other two. Pete, you can load the ice blocks and Ilene, if you like you can slide then to the front of the wagon. If the ice is not too heavy for you Ilene, we can stack these about three rows high. "I can do that, Ilene replied happily!

Ilene tried to think of a way to lift Pete up, as the three worked away. "I wonder how you could lift these, if you didn't have ice tongs, Ilene questioned.

"A lot of manual lifting and broken bones, Jonathan suggested. When there was no room left to stand on the back of the wagon, Ilene jumped down, so the last of the blocks could be loaded from the ground. "There we go a load, Ilene happily offered the obvious. Here is a hug for you Pete and a kiss of thank you. Ilene gave a great hug and a kiss on the cheek, but it brought no reaction from Pete. "Hey, what's for my hard work, Jonathan asked? Ilene fulfilled Jonathan's request. I can't wait until the next load, Jonathan laughed. How about you Pete? Pete still gave no response.

The three climbed up on the wagon and headed to Ilene's ice house. There was no meat, no milk or even any ice left in the ice house. "This is about as empty as you can get my friend, Jonathan offered the obvious. I don't know if we can even get two loads in here, Jonathan suggested, when the load was almost finished. The three were back on their way for another load, when Jonathan drove the wagon around to the harness box on the side of the small barn. Stay tight and I will grab something. Jonathan quickly went over to the small barn grabbed some short four foot boards and threw them into the wagon box. "What are those boards for, Ilene asked? I just thought they were extra's. "You are right about them being extra's, Jonathan offered in agreement. It was Pete's idea about you getting water from the lake. "Really, Ilene questioned? Thanks for thinking of me Pete! That's worth another kiss on the cheek, Ilene suggested, as she placed the highly sought after kiss. "Hey, that should only be if Pete tells you how his idea works, Jonathan suggested, with another one of his hearty laughs.

"How does your idea go again Pete, Jonathan asked? Jonathan gathered the short boards from the wagon and handed them to Pete. Pete just stood there with the boards leaning against him. Let me see, Jonathan mumbled? Cut an ice block and sit it on the edge of the hole? Jonathan cut an ice block and sat it close to the edge of the hole. "No, Pete offered a single word! A foot back on the north side. A three foot by three foot hole!

Three blocks on each side by three blocks high. Lay the boards over the hole and leave the south side open to access the hole for water.

It will not freeze over as much. Jonathan worked about quickly performing the given instructions.

"Well Peter, you are a hero and you saved my life, Jonathan touted! Tell your friend Ilene what happened on our freight trip. Pete said no more, but just picked up another saw and started cutting more blocks of ice for the wagon. Ilene took her ice tongs and grabbed an ice block. With a hefty pull, she almost slid into the lake. Pete grabbed Ilene by the arm to prevent her from going in the water. Ilene caught her balance, but she was having her heart beat out of her chest. "I have a rope on my ice tongs to pull out a block of ice, Ilene confessed. Now I remember why! Ilene gave another hug to Pete. I am a bit scared, so give me just a minute. It was probably two minutes, before Pete suggested that they get back to work.

The whole situation took place with Jonathan busily working on his project to the other side of the big ice hole. Pete cut and lifted the ice blocks out of the hole for Ilene to drag to the wagon and load. After a short time Jonathan sounded out, "Come see your water retrieval hole Ilene. "It looks grand, Ilene proclaimed! "It would work even better if you cover the boards with a bit of snow for insulation, Jonathan instructed. Project done, back to icing! Ilene went back to standing in the wagon and loading, while Pete brought the ice blocks to her.

Jonathan stopped sawing for a rest break offering the question "Pete, did you tell Ilene yet? Pete said nothing. "We were coming back from Minneapolis with our freight. We were maybe half way back when two guys pulled guns on us to rob us of our wagons and supplies. I was in the lead wagon and they had their rifles pointed at me. We had rifles and revolvers under the wagon seat boxes, but that would be almost impossible to reach for them. Now Pete, always trying to be more prepared was wearing his holster with his revolver loaded and ready. However, Pete is the one that has always said,

"If I shoot and kill someone, just put me in my grave! Just as soon as the robbers told us to stand up and get off the wagons,

Peter shot both of them. When I stood up, I blocked their view to Pete. He shot them both, before they could fire a shot.

We loaded them on top of the freight wagons and took them into town. It happens that they both were wanted men. Even to the point that they had bounties on their heads. We were caught up in town for a night, before everything was sorted out. "I can feel for Pete, Ilene offered in sympathy. It has to be a very hard and terrible thing to shoot someone, especially if they die. Ilene walked over to Pete and placed a kiss on his lips. Live Pete, we need you! "I want to live too, Jonathan offered with a laugh!There is enough ice to fill your ice house, so let's go unload and come back for a load for our ice house. The three went quietly up on the wagon and to the ice house. The little ice house was soon filled. Probably more than it had ever had in it. Then it was back to the lake for another load.

Pete pulled an ice block out quickly and it was followed with a big slush of water onto the ice. "Careful pulling blocks out like that, Jonathan warned! Too much water on the ice will make the edge too slippery. Let's take that last block out and move to the other side where it's not as slippery. No sooner had Jonathan given the warning, when Pete slipped and went into the water. Jonathan quickly grabbed a pike pole with a loop on the end and reached for Pete. The first attempt missed Pete's arm, as Ilene jumped off the wagon and rushed over to the disaster.

"Pete, Peter, Ilene screamed! Jonathan couldn't reach Pete anymore with the Pike pole. Ilene ran to the wagon seat and snatched up the rope she had brought. The lassoing of goats had not been in vain all these years. Within seconds the rope was whistling in the air and flying towards Peter. It was a catch around his neck and one arm. It didn't matter, as Ilene pulled with all she had. Jonathan reached for Pete's arm again. The second attempt made it over Pete's arm.

It went over his arm and Jonathan pulled it tight. Pete was quickly pulled from the water, by the two. Jonathan picked Pete up and ran to the back of the wagon and shoved Pete in.

"Hold onto Pete and try to keep him warm, Jonathan shouted! I am driving fast for the trading store.

Ilene quickly unbuttons her coat and wrapped her body and coat around Pete. She pushed her face close to his as she lay on top of him. She could feel the dense coldness beneath her body. In just a few minutes the cold had enveloped her. She was shivering as much as Pete was. Trading store words from Jonathan's lips finally hit her brain. It was a chill greater than the cold coming from Pete's body. Ilene clenched tighter to Pete, for herself.

It didn't take long to get to the trading store. Ilene quickly tried to move the limp Pete. It was Jonathan's quick movement, which snatched Pete up. The door of the trading store was opening up; by the time Jonathan reached the door. The only problem is that the door wasn't opening up

53

quick enough for Jonathan, so his mass moved it open a bit quicker. It caught mother Alice by surprise, as she went stumbling backwards. "Hypothermia, hypothermia, Jonathan shouted! Ilene quickly closed the door and just stood back with her half wet clothes. Her shivering made her teeth rattle, a she watched Jonathan strip clothing from Pete and mother Alice running to some other location in the store.

Mother Alice was back with towels and blankets. Pete didn't seem to be able to stand on his own. Jonathan half held Pete up as the two quickly rubbed him dry. A mat was thrown down in front of the fireplace. Pete was wrapped in a blanket and placed on the mat. He was covered with several more blankets. Just as soon as the last blanket was placed, Jonathan came running at Ilene. A quick arm around her and she felt like she was flying towards the fireplace. "You are wet and shivering, Jonathan shouted as he hurried Ilene to the fireplace. Mother Alice was adding more wood to the fire. Jonathan quickly removed the wet coat and scarf.

Ilene stumbled backwards thinking Jonathan was going to undress her as he did Pete. "Come with me, mother Alice spoke quickly! Mother Alice's arm was around Ilene and rushing her around a corner and up a stairs. Get your wet things off, mother

Alice directed. Mother

Alice grabbed a towel from a shelf and tossed it to Ilene. I will get you some dry clothes, she offered as she disappeared. The wet clothes were off and the towel for drying was held close as mother Alice came back into the room. When, you get these dry clothes on, come down to the fire. Are your boots wet, mother Alice asked? "No, Ilene replied! "Ok, just put them back on to help warm your feet by the fire. I will go make some hot drinks.

Ilene quickly got dressed, while she shivered and of course scanned the bedroom. It was a wonderful place. The wet clothes were gathered up to dry in front of the fireplace. The clothes were placed over the back of some chairs that had been placed appropriately. Pete was lying on the mat with his eyes closed. "Is Pete going to be ok, Ilene asked? "I think so, Jonathan offered with uncertainty. "Here is some hot coffee, mother Alice offered, as she returned with two cups. "Thank you Alice,

Jonathan offered with appreciation. "Thanks, mother Alice, Ilene added for her cup. "Come on Pete; get your head together, mother Alice protested! "It's just an accident, Jonathan informed. "Poor son, you have changed so much since your freight haul, mother Alice offered in sympathy. There are too many ways to get hurt out here, if you don't have your wits about you. Out here is shoot or be shot! There is always a lazy somebody waiting to rob you. It's probably a matter of time before someone tries to rob this store. Mental fatigue!

"How are you doing sweetie, mother Alice requested? "Some days good, some not, Ilene replied. Are you warming up, mother Alice requested? "Yes, thank you, Ilene whispered. I will have another coffee please? "Of course dear, mother Alice responded. "It is very good, Ilene complimented. Mother Alice reached for Jonathan's cup to get two cups of coffee.

"The ice is a good money maker, but is it worth it, mother Alice mumbled as she walked away to get the coffee.

Mother Alice soon returned with the two coffees. "That is quit an ordeal for you to lose both parents so close together, mother Alice questioned? How did you get through all that?

"Pete and Jonathan showing up at just the right time, Ilene remarked.

It may also be by the hand of God if you believe so."I would have been mad at God for something like that, mother Alice confessed. "Oh, it crosses your mind, Ilene offered.

It wasn't long and papa died, so I buried him on the hill behind the house, at mama's request. I didn't know what to do and really became quit terrified. I had no problem digging the grave, but I couldn't put the dirt back on top of papa. Mama instructed me to put a blanket over him and it would be alright to then put the dirt on him. I got it done, but I cried all the time.

"It was just a day or so when Mama got sick and I stayed by her trying to get her temperature down. After a day or so she started to get cold. Mama told me that this may happen and that I must bury her by papa. I dug the grave again! There was just no putting the dirt on mama, even after I had covered her with a blanket. I took a blanket and wrapped myself with it and tried to pull the dirt in on both of us, but it was just impossible!

"There were tears running down my face, but I just kept taking deep breaths. "I kept hearing rise up and live, but there was no one around me. I stood in the grave and looked out across the meadow, but there was just no one around. As I climbed up out of the grave and began to shout, "I can't do this! I can't do this! The next thing I knew, I was running across the meadow towards the woods. I froze stiff in my tracks, when I saw a black bear stand up in the edge of the woods. There was contemplation between running straight towards the bear or quickly returning to cover up my mama, before the bear came to find her.

"The bear took off into the woods, so I just turned around and walked back to do what had to be done. It was a one shovel, then thoughts, one shovel and thoughts. It was very late into the night with the moon shinning overhead. The moonlight completely revealed the two mounds of dirt.

So many thoughts went through my head, but it wasn't about anything in the future, it was mostly about when I would get sick and how would I bury myself? There was enough room between mama and papa,

I thought. Finally I went into the house and retrieved a blanket and lay down between the two graves. A couple of the goats came over and lay down beside me and there I fell asleep.

"The next day I made a couple of crosses for mama and papa. The goats came by and begged to be milked, so I did so. This distraction and that came by, so I was busy. I went and found some wild flowers and planted them on each of the graves. I seemed to cry at every movement.

"I dug a third grave and made my bed in it, thinking I would be gone in a day, Ilene instructed. I never got sick, but I had the plan for it. I had the grave for me, but it just never happened. I memorized many bible verses, so, I could recite them when I felt it. There was a great moon in the middle of the night. It took the black grave I was lying in and totally lit it up. I crawled up the ladder a bit and saw a great stag standing on the ridge and starring at the moon. For whatever reason, my mind said to me that God was glorifying himself. In the morning,

56

there was a strange face looking into the grave at me. "Are you sick, the voice from the face requested? "No, I replied! "Then come forth and live, the voice commanded! It was Pete! "That sounds like something Pete should hear, mother Alice instructed!

Rise up and live

Pete could be heard and seen stirring a bit. "He must be feeling better, mother Alice surmised. Ilene stood up and felt her clothes. "They seem good and dry, so I had better be off, Ilene suggested. "Don't want to stay for some supper, mother Alice questioned? "I like to get my chores done before dark, Ilene replied. "Keep the clothes on that you have on, mother Alice insisted. You can just carry yours home. Never forget that you can come live with us and work with us in the store too. It would pay better than tending your goats. "You are very kind, Ilene offered. Mama and Papa are in the valley and I somehow feel obligated.

Ilene picked up her clothes and walked over by the mat, which Pete was laying on. Pete's eyes were closed as Ilene stood looking at him. "Are you sick, Ilene requested in a loud tone? "No, Pete replied with his eyes still closed. "Then rise up and live, Ilene commanded! "I can't I am naked, Pete replied with his eyes still closed. "Too late, Ilene whispered!

"I will give you a ride home, Jonathan offered. I still have the team standing outside. "Thanks mother Alice, Ilene offered as she left. "Come again, mother Alice shouted after the two. The idea gave Ilene a chill down her back, but then she had survived today? "That was funny, Jonathan offered with a laugh, as they climbed up on to the wagon seat. "How's that, Ilene questioned? "I never knew that Pete found you in the grave, Jonathan confessed. Are you sick? No! Then come forth and live! Jonathan laughed as he drove the horses. Now you got to say it back to him. That's extra funny. We will see how he feels about that tomorrow, when we start hauling ice.

Would you like some help with chores? "If you like, Ilene replied with a smile. Do you have anything to carry eggs in? "Well, not really, but maybe in my coat pockets, Jonathan suggested, with another laugh. "I don't have money, but I have a lot, a lot of eggs, Ilene reflected with a laugh of her own. "Nice laugh, do it more often, Jonathan suggested. If you were a couple of years old, I would ask you to marry me, Jonathan confessed, as he looked at Ilene. Are you sure you are only thirteen? "Born in 1879 and its 1893 now, Ilene instructed! "Well you're headed to fourteen, but you look eighteen to me, Jonathan offered his feeling.

Jonathan gathered up a bucket and a water barrel to go get them filled for the stock. It was the hard part of chores in the winter. He had to gather up all the tools that were left from earlier in the day. Jonathan saw the water hole project he had made earlier, as he drove the team up to the side of the lake. "This is a nice job Jonathan, If I have to say so myself. I will be the first one to try this out, he instructed himself. Jonathan removed the boards to see if there was any freezing. There are barely any ice crystals. Nice! I wonder if Ilene has a goat skin to place over the boards. That would really help. Let's see, if I put the barrel up in the wagon, I will not be able to lift it back down. Jonathan put the barrel on the ground and tied a rope around the middle and back to the axle. It's slippery, so it should just slide along the ground, if I go slowly. The barrel was filled and the test tried. "It works, Jonathan boasted with an added laugh.

Jonathan came driving the team right up beside the small barn. "Water delivery, Jonathan laughed, as he untied the rope. "That is clever, Ilene suggested, as she shoved some hay into the small doors to the hay bunk. It is really handy to put the hay into the bunk, through these small doors also. "I tried out the new water access for winter too, Jonathan advised Ilene. It works really well too. Pete had a good idea.

If you had a goat skin to lie over the boards, than some snow, it would really help. "I do have one, Ilene admitted. I brought the eggs up to the house, so come around with your team and get some to take home.

Jonathan knocked on the door. "Hello, Ilene's voice sounded out! I mean come on in. Jonathan steeped inside the house. I don't know if I have heard anyone knock on the door. I wasn't sure, what to say, Ilene laughed. "What's this, Jonathan asked? "It's a basket, Ilene offered sincerely. "Not bad, Jonathan replied with a laugh. A pair of jeans with the legs tied off short. A piece of rope through the belt loops to draw it closed. It's a bunch of eggs ready for transport. Nice, Jonathan smiled as he picked it up to test the ability to carry the eggs. "That's three dozen eggs for you sir, Ilene laughed. "And a pair of Levi's, Jonathan smiled. I will see you tomorrow for icing. Ilene rushed over and gave Jonathan a hug. Thanks for the winter water access, Ilene offered. I hope Pete is better tomorrow. "If he is not, I will use the magic words, Jonathan suggested. "Are you sick! No! Then rise up and live!

It was a little surprising to see Peter with Jonathan the next morning. I found my heart leap inside my chest though. It leaped even more when Peter sounded out his usual self. "Good morning Ilene, Peter sounded out, as the wagon pulled up in front of the house. "I am not sick, I am alive and well! "A good dunking in the lake yesterday has brought Pete back to his old self, Jonathan proclaimed. Well, it was actually yesterday when you were at the trading store.

"Let me see, how did you say that phrase, Jonathan pondered? "Are you sick? "No, Pete replied with his eyes closed. "Then rise up and live, you commanded! "I can't I am naked, Pete replies with his eyes still closed. "Too late, you said! That will be funny the rest of my life.

"Just curious, Ilene stated? If you were conscious, why did you keep your eyes closed, when I spoke to you? "I was naked, Pete protested! "You were under six blankets, Ilene laughed. Jonathan laughed and added,

"A memory for a life time! "A sad and scary time, but now we can laugh, Ilene suggested.

I really like being with you two. "Come live with us, Pete requested, as he took a hold on Ilene's arm? "I can't Peter, Ilene responded, as she patted Pete on his clasping arm. Maybe one day?

The next two weeks went by quickly hauling ice to the icehouse. "These are two of the best weeks ever, Ilene offered, as the last block of ice was placed in the icehouse.

"Hold out your hand, Jonathan requested of Ilene? Ilene didn't know what to expect, but she trusted Jonathan, so she held her hand out.

Jonathan plunked twenty silver dollars into her hand. "Wow, I have never had this much money, Ilene gasped with joy! Need any more ice? Jonathan laughed, "Not until next year!

"Well, I best get back to my work, Ilene suggested. I want to get the hay slacks hauled home, before the weather turns. "We will be there in the morning and help you get the job done, Pete offered. "Yes we will, Jonathan added, as he turned the team around to take Ilene home. "I am so glad God created the two of you, Ilene suggested.

The third morning Pete and Jonathan showed up, it was Pete who jumped down from the wagon with a shout out, "We have a surprise for you Ilene! Ilene was snatched by the hand and taken around to the back of the wagon. Look, two quarters of beef. The two found themselves jumping up and down in celebration. "Let's go put them in your icehouse, Jonathan offered with his laugh. "We have never had that much beef on this farm, alive or processed, Ilene confessed. I may not need the two wether goats I have. By the end of the third day the hay was all hauled in close to the small barn. It was none too soon as the snow started to bluster in. The two wether goats were loaded into the wagon. Twenty silver dollars were forced into Ilene's hand, under great protest. It was a few quick hugs and thanks as Pete and Jonathan hurried off home.

Hard winter brought about an unusual amount of extra work. It was the chopping of ice and snow away from the doors to just them open. It was scooping snow away from the hay to just get it into the barn.

It was many times of hitching Sam up and pulling the wagon sled thru the snow, to keep a path open to the lake for water. The water hole made by Jonathan from Pete's idea was a big help, but still had some ice to be removed. There was even snow to be scooped out of the coral. Then it was the barn cleaning with the wheel barrow. It brought about a great temptation to take mother Alice up on her offering of living with them.

When the family was the three of them, the work load was much easier.

The work load seemed to be lighter when the baby goats started to be born. Maybe it was just the excitement and the standing and watching of them. Maybe it was the skipping of the work and spending time with them. Spring was needed real bad for more reasons, than one. It was an endless stream of twin baby goats. The fifteen nannies had twins and three nannies had triplets. It was quite lopsided with thirty doeling and nine buckling. It was Peter that had insisted in not cutting any of the buckling. More people will want to start herds he thought. Jonathan and Peter owed here two new bucks, so this may be a perfect year to start a new herd. The babies from the four nannies Jonathan had purchased were also hers.

Ilene stood in the midst of her grand herd of goats in early June. It was a contemplating of what she was going to do with some of her goats. The new little nibblers were eating a lot of grass. The other side of the creek was very nice with grass, but that was the winter feed. As she stood there in thought and gaze at the winter feed across the creek, she saw something she had never seen before. It was herd of cattle in a large number moving through the tall grass, eating and trampling it. Without hesitation she quickly wadded across the creek up to her waist. "Get out of here, get out of here, Ilene shouted. That wasn't going to do any good at all, she could see.

.Ilene took her sling out and whirled a stone at the closest animal. It struck the animal in the head, but it just bucked and ran a short distance away. Soon a rider came charging at her on horseback. It bumped her and sent her flying backwards. "Get your cattle out of here, this is my land, Ilene shouted. "I am going to teach you and your goats a lesson, the stranger growled, as he started to dismount. Ilene jumped up and quickly placed a stone from her pocket into the sling. She turned to start running, but only intended to get a short distance away. Whir, whir with a little snap! The stone hit the stranger in the head. He fell like a large rock. Another rider came charging over towards her. Another stone was placed in the sling. "Get your cattle out of here, Ilene shouted! "You killed my boss, the rider shouted back as he leaped from his horse.

The rider bent over the first and then picked him up and pushed him over the horse." If he dies you die, the second rider shouted! The two quickly left, but the herd of cattle continued to munch and trample. She needed more noise to scare them away. The sling was shoved back into her pocket pouch. Without hesitation she quickly waded back across the creek. Then it was a run to the house.It was grabbing Papa's

Winchester and dumping a box of shells into her pocket pouch. The rifle was quickly loaded and she was on a run to the creek. It was wadding across to where the cattle were still munching and munching. There were two more riders back of the herd, doing nothing. Ilene ran towards the herd and fired the Winchester again and again. The cattle quickly turned and started running towards the riders. Ilene quickly reloaded and continued to fire the Winchester. The animals were on a full run down the valley.

The herd was gone for now, but how was she going to keep them out? As Ilene stood there contemplating her problem, Pete came rushing down on his saddle horse. He rode up quickly to Ilene and leaped from his horse. "What's going on, Pete shouted? "Riders and a herd of cattle came into my valley and were destroying my winter grass feed, Ilene chimed almost in tears. Peter offered an arm around Ilene and stood looking at the situation.

"It's more cattle, needing more grass for more greed, Pete confessed! We could build a fence from the bluff to the creek, that's only about one hundred feet. I don't think they will cross the creek and climb up the ridge? "Do I have enough money to buy the fence for this, Ilene asked? "It is not much, so don't concern yourself, Pete replied. There are some good Aspen just there on the other side of the creek, Pete pointed. We will cut about twenty posts and carry them across the creek. It doesn't seem to be too deep, as you are wet only to your waist.

"What do we have here, Pete questioned, as he pointed further down the valley? It looks like a Calvary Troop or Squad? "I think I killed someone, Ilene confessed? They are coming to kill me! Ilene started to take steps backwards. "No one is going to kill anyone, Pete assured! Pete quickly put his arm around Ilene. It is ok; you were just trying to defend your property.

Give me the Winchester, Pete suggested, as he removed it from Ilene's hands. As the troop got close, Pete sounded out, "It's Captain Bates and his troop. The troop came to a halt on the captain's command. "Captain Bates, U.S. command for this territory! Peter Rock, I know you. Who is your friend? "Captain, this Ilene Rasmussen, Pete introduced! I can see your hayfield run down by a herd of cattle from the Smith ranch. It's another hungry cattle rancher running his herd where ever he wants.

The trail boss has a lump on his head and I was told from one of the hands, that you did that? In your words, what happened here Miss?

"Well Sir, Ilene began, I took out my sling out and whirled a stone at the closest animal. It struck the animal in the head, but it just bucked and ran a short distance away. Soon a rider came charging at me on horseback. It bumped me and sent me flying backwards. "Get your cattle out of here, this is my land, I shouted. The man on the horse said, "I am going to teach you and your goats a lesson! He started to dismount, so I jumped up and quickly placed a stone from her pocket into the sling. I started running, but only intended to get a short distance away. I threw a stone at him. The stone hit the man in the head. He fell! Another rider came charging over towards me. I placed another stone in the sling. "Get your cattle out of here, I shouted! "You killed my boss, the rider shouted back at me, as he leaped from his horse. He bent over the first and then picked him up and pushed him over the horse." If he dies you die, he shouted at me! The two quickly left, but the herd of cattle continued to munch and trample. I needed more noise to scare them away. I shoved the sling back into my pocket pouch. I quickly waded back across the creek. Then I ran to the house.

I grabbed Papa's Winchester and dumped a box of shells into my pocket pouch. I quickly loaded the Winchester and I was on a run to the creek.

It was wadding across to where the cattle were still munching and munching.

There were two more riders back of the herd, doing nothing. I ran towards the herd and fired the Winchester again and again. The cattle quickly turned and started running towards the riders. I quickly reloaded and continued to fire the Winchester.

The animals were on a full run down the valley. All the shots were into the air and not at the cattle or the riders.

"Where are your parents, Captain Bates requested? Ilene stared at the ground. "Captain, Ilene's parents died from Influenza last fall, Pete informed! Ilene's Papa was a captain in the union army. He homesteaded this one hundred sixty acre farm, when he left the army. It's only Ilene at age thirteen trying to make a living on this farm and stay close to the memories of her parents. "Good God, Captain Bates shouted! Restitution! Do you know where your boundaries are? "I believe I do Sir, Pete replied! It's the entire valley, from the lake south to the end of the valley. We did the survey, for our purchase and building of the trading store. It then went from this ridge on the east to the river on the back side of the ridge on the west.

"I will see that the Smith ranch puts a fence in at the end of this valley. It will go from the bluff on the east to the ridge on the west. That includes crossing this creek with a fence. They will put a gate on the southeast corner. They will cut and put up the hayfield east of this creek also. Plus one thousand dollars! I am tired of these cattle ranchers doing whatever they want. I will be back here tomorrow to see that they get started. I will be by here ever day to observe the work and that you get your money. Are you in agreement with this Miss? "Yes Sir, Ilene agreed!

"Do you have enough fencing, wire, gates and posts, Peter Rock, Captain Bates asked? "Yes Sir, Pete replied! I think the fence should be woven wire with three strands of barb wire above. It is because of the herd of goats, Ilene has. "Fair enough, Captain Bates agreed, as he turned his troop around to leave.

Captain Bates was a man of his word, showing up the next morning. There was horse drawn hay cutters used the next morning to quickly cut the hay in the meadow valley. A group of workers had the fence put in by sun down.

One thousand dollars was handed to Ilene by Captain Bates. Captain Bates informed Ilene, that the hay had to cure for a day and then it would be put into stacks on the east side of the creek.

He would be back in two days to make sure it was done.

It was two days later when Captain Bates came with his troop. There were a handful of men with another machine drawn by horses. It kicked the hay lying flat on the ground into a row. Then another machine pulled by horses followed over the row of hay and made it climb up to the top, then fall onto a flat wagon. Men with forks stacked the hay on the wagon. The wagon was unhitched from the loader and a new wagon was attached to the hay loader. Horses would be hitched to the flat

65

wagon of hay and haul it to the east side of the creek, where stacks were made. The whole meadow valley was stacked by sun down. It was beyond belief.

All of the equipment, horses and men began to leave, except one riding towards her. He was riding hard at Ilene. A fear came over her as she stumbled backwards. It was a quick finding of the sling and a stone from the leather pocket pouch. It was two swings and near a release, when the rider put both hands into the air, as he finished riding towards her at a slower pace. "Do you want to sell this land, the rider requested? My boss, Mr. Smith requested me to ask you. He will pay you five thousand dollars for this land. That is more than it is worth. "I live here and my parents are buried up on the hill, Ilene informed the rider. Ilene pointed to the top of the ridge beyond the house. I feel, I must live my parents dream and so I shall. My answer is no! "You are young and foolish, the rider shouted! "I am young, but not foolish, Ilene shouted back! I love and fear the lord my God. That is the beginning of wisdom! The rider turned without a sound and hurried after his fellow workers.

Ilene stood there and starred at the nine stacks of hay. Beautiful stacks of hay she thought. She had only every done three stacks and they were not as large. To have that equipment and help made so much difference. Thank you Heavenly Father! Help me to not be foolish!

I am Sixteen

Ilene never knew what day of the week it was or for that fact what time of the day it happened to be. The sun came up and it was chore time. When the sun started to set it was chore time. You just tried to get as much work done between the two jobs. She didn't even know what month it was. It was spring, summer, fall or winter? When it was well into fall and the leaves had fallen, it was her birthday. Now it was also the time when her parents had left her.

The mist had started to pour in off the lake and into the valley. It was like boiling water at times. Pouring in over the creek and working up the hill. Then a bit of frost would start to bite the grass. Ilene found herself standing in the mist feeling the coldness, when a voice called out,"Hello, hello! It sounded like Pete, Ilene thought. "Hello Peter is that you, Ilene called back? "Yes, it is Pete and Jonathan too! "We are near you, but we can't see you, Pete called out again. Ilene could hear water splashing as a wagon and team were pulling through the creek. Suddenly Pete came out of the mist, just feet away from her. He was leading a small Sam. "It looks like a little Sam, Ilene remarked! "Happy Birthday Ilene, Pete replied! It is only October 4th and not November 20th, but Happy Birthday early. Little Sam is yours. He came from the same mother that Sam came from, so we thought it would be grand for you to have him. His mother will not have any more colts.

"I am leading the team by hand, so I will not run you over, Jonathan called out. There was a tinkle of a chain, but he could not be seen yet. Without much notice the team and Jonathan were standing right beside the two. "We have ten sacks of grain, Jonathan instructed Ilene. I am guessing you want them in the house like before? Early Happy

Birthday, Ilene, Jonathan sounded out with his usual laugh. We will come back on your birthday and bring came. Sweet sixteen, Jonathan shouted! "Sweet sixteen, sweet sixteen, Pete added!

"It seems like every time we come out here, we still owe you, Pete informed Ilene. "So we have the two new Billie's, we owe you. We have the six doe lings from the four nannies. We sold the three Buckling from the nannies. We got a hundred dollars for the three, so that's why we brought the ten sacks of grain. The lumber we have is to build a stall right beside Sam. We have a bunch of leads to tie the goats up and hopefully lead them back home. I have a pasture for them at my place. I am going to keep them. Did you keep three milking like we discussed, Pete asked? "Yes, I have milk coming out of my ears, Ilene laughed. I have even been letting some of the smaller goats drink. "We will leave one of the milking nannies with you for milk, if you like, Jonathan suggested. "Yes, please, Ilene offered with appreciation!

"We have to get these goats home, Jonathan announced. However, we will be back with another surprise, even if it is so thick out here to see. "Happy early birthday, Pete shouted, as the two vanished into the mist. Ilene thought about the couple of short words that made her head dance with thoughts of wonder. "Coming back, Ilene whispered into the mist, as she walked to the small barn to see her new additions. What were those two up to? Ilene found her head guessing at all the possibilities. Was it more early gifts perhaps? October 4th was today? Ilene thought of dropping a bean into a jar to keep track of the days. It made her smile at the idea of knowing what day it was.

"Hello, Little Sam, Ilene offered as she walked into the small barn. Now there was a gate from Sam's stall into Little Sam's stall. Then there was another gate to the goat pen. Now there were thirty-six doe lings, one nanny and two new Billies.

This was the possibility of a lot of goats. A new herd bigger than any the farm had ever seen.

Old Billy and the seventeen nannies were gone, leaving a lot of room. It was a bit sad, but if Jonathan was going to keep them, it felt good.

A bit of work had to be done, but not to get too far away from the house, Ilene pondered. Get vegetables into the root cellar was a good plan.

That job had to be finished. Cutting firewood would be for another day. It was five hundred dollars of credit for the goat herd and she had a new bigger herd. "Happy, happy Ilene sang to herself while she went to the garden with a shovel and wheel barrow. I am almost sixteen!

Two hours had past, before she heard the familiar sound of tingling chains on a wagon and team approaching. The mist had lifted slightly, from a soft breeze. Ilene looked toward the creek and saw the wagon driving under the canopy of mist. She had a load on the wheel barrow, so she headed to the root cellar behind the house. The shovel was added to the load this time and a more brisk push was added for power. The meeting of the three was simultaneous at the side of the house.

"So I have had a lot of excitement in my head for the last few hours, as why you two were coming back, Ilene spouted with joy. "Oh, but isn't it wonderful to have such anticipation, Pete boasted. It's half the fun! "It's a date with the two most handsome fellows in the area, Jonathan offered with a gleam of happiness. "Look at what we have in the wagon, Pete offered with a tone of excitement! New fishing rods and gear, that we started carrying in the trading store. One for each of us! New bait bucket with minnows. There is a tackle box for each of us, with all the best stuff. "The three of us are going to spend this afternoon together fishing, the two announced together, with yips of joy.

No time was wasted for the three of them to find a spot on the lake. "Ok, I see all the items, but I don't know what is in the basket you are carrying Pete, Ilene questioned? "Oh, more surprises, not yet revealed, Pete offered in a smiling, clever look! I will show you in a bit, Pete offered.

"This will be a learning process for all of us, Jonathan admitted. The three were instructing each other and Pete was giving special attention to Ilene.

We are cheaters, Jonathan admitted! Pete and I have been practicing casting a number of times at the trading store. Probably for the last month, since we got this product into the store.

Pete braced his rod in a rock with the line cast out. The basket was opened up and Pete spread a red and white cloth on the ground. "It's a picnic, Pete shouted as he did so. A tasty apple pie baked by my mother.

69

Equally excellent fried chicken, again made by my mother, Pete admitted. Potato salad, by mother of course! Lemonade, made by me, Pete sheepishly shrugged! Pete propped Ilene's rod in some rocks like he had done. Then a plate of potato salad, chicken and mini dill pickles was handed to Ilene. Ilene gave Pete a kiss on the cheek. "You must like me, Pete questioned? "I do, Ilene admitted! "Oh, I do, Jonathan spouted with a laugh! I wish I knew of someone that liked me? Ilene stood up from her eating and walked over to Jonathan and placed a kiss on his cheek. "You like me then, Jonathan announced! "I do, Ilene admitted! "Oh, another I do, Pete laughed!

"We were going to do this on your birthday, Pete confessed. However, we thought it may be too cold, besides it may give us twice the fun to plan another day. Your sixteenth birthday is no going to be forgotten by us! The picnic went with its fishing, eating and banter. I have never had so much fun, Ilene boasted! "Me too, Pete offered! "Me three, Jonathan chimed in! What could be more fun? "I can only think of one more, thing, Pete confessed! Wait, I have another fish, Pete shouted, as he reeled it in. This is not the one more thing! Pete put the fish on the stringer and gave a look at Jonathan. Jonathan reeled his line in and lay his fishing rod down. "Here, let me help you, Ilene, Jonathan offered, as he took Ilene's fishing rod. Just as he took the fishing rod, a fish took hold of Ilene's line. "Oh sure, now there is a fish, Ilene shouted! It's big too, but we will just say it is yours, Jonathan laughed! The fish was landed and added to the stringer.

Ilene watched with excitement and laughs of joy. Ilene turned around and saw Pete on one knee with a small box in his hand.

"Are you hurt Pete, Ilene questioned? "No, Pete offered! "Then rise up and live, Ilene suggested. "In a minute, Pete offered! "I love you Ilene! Will you marry me? Ilene stood starring at Pete. "I will marry you Peter, Ilene replied very sober. There were tears of surprise and joy coming from Ilene. Peter stood up and offered Ilene a kiss, of everlasting hope and joy. A hug pursued for a lasting moment. This was the one more thing to make this day better, Pete admitted! Jonathan came over and hugged the two together. "I am so happy, Jonathan admitted! The two best people I know and love.

Will I Live One More Time

The next two weeks were fun for Pete and Ilene, as they saw each other almost every day. Of course it thrilled Ilene with the idea, which they would build a home up on the hill overlooking the valley. A new barn was planned upon the top of the hill also. A bridge would be built over the creek to access the town more easily. The trading store needed all the hands it could get to operate.

When the snow came, the mist would dissolve from the valley. Winter warned of the time of change coming. Ilene recognized the changes of the creek each day, as she now had to tie her rope to the bucket and toss it out into the creek to fetch a bucket of water. The thin ice near the edges made it impossible for the goats, Sam and Little Sam to reach the water safely. Ilene found it a blessing that the stock didn't drink as much in the winter. Another blessing is when Peter came over to help with the chores.

Ilene's senses were in so much thought of her coming sixteenth birthday and Peter's visits, that there seemed to be no other concerns. Work still had to be done each and every day. The mist of the day never came, but the snow storm offered its appearance in replacement of it. Ilene thought the barn should be quickly cleaned before it became more difficult. Sam was let out of his stall and into the coral. The wheel barrow was placed by the door and the cleaning was quickly under way. Suddenly there was a squeal from Sam. Ilene turned slightly to see what she might be able to see. Sam came slamming into the stall out of the white out of snow. Ilene went crushing into the front of the stall. Her head and shoulder were slammed into the manger. The fork handle broke off, thrusting a broken piece into her thigh.The pain was intense, as she fell to the ground. Her last thought was seeing Sam turn and rear into the air, just outside of the door to the stall. Ilene lay there for an unknown amount of time. It was only one eye opening to see what was going on. The other eye wouldn't open. The one eye saw a lion lying on the ground about eight or ten feet away. The lion lay starring back at her with a mouthing snarl, but no sound came from it.

Ilene burst into a sense of fear, with her heart rate beating out of her chest. She grabbed at the side of the stall with one hand as to attempt to stand up. It was a dizzying futile attempt. One arm, one leg and one eye were surly lacking what was needed. The lion made no attempt of movement at seeing here struggle. Even the one eye sight of that gave no comfort to Ilene. It was going to be an inch by inch effort to get up.

Little Sam and the goats may have been terrified at some point, but now they were very calm. After several minutes, Ilene got her one good leg under her. There was no clue as what to do about the piece of handle sticking thru her leg. Half of her body was throbbing with pain from her head to her foot. She had to get to the house or freeze is the entirety of what she was thinking.

The lion continued to stare at her and mimic a snarl with no sound. The problem was that the lion lay just outside the door. She had to go very close to get by the animal. There was just no way for her to go thru Little Sam's stall and then out thru the goat door. The goat door was locked from the outside anyway. With a great effort Ilene balanced herself as she attempted to pick up what was left of the broken fork. The second attempt retrieved the foreshorten fork. It now was about three feet long, rather than the original five feet. It was a little better to help balance here broken body.

The balancing was not clearly on her mind however it was protection to pass by the lion. The small one inch hops towards the lion made her head go swimming in a dizzying torrid of pain. The lions paw moved ever so slightly, as Ilene made another attempt at hopping toward

the doorway and the lion. Ilene made an attempt for a better look with her good eye, with a slight tilting of her head. Her dizziness made her unsure of what she might be seeing. As she finally reached the doorway, she starred down at the lion. Whatever had happened, the lion was just laying there and still starring at her. It had not moved its head

72

in anyway. It was severely injured from something that had happened between Sam and it. Ilene raised the fork up and thrust it into the chest of the lion, just behind the left leg. A one hand thrust wasn't a lot, but with a little more pressing of the one hand and a balancing against the door jamb was enough to place the fork deep into the lion.

Ilene hopped around the lion and leaned against the coral fence. She couldn't move the lion or shut the door of the barn. It was a one inch by one inch hop to get along the coral fence to the gate. Sam couldn't be seen anywhere. There was a top portion of the coral fence broken at the far end of the coral. Sam must have tried to jump over, but made more of a plowing thru it instead. Once she was out of the coral she could continue her inch by inch movement along the fence and back to the outside of the small barn end. The harness box on the end of the barn was soon approached. Was there anything in it to help her get to the house, she questioned in her head? Just to have a look took every capability she had to look. The door cover was finally opened to reveal the walking stick, which her Papa had given her. The smooth hickory stick of about five feet was a welcoming sight. Emotionally more than physically!

The walking stick was used to help stabilize her awkwardness. The lid was let to gravity and bangs itself shut. Ilene used the side of the barn and the walking stick to move inch by inch along the barn. Finally she reached the end of the barn and was left starring at the fifty feet to the house. There was nothing left to support against. The blowing snow and wind were now more evident. Ilene gritted her teeth to fight against the wind and it wanting to just blow her over.

The pain was about to knock her over, now the wind and snow wanted their share. "Peter, Peter, Ilene whispered threw her gritted teeth!

"Father in Heaven, where is my help now, Ilene whispered threw her clenched teeth? It was eternity to reach the side of the house. It blocked the wind and snow, offering some reprieve. It was along the side to the front of the house. Then the door was finally opened. A few more hops and she was inside the house. "Now what, she questioned verbally? Over to Mama's chair by the fireplace, she thought. With the assistance of the walking stick she was able to pick up a few pieces of wood and drop them into the fire. Dizziness and nausea seemed to be gripping her

73

with a rush. It was a slow attempt to sit into the chair, but the result was gravity pulling her down harder than expected.

"How can I get this piece of wood out of my leg, Ilene whispered to herself? It's a storm out there. Peter, can you come please? Father in heaven, have mercy! Then no thoughts came any more.

Pete and Jonathan stood talking and starring out a window in the cozy trading store. "There is sure nothing going on today, Pete offered. "Before or after a snow storm, Jonathan replied with the obvious. Suddenly a horse came walking into sight in front of the Trading store. "A horse, no saddle or rider, Jonathan questioned? Pete quickly got dressed and stepped outside to lay a hold on the horse, before it could continue on. "Jonathan, it's Sam, Pete yelled back at the friend standing in the doorway! "Throw a saddle on Sam and go out to see Ilene, Jonathan yelled into the wind! The two grabbed a hold onto the bridle and quickly moved around to the back of the store.

"What are these cuts, Pete yelled into the wind towards Jonathan? Are these cuts barb wire? Jonathan walked over to Pete to see what he was talking about. "There is a scrap on one leg, Jonathan suggested. These cuts on the neck and rump look more like an animal. They are perhaps from a lion. Get your horse Pete and leave Sam in a stall. Pete soon had his horse ready to go. Jonathan had just arrived and had not unsaddled his horse in the stall of the barn. Jonathan led his horse to the back door and yelled into the Trading store, "Alice we are going to check on Ilene!

There was an ok, as Jonathan slammed the door shut. The two were riding close as they made their way through the woods and down to the gate at the end of the valley. The gate had been deliberately propped open for there was no need to close it in the winter time. It was a slow movement along the fence to the creek. It was a treacherous crossing of the creek and then a blinding movement forward towards where the house should be. A movement along the creek, but hopefully not riding into it. A direct ride into the Northerly wind was like having their faces bit.

The house was located and the horses were securely tied, so as not to be lost in the driving wind. Jonathan started to knock on the door, but Pete pushed on by with a shove into the door, as he was in a great hurry.

Snow was quickly brushed away, as Pete began sounding out, "Ilene, Ilene? Ilene was in sight, even before the words had dropped. It was more of Ilene sitting in a chair and not moving.

Pete was ready to offer a hugging motion, but Jonathan grabbed Pete by the shoulder with a loud suggestion of, "Careful, careful! Let me check for a pulse! Jonathan placed his finger to the side of Ilene's neck. Nothing, Jonathan announced! "Sweet Jesus, Pete yelled! "Hold on, Jonathan offered quickly! She is still warm. Jonathan slowly opened the front of Ilene's coat. He carefully put his head to Ilene's chest to listen for a heartbeat. She has a heartbeat, Jonathan offered! Ilene has a piece of wood thru her leg and her face is all bloody. Her left arm may be out of its socket? We need your mother here fast, Pete. Pete you go get your mother as quick as you can. I am going to the lake and get water. We need to heat up some water. Tell your mother what we can see. Tell her we think that Ilene has lost a lot of blood.

Pete was out the door, before the," Be careful, from Jonathan could really be heard. Jonathan began to stoke up the fire. "We need your mercy here and now Father in Heaven, Jonathan requested as he built up the fire? Jonathan grabbed a bucket, which had water in it. He poured it into a large empty pot hanging in the fireplace. Then he quickly left the house to get the wagon sled.

He quickly located the wagon sled with the water barrel still on it, beside the wood pile. The barrel was empty for obvious reasons. It would be frozen up in a short time. It was still on its wheels and not on its runners. An ax was planted into a large wood round beside the wagon sled. Jonathan walked around the wagon sled with the ax and tapped on each wheel to see that it was not frozen down. "No time to harness up, Jonathan whispered to himself. The ax and the bucket went into the wagon sled and he tied a rope on the hitch, then onto the saddle horn. It was an easy move, but what about water in the barrel he wondered?

It wasn't easy finding his new invention of ice blocks and water hole on the lake. Once he found it and removed the pine branches, goat skin, boards, it only had a thin coat of ice in the hole. "Nice, Jonathan whispered to himself! Jonathan decided to only get a half barrel of water and covered his invention back up. The half barrel of water moved easier than he thought it would. Going back to the house was easier than before. The blowing wind and snow seemed to coax him back to the house. Jonathan quickly tied his horse to the south side of the house. Then it was water into the house and the filling of the big pot. The fire was stoked up again to hurry the warming of the pot of water.

Pete and his mother Alice were not there yet. Jonathan was at a loss as what to do next. He would search for some cloths to clean and perhaps some bandages, he instructed himself. A short piece of rope for a tourniquet was something he had seen Alice do before. The piece of wood thru the leg was fairly high in the thigh, but there was just enough room to get his tourniquet tied in place. There was absolutely no sound or movement from Ilene, as Jonathan did what he thought he could do. "Why don't you have anything on her head, Jonathan whispered to himself? Jonathan scooped up a bowl of cool water to start cleaning some blood from Ilene's face. It only took a few wipes before the water looked like all blood. The long blonde hair was totally matted with blood. It seemed to be hard matted on an area of her head, so he thought it was good to leave that part to help keep it from more bleeding.

The quietness of the small house was suddenly split with noise of Pete and Alice bursting into the room. "Let me see, let me see, Mother Alice requested? Open the saddle bags and get all the stuff out on the table, Mother Alice calmly requested? Give me the scissors? We need to cut this coat back and then the pants. Assist me, but don't pull on anything. Nice tourniquet, Jonathan! Thank you Alice, Jonathan whispered! I was not sure what to do? Severe bleeding in the limbs needs a tourniquet as soon as possible. You will bleed to death in a short time. Other body parts need pressure. Cleaning around this head wound and leaving the very matted part untouched was a good idea. We will leave this tourniquet on, until we get this wood out of her thigh. What is this, a fork handle, Mother Alice questioned?

"It looks like it could be, Pete replied. Good thing Ilene is unconscious, because this looks painful! "Maybe, Mother Alice suggested! "Maybe, Pete questioned? "She has lost a lot of blood, Mother Alice stated the obvious! I think I would be happier if she was awake and yelling. It looks like this piece of wood went into the leg from the outside, so we will take it out in the same direction. Cut me about ten pieces of that bandage wrap. Make them about three feet long. Open one of the bottles of Carbolic acid. Fold the wraps back and forth over it, so they are about four inches long. The piece of wood should be checked for slivers before pulling it through. Then put Carbolic acid on it to help prevent infection. Then we pull it out slowly, like this, Mother Alice instructed as she did so. Carbolic acid is then poured on either side like this, and then you pack each side like this, Mother Alice demonstrated. Ilene gave not a peep or movement. Then you can wrap the wound with the bandage several times fairly snug, but not too tight.

"This left shoulder is out of place a bit, Mother Alice pointed out. Let's cut this shirt off, so I can pull this arm back into place. Pete, you can hold Ilene by the arm and chest, like this, Mother Alice demonstrated on Pete. Hold her back firm in the chair, so I can give a good pull on the arm. "Wait, Ilene is naked, Pete protested! "Let's see, naked or dead, Mother Alice offered sharply! You fight for this girl! You are going to marry her in a few months.

Pete quickly moved around behind Ilene and wrapped his arms around from behind with a firm hold. Mother Alice moved the arm slightly and gave it a steady pull. A slight pop was offered from the shoulder. That was an easy one, Mother Alice proclaimed. Give me one of the slings from the table, so we can give this arm some support.

"It is going to be easier to clean this head wound if the hair is not so long, Mother Alice instructed. I know you said, Pete, that Ilene has had this long hair since she was little. You make the call to cut it Pete? "Better short, until it heals, Pete whispered. Sorry Ilene! The hair was slowly cut for need and respect. At least I am the one to cut it, Pete offered in an apologetic manner. "Ok, I will slowly clean this and put some carbolic acid on it, when I am done, Mother Alice instructed.

"I rode Sam out here, Mother Alice informed Jonathan. There is some antibiotic suave there on the table. Put Sam in his stall and apply that to all his cuts. "I will go out and check the barn, before I do that, Jonathan suggested. Jonathan bundled up and went around the house, then the barn, then the tall fence to the coral gate. Jonathan didn't see anything until he stepped on the cougar with the fork stuck into it. "Whoa, whoa, Jonathan shouted in surprise!

Jonathan went by the Cougar and into the barn. There was little Sam munching his hay. Goats were eating hay or lying down. They all were calm with no awareness of the Cougar of any kind. Jonathan went to stand by the Cougar again. "Well, Mister Cougar, you have caused considerable problems, Jonathan informed the Cougar. I will get my horse and rope and give you a pull out to the woods. It was back to the house and to inform the others as to what he had to do.

The silence in the small house was broken again, as Jonathan burst into the house quickly. "There is a Cougar with a fork plunged thru it lying by the barn door, Jonathan informed Pete and Mother Alice. I have to drag it out to the woods. "Yes, you do, but not until the blowing snow goes down, Mother Alice instructed. I didn't even think we could find our way over here a bit ago. Just drag it out of the way for now.

Get Sam in his stall and apply that suave. Is there enough room for the other two horses? "I will put the other two in the small lean, Pete instructed.

"Lay that sheet I brought down on the bed, with the blankets folded back, Mother Alice instructed. I wanted to make sure we had very clean surfaces. Then carefully pick up Ilene and lay her down over there. We will stay here until the storm goes down. We will see what tomorrow brings. Doctor Johnson is too far away to get Ilene too. Its twenty miles to his office and then he might be in another town. I don't think Ilene could do a rough ride like that. "Well mother we are glad you can doctor us, Pete offered enthusiastically.

Jonathan and Pete picked up Ilene carefully to move her over to the bed. "Ilene is a little naked, Pete informed Jonathan of the obvious. "She is almost your wife, Jonathan replied with a smile. You are a lucky guy! "She is such a sweet pretty thing, I hate to see her like this, Pete confessed. It brings tears to my eyes, Jonathan!

The horses were unsaddled and the saddles were brought into the house. The small lean was just perfect for a couple of horses. Pete and Jonathan latched a hold on the cougar and drug it out away from the small barn. It didn't look like there was any evidence of the cougar, but Sam showed some disagreement of that when Jonathan tried to bring him back into his stall. Jonathan had to tie Sam to a post inside the stall to keep him in the stall. Suave was applied to his cuts on his neck and rump. "Sorry old boy for your ordeal, Jonathan calmly spoke to Sam. You may be the very reason that Ilene lives or dies. Sorry to say that it goes both ways, but you may well be the reason she is broken up. You may also be the reason that the cougar didn't eat her too. The idea of Ilene not making it doesn't make me care for you any less. Jonathan gave Sam a hug as he had done many times before. I can feel you shaking Sam. You can still smell the cougar, can't you?

Jonathan's moment was quickly interrupted, as the small hay filling door was popped open to put the hay into the bunks. Jonathan left to carry water from the barrel he had went to the lake earlier. It was his unspoken hope that there would be enough water in the barrel for tonight. It appeared to be so as the chores progressed.

The chickens were the last, as Pete seemed a bit short of where to gather the eggs into, so they just went into his pockets. It was a careful walk back to the house to preserve them.

With the eggs unloaded into a wire basket on the table, Pete walked over to the end of the bed where Ilene was lying. Mother Alice was sitting in a chair beside the bed near Ilene's head. "Any success, Pete asked? "Not a movement or a peep, Mother Alice replied. She is breathing steady and seems to be comfortable. Thank God for that!

"Thank God, Pete protested! "Absolutely, Mother Alice snapped back! "She could have died from this and still may, Pete inserted! "Peter, Peter, you should know better, Mother Alice insisted! I don't know everything that happened here, but that cougar could have eaten Ilene. Most of this looks like Sam probably caused this, but it also looks like Sam resolved most of this. It Sam hadn't gone all the way to the trading store, we wouldn't have come over here to help.

"Ilene doesn't look like the same person at all, Pete confessed. "You two committed to each other into marriage, so that is the way it is going to be, Mother Alice insisted. For better or for worse! She was fighting for you, when you fell into the lake. She was the one that got a hold on you, to get you pulled out. "Of course, of course, Pete offered in defense! I just meant Ilene looks like she has really gone through it. I feel so bad for the state she is in. She really is better off sleeping or being unconscious, right? Because of the pain she will have right?

"Perhaps, Mother Alice offered! I have some soup cooking for supper. It has a nice broth in it. We need to get some of that into her. She has a lot of blood that needs to be replaced. Dehydration and such! We will keep it on the fire and wait until she wakes up. You two go ahead and eat. There is a loaf of bread on the table from home.

When the wind goes down, Jonathan and I will get back to the trading store. You will just stay here and look after Ilene. There is plenty of carbolic acid, wraps and suave. Did you two remember to milk the one nanny she has? "Oh no, Pete replied! Grabbing his outer clothes quickly, while Jonathan lit a lantern from a shelf.

"Here is a bucket and a lantern, Jonathan offered with a big grin. Pete rushed out the door into the blowing snow, as he mumbled, "How does Ilene do all this morning and night?

It was a fair amount of time when Pete finally came stumbling back into the house. "Look baby sister, your man is in from doing the chores, Jonathan shouted out. Pete quickly placed the milk bucket and the lantern on the table and went over to see Ilene. "Ilene, you are awake Pete questioned? "Yes, Peter, Ilene offered in a soft voice. Peter offered a quick kiss, as he knelt down on the floor beside the bed. Ilene's good hand was slightly out from under the blanket, so Peter clasped a hold on it. The action of lifting the hand and arm brought a bit of a draft to Ilene. "Oh, a bit of a draft, Ilene softly protested! I seem to be a bit naked under here. "Sorry, Peter apologized! He quickly placed the arm under the blanket and tucked it in.

"Well, I guess you have seen me then, so no surprises on our wedding day then, Ilene offered in a tease.

"How, are you feeling, Peter asked? "My leg feels the worse, Ilene confessed! My head hurts, but I can see out of both eyes. My arm hurt more before I came into the house. Mother Alice told me she had to put it back into the socket. I thank god for you all! "Hear that Pete, Mother Alice broke in! Lets' get Ilene propped up and you can help her eat some of this broth.Pete placed another pillow behind Ilene to help her sit up a bit for the ease of eating some broth and perhaps a bit of soup.

The blanket on her seemed to slide down a bit, offering a bit of private moment. I will pull the blanket up a bit more, Pete offered. "Thanks Peter, Ilene whispered. I love you Peter! Peter slowly fed the soup to Ilene. "This may sound silly, but this feels romantic, Pete offered with a smile.

Everyone found a place to settle in for the night with hopes of getting some sleep. Pete chose a place beside Ilene, even if it was on top of the blankets. It was not a bad choice, as Ilene made a request of, "Kiss me good-night? "Of course and every night I am near you, Pete offered in agreement! "I am overwhelmed with emotion for some reason, Ilene whispered to Pete. I thought I was going to die a few times during all of this. Then I passed out or went into and unconscious state. I didn't know what was going on during that time.

"When Sam came running into the stall and crushed me against the front of the stall, I had so much pain and not a clue as why he did it, Ilene confessed. It must have knocked me out for a bit, how long I don't know? Then I opened my eyes, or at least one of my eyes. I lay there starring into the eyes of the lion. It kept opening its mouth and snarling at me, but no sound came out. I waited for it to jump on me, but it couldn't move a muscle. I struggled to stand up, which seemed almost impossible. I had to get by the lion to get to the house somehow? I took the broken fork and slowly hopped towards the lion, while it tried to snarl, but couldn't. I was about one foot away from it as I passed thru the doorway. With my one good hand I stabbed the lion right behind its left leg, into its chest.

I hopped on by it, feeling sorry for it. It took me a long, long time to hop to the house. I collapse into Mama's chair and the last thing I remember was thinking I was going to join Papa and mama. Peter, can you hold my hand until I fall asleep? "Yes dear, I surely can, Peter offered!

The next morning Mother Alice and Jonathan had to get back to the trading store, but Pete was going to stay with Ilene until she was better. May be longer? "Peter, give Ilene the privacy she needs, Mother Alice advised! "Yes mother, Pete responded! Pete didn't really know what his mother was instructing him to do. "Place a warm wash basin beside the bed for Ilene to wash up as you go out to do the chores. Keep on using the carbolic acid and suave twice a day, Mother Alice instructed. If you get a smell from the leg, come get me right away. If Ilene is feverish and has sweats, pack her in some ice.

Pete repaired the coral so that the horses and goats could get outside. It also made it easier to clean the small barn. Pete wanted to do the best job he could, because these animals were Ilene's. Going to the lake and hauling enough water back seemed to be a great feat to Pete. "How did Ilene get this done, before she had Sam, Pete found himself asking several times out loud? Her explanation was using old Billy to pull a small sled with the barrel partly filled. It was maybe only a third full? The stock was locked up at night for their safety.

Well Enough to Bathe

It was the day before Ilene's sixteenth birthday, when Pete got up a little earlier. The chores were done, except for going to get the water. Pete was anxious as he brought the milk in one bucket and the eggs in another back to the house. He quickly entered the house and found Ilene washing her hair by the table, as naked as one could get. Her hair was totally soaped and she was caught by surprise. "Oh, oh, Ilene shouted, as she hopped backwards on one foot and came to a sudden seating position as she bumped the back of her legs into it. "It's Pete, sorry, I have eggs and milk, Pete quickly advised Ilene.

Pete quickly sat the items down on the table. Pete quickly grabbed a towel from the table and placed it around Ilene's shoulders. "I wanted to wash my hair and take a bit of a bath today, Ilene instructed. I think I jammed my leg. Is it ok? Pete grabbed a cloth and patted the wound dry. "It looks ok, Pete advised! He touched the leg and looked more closely. "I am so naked, Ilene responded! Pete kissed Ilene's soapy cheek. You are so beautiful and so sweet! I have seen all of you and I should know. Let me help you finish washing your hair. "Ok, Ilene agreed!

Pete helped Ilene up with anticipation of helping with the washing of the hair. It was a complete surprise when the soapy hair Ilene dropped her towel and planted a passionate kiss on Pete. I love you Peter, Ilene whispered! I couldn't be happier! "I am a bit excited, but I have truly loved you from the moment I saw you three years ago, Pete replied! Ilene was washed and dried. "There is my mother's blue dress in that corner closet, if you want to get it for me, Ilene requested? There are some under clothes in a crate on the floor of the closet, if you want to reach them for me? The bra is a bit tight, but it will have to do. I will not be able to wear a shirt until I get my arm out of this sling. The Levis you got for me will have to wait until this leg is quite mended. I need you to help me get dresses too! "Of course, Pete offered!

"We can take this sling off for a bit, so we can get you dressed, Pete offered the suggestion. I think keeping the sling on helps keep you from using the arm until it is ready? How is your leg now? "Fine I think, Ilene replied? "Well, here is a surprise for your birthday, Pete offered. A couple of days ago, when Jonathan was here, he brought a new coat, scarf and mittens, because yours became lost and well cut up by me. Pete handed a brown paper wrapped package to Ilene as she sat on the edge of the bed. Pete held the brown package steady, while Ilene used her one good hand to open the gift.

"Mother made Jonathan stand back while I helped her work on you. I cut your coat off. I cut your shirt off and I cut your Levies off. Then I cut your hair because it was so dried up with blood. We had to see your injuries as soon as we could to help you. My marrying you had a lot to do with it all. I could see you, but Jonathan could not out of respect. Ilene took a hold on Pete's hand and placed it on her breast. "Feel my heart and know how happy I am, Ilene requested? I wondered about what to use for a coat the other day? I knew my coat had to be cut.

"If you feel up to it, mother wants to give you a birthday party tomorrow at the Trading store, Pete instructed? You can ride Sam and I will lead him over there. "Pain or no pain I wouldn't miss that for the world, Ilene expressed with a smile. Help me up, so I can try this coat on, Ilene requested? It is a beautiful blue coat. I just love the look. Button it up for me please? Pete began to button the coat, but had a problem in the chest area. "Crazy breasts, Ilene blurted out!

Why so much? Why so big? "Feed babies and look sexy for your husband, Pete offered with a laugh! "Well, if they keep growing, I may tip over, Ilene offered with a laugh back and a light push back on Pete! "You can wear it over to the store and see if there is one that fits better, Pete suggested. Mother can help with that.

The next morning after chores were done, Sam was saddled and the two prepared to leave for the Trading store. "Loving you Peter, makes me brave, Ilene confessed, as Pete helped Ilene up on Sam. I was scared the first time I left the valley, but it was for you Peter. It was the idea of losing you from the drowning incident. It still gives me a chill. Today I am not scared, because I am with you. happy to be with you, more than for my birthday. Does something become fearful, just because you have not done it before? May be its just me?

"It sure is a nice day, Peter proclaimed. November 25th, 1895 is your birthday, Miss Ilene. You have been alive for sixteen years. Pete talked on as he led Sam along the creek. The snow is a bit squishy as it warms up. Perhaps the snow will melt away? "We will have to be careful and watch for ice melt on the lake, where we get the water from, Ilene suggested. "I agree, if it stays warm, Pete replied.

"Who is the president, Ilene requested out of the blue? "It's Grover Cleveland, Pete offered with a smile. Why do you ask, Pete inquired? Papa use to talk about who was president quite often, Ilene instructed. Rutherford B. Hayes was president when I was born. James A. Garfield was president in 1881. That's all that I know, but Papa told me it was very important to know who the president is. They are the leaders of this country. I would like to know what is going on out there, Ilene offered, as she pointed to the unknown with her good hand. I suppose you have to know a lot to take care of the Trading store? "I am learning all the time, but it is my mother that is really smart, Pete confessed. I don't know what I would do without my mother? She is everything to me! I feel really bad that both of your parents are gone, Ilene.

"Thanks for your compassion, Ilene replied. It has been two years and some, but I sometimes miss them like it's only been yesterday.

I am so glad we are staying in the valley when we get married in a couple of months. I wish we were getting married today, Ilene offered with a smile, as Pete looked back over his shoulder. Love you Peter! "Double that love for you my dear, Pete responded! "My dear, my dear, Ilene sounded out! It gives me Goosebumps!

"We have a coral behind the Trading store, Pete sounded out as the two approached the store. It is a good thing to let Sam have some hay and water while we are here. It's nice out, so I think I will just throw the saddle over the fence rail. I am going to let you off at the back door of the store, Pete instructed as he stopped Sam by the door. Wait right here while I put Sam in the coral, Pete suggested, as he helped Ilene off the horse. It will take but a minute to get Sam situated.

Ilene leaned against the log store, as she watched Pete unsaddle Sam. Remove the bridle and lay it over the saddle. Ilene observed four horses in the coral. One was Pete's, one Jonathans and the other two were unknown to her. "I know two of the horses in the coral, but who do the other two belong to, Ilene asked, as Pete came walking close? "The other two horses are being boarded here, Pete replied. We get twenty-five cents a day to board a horse, if we keep it longer than a week. Otherwise we get thirty-five cents a day. Most of the time people just board for a day or two. We have two extra rooms to board for people. There will be three rooms to rent, when we get married. That should make mother happy, Pete offered with a laugh. Pete scooped Ilene up in his arms and offered a kiss, as they went through the door into the store.

"Mother, mother, Pete called out as he carried Ilene towards the store front? "In the store Pete, Mother Alice shouted out! "Happy Birthday daughter to be of mine, Mother Alice boasted with pride! Mother Alice came over to offer a hug to the two standing in front of the fireplace. Happy Thanksgiving too, as tomorrow is Thanksgiving! "Thank you, Ilene replied! Happy Thanksgiving to you too! I got some Goosebumps from the idea of being your daughter.

Another hug please, Ilene coaxed as she hopped on one foot? This hug feels so wonderful; don't let me go, Ilene laughed. "Let's get you set up here in this chair by the fireplace, Mother Alice insisted.

"We are celebrating Thanksgiving today, along with your birthday, if that is ok, Mother Alice requested? "Very nice, Ilene agreed! We always called Thanksgiving, Prayer Day! Our celebration was praying around our table.

Each of us would offer a thanks or prayer. We would rotate around the table until each of us had seven prayers. "Let me help you off with your coat. "It is a lovely gift, but may I make a request, Ilene whispered? "Yes dear, what is it, Mother Alice asked? "Ooh, the dear sound, gives me Goosebumps, Ilene stated! It's a lovely warm sound! My breasts are too large for this coat! "Right to the point, Mother Alice reflected with a smile! I guess you just have matured quicker than most. Mother Alice took the coat and hurried away to the far end of the store.

"Let's get you off your leg and sitting for a while, Pete suggested, as he helped Ilene to sit down. Now we can have a cup of coffee, Pete suggested as he walked over to a coffee pot sitting on top of a wood stove at the other end of the store. "Yes please and thank you, Ilene offered as Pete walked on. Mother Alice came popping back from her disappearance in the store. "I have something that I think will work, Mother Alice spout out as she quickly approached Ilene. It's red though, she questioned? It has a couple of embroidered flowers on it too. "It's a lovely coat, Ilene suggested as she struggled to get up. Mother Alice helped Ilene to get the coat on. Can you button it for me please? "Oh, it's going to fit just dandy and you will look so smart too, Mother Alice confessed. "Smart, Ilene questioned? "Beautiful is a better word, Mother Alice revised. "Too beautiful to wear out to do work, Ilene questioned? "No, not at all, Mother Alice suggested! I have leather, but it is not as warm. "Thank you so much for the red one with flowers, Ilene offered. I prefer warm! Is it ok to trade? "It is quite ok to trade, Mother Alice suggested. If it doesn't fit, it's no good to you.

"Come over to the counter and take a look at what I tried to do, mother Alice coaxed Ilene with a slight tug on her sleeve. It is a three tier birthday cake, which

I know is quite unusual. I wanted to have a practice shot at your wedding cake, so I thought I would try it out for your birthday. I got the three tiers only because in my mind a wedding cake should be three layers high. I wish it could be even grander, but my talent has limits. "I think it is wonderful, Ilene offered with a smile. I never even thought about having any wedding cake.

Mama tried to make me a birthday cake a few years ago, but it ended up having a biter frosting of cocoa on it. We ate it and we laughed. You are so sweet Mother Alice!

"Here is a coffee if you like, Pete offered on his return from the other end of the store. Pete handed one coffee to his mother and then offered a hand to Ilene for sitting down, before giving the second coffee to her. "The coffee smells so good, Ilene offered, as Pete walked back to get one for himself. What is the other lovely smell, I detect? "The turkey I am sure, Mother Alice suggested. Jonathan went out hunting and got us a turkey for our supper. He is upstairs getting cleaned up. Would you like a lovely bath and a soak for your leg, when he is done? "Well, Pete helped me with a sort of bath yesterday, Ilene confessed.

"Helped you with a bath, Mother Alice asked with a surprise? To the point again, my dear! "I was washing my hair by the table, when Peter came in from doing chores, Ilene explained. "Oh, washing your hair, Mother Alice offered calmly? "Well, I was totally naked and my hair was all soapy, Ilene added. "Peter, Peter, Mother Alice offered excitedly, as Pete began to sit with his coffee! "I didn't know, Pete offered in defense! I grabbed a towel and put it around her top part. I helped Ilene finish her hair, while she held the towel with her one good hand. I kissed her on her soapy cheek and said I loved her. Besides we will be married in a couple of months?

"You are not married yet, Mother Alice instructed! "Everything is just fine, Pete offered calmly. Ilene is just being taken care of. "Perhaps, Mother Alice suggested! I just want you two married by Preacher Brown, whenever he gets here. A marriage consecrated by God is a union between a man and a woman that is blessed and sanctified by a higher power. It is a sacred covenant with divine participation. It is a signification of commitment made not to just each other,

But also to God, with the expectation of divine guidance and support throughout the marital journey.

"Besides Preacher Brown, may just show up at any day. He knows we want him to marry you two. It is really up to the weather? This time of year is a lot of Christmas requests too.

He can only do so much! The economy has not been good for several years. Perhaps he will want the ten dollars, Mother Alice smiled! He usually gets five dollars, so a ten may put you on the top of the list. Just wait, for me please?

The door of the Trading store suddenly opened with the entrance of a man and a woman carrying various things. "These lovely two are Jonathan's parents, Mother Alice introduced. They farm about a short mile away. Patty and Bo Williams this is Ilene Rasmussen from the valley below. Bo came over to Ilene and kissed her on the forehead. "We know a lot about you from Jonathan, Bo advised. It is so wonderful to finally know you face to face. "Happy Birthday Ilene, Patty offered, as she handed a wrapped gift to Ilene. "I am very happy to know Jonathan's parents, Ilene replied. Jonathan is a dear!

"Thank you so much for the gift, but you surely didn't need to, Ilene professed. May I, Ilene request? "Please go ahead, Patty suggested. Ilene began to un-wrap the small package. "Oh look, it is pictures of Jonathan, Peter, one of Bo, Patty and Jonathan together, Ilene announced with a display of each. Here is one of Peter and Alice together. I didn't know you could do this, Ilene confessed? "They are Cabinet cards in frames, Patty explained. "They are four and a quarter by six and a half in size, Bo further described. They are new to us, but wonderful to have.

"I don't think I can beat that, Jonathan laughed as he came walking into the room. Jonathan handed a gift to Ilene. Open up, Jonathan suggested with another laugh. "I am so surprised, because I never expected gifts; Ilene smiled, with a bit of a red blush coming to her face. The wrapping was soon pulled back with the revelation of a silver coffee pot and six silver cups. This is so grand; I don't think I know how to even use them. "You would make coffee in your regular pot and then pour it into this server. Then pour it into a cup for each guest,

Mother Alice described. "It is something for your new house next summer, Jonathan announced.

"Let's just add to the theme, Mother Alice, offered with a laugh. Another gift was handed to Ilene. Ilene's hands began to shake, as she started to open the gift. "This is starting to be a bit overwhelming, Ilene confessed. I am very proud to say I love you all very much! The package revealed two silver candle sticks and a porcelain basin with a pitcher. "Oh, Mother Alice this is beautiful beyond words, Ilene chimed. "I am glad you like it dear, Mother Alice responded! Mother Alice reached over and kissed Ilene on the cheek. I am going to get the daughter I never had! I am so happy!

"Well Pete, the floor is yours, Jonathan anxiously suggested! Pete bent down on one knee and opened a small box and tilted it towards Ilene.

Ilene, will you marry me, Pete requested? "You know I will, as I have already said yes, Ilene smiled as she opened her arms to Pete for a hug. Pete relied with the hug and a kiss. Pete leaned back and pulled the ring from the small box. The ring was slid onto Ilene's finger. "A perfect fit, Pete announced! "What are the little colored bits, Ilene questioned? "Colored bits, Pete laughed! The clear one is a diamond. The two green ones are Emeralds and the two red ones are Rubies! "So lovely Pete, Ilene whispered, as she looked at the ring very close. Pete slipped the ring on Ilene's hand. Now you can show it off, Pete smiled proudly! Ilene held her hand out for each to look at it very close. "Pete has had this ring for a very long time, Jonathan revealed.

"We don't have enough room for all the food on the table, so we will just line it up on this counter, Mother Alice suggested. Let's carry the kitchen table over here by the fireplace, so Ilene can set here in this better chair. The food was lined up and the furniture was moved around to make it just perfect. I liked the idea of taking turns seven times in thanks or prayers around the table, like Ilene's tradition. So the six each had a turn of thanks or prayer and rotated until each had seven turns. "This is nice, Ilene suggested! I hope we get to do this every year? "Especially in your guy's new house, Jonathan laughed!

There was much discussion about the coming wedding and the building of the new house. The inventive Jonathan offering many ideas of water pumps in the house.

Then it was the sinks, tubs and maybe an indoor outhouse, which brought about many laughs and ideas. It was then a barn for stock, hay and grain. The tuff questions of where the best place in the valley to build really was? The idea of building a bridge across the creek was the real conquest if the house was to be built on the hill. Ideas were written down and sketches were done. It was great fun and all agreed to help build and even buy materials. It all had to end and send everyone home to do chores. The items were packed into bags and placed across Sam with a balance act offered by Ilene on the trip home.

The weather stayed mild in the coming weeks. Ilene improved day by day as she helped with the chores. It was a slow process as she hopped around with her Hickory walking stick. Pete seemed to always have surprises to offer. Ice fishing with their fishing rods, which brought about very good results. Jonathan was even brought in on that. Taking a ride in the wagon sled was a favorite, especially with a new product introduced by Pete, called hot chocolate. It also included going to the Trading store to help Mother Alice with various jobs. There were a couple of snow storms, which made them, hunker down for a few days.

The night time however brought about great temptation of lying in bed and exploring each other. The sweet kisses and caresses were performed by both, but the deep intimacy was held back for the marriage night. It was all they could do at times to complete a stop and contain themselves. The word torture was sometimes confessed!

Robbery

It was just prior to Christmas when Jonathan asked Pete to help clean out the barn and stalls. It had been nice, so it was a good time to get that done. The wagon had to be loaded with the manure and taken out to the field and spread out. The chores were done and a hug with kiss was given to Ilene. Good-bye my sweetness, Pete whispered! Pete went out to saddle Sam and Pete was on his way. The process was sent into reverse as Pete reached the coral at the back of the Trading store. Sam was unsaddled and bridled and put into the coral, while the two began cleaning out the barn. The hours ticked by as the two talked some or worked quietly.

The two were totally unaware of what customers or visitors were passing through the store. People were always coming and going. There were two masked men inside the store. "Give us your money, one demanded! Alice opened the cash drawer and handed forty dollars to the demanders. "A store like this, you have more than that, one thief demanded. We keep our money in the bank, twenty miles away, Alice offered calmly. "You lie, the other thief growled! He rushed behind the counter and shoved Alice aside. The drawer was pulled out for investigation, but nothing was found. Alice pressed against the wall with her hands held up. Her eyes went to the holster with Jonathans' revolver in it. "Take what you want and scat, Alice calmly suggested. "Who else is around, a thief requested? "I am expecting my son and his friend at any time, Alice instructed, as she knew that Pete and Jonathan were out back.

"Maybe they will just find you dead, if you don't come up with some more money, the thief growled at Alice with his revolver pointed at her. "Let's just get out of here the second thief requested? "Not without more money, the first thief demanded. "I am leaving Tim, the second thief instructed as he walked towards the door. The first thief started to follow, but turned quickly as Alice started to put her hands down. The first thief shot Alice for whatever reason of her slight movement. "Why did you shoot her the second thief yelled as he ran for the door?

The gunshot was heard outback. "What's going on, Pete yelled? "I think it came from the front of the store, Jonathan replied! Pete was still in the habit of carrying his Colt and it was out of its holster before the echo could fade. Pete went running to the front of the store; as he threw open the coral gate. "I am right behind you, Jonathan shouted after Pete. Pete went flying around the corner of the store without hesitation. Pete was ready to shoot whatever confronted him.

A shot sounded out and Pete went stumbling backwards, landing at Jonathan's feet. Jonathan quickly snatched the revolver from Pete's hand and fired at the two fleeing thieves. One was masked, but the non-masked one Jonathan recognized as he fired until the Colt was empty. Pete stared up with empty eyes at Jonathan. "Tell Ilene, I am sorry, Pete offered through gasping gurgling breaths! "I will tell her Peter, Jonathan whispered quickly! Pete was gone, as he went limp.

Jonathan quickly scooped Peter up in his arms and prepared to carry him into the store, as Sam went racing behind him. Jonathan turned with tears in his eyes to carry Peter into the store. A glance at the spooked horse showed Sam turning off the wagon trail and down the path to the valley. After a clambering motion to get the door to the store open, Jonathan yelled out, Alice, Alice? Jonathan laid Peter on the floor and shouted out again, Alice, Alice?

It was a slow walk to the counter, as he looked around the store. He started to walk to the stairs in the back of the store to explore the upstairs, when he spotted Alice lying behind the counter.

He rushed over quickly, but the great pool of blood already told the story. "Oh Alice, sweet Alice, not you too, Jonathan whispered! Jonathan felt for a pulse and then a heartbeat, but there was no hope found. Jonathan scooped Alice up and carried her over to lay by Peter.

As Jonathan stood there starring down at the two, the tears became a flood. An uncontrolled sound of sorrow became an angry yell of loss.

93

"Alice, Peter, Jonathan yelled over and over! A future of joy fell into a pit of darkness. The yelling stopped with a great question of what now? "Ilene, Jonathan whispered? Had Sam run all the way to the little house in the valley? It wasn't far away and he knew the way? The two thieves that rode away, he thought he had hit them both with Pete's revolver?

Jonathan ran to the counter and searched behind it, to quickly find his Colt revolver. A quick grab for an extra box of cartridges was next. Then it was out the back door to quickly saddle his horse. Just as soon as he reached the front of the store, he saw Sam and Ilene preparing to open the Trading store door. "Ilene, Ilene Jonathan shouted out! It was too late as she opened the door still looking at him. A slight turn of her head to the inside of the store brought out screams of terror, unbelief and unknown emotions. Jonathan leaped from his horse and ran to the open door. It was a quick hug and a movement of Ilene back out the door of the store. It was too late to save Ilene from what had happened. However there never was any way to save her from this. It was just Jonathan hugging Ilene close and letting her sob against his chest. It was more tears for Jonathan, even if he wanted to be strong in some way for Ilene. The two stood there half leaning against the front of the store for a long time. It was Bo and Patty Williams pulling up in front of the store with their wagon, which brought a tone of reality to the situation.

A half of a wave by each of the new arrivals was dropped short as they realized something was amiss. The two scrambled down quickly from the wagon with a run towards the two as soon as their feet hit the ground. It was a four way hug without words yet even being spoken. After a couple of minutes, Jonathan whispered, "Peter and Alice are gone! "Sweet Jesus, Bo replied!

"Was it a robbery, Patty asked, through tears of surprise? "I have always been afraid of that happening, Bo implied? Do you have any idea of who might have done this, Patty questioned?

Jonathan hesitated in a response. Soon the crying stopped and the three looked at Jonathan without speaking. "Yes, I do, Jonathan finally offered in a quiet voice. Pete was right in front of me as we ran around the corner of the store, right here. Jonathan looked at the ground, where they were now standing and pointed to the blood on the ground. "They

94

still have a troop stationed at Eagle corner, Bo stated! Its twenty miles, but we could be there by dark, unless they are out on some kind of rounds right now?

"I grabbed Pete's Colt and emptied it on the two as they fled away, Jonathan instructed the three. I think I hit them both? Maybe even a couple of times? "We need to get after them right away, Bo insisted! "We need to say our good-byes, Jonathan suggested! "Where, would they want to be buried, Patty asked? "They never talked about it, Jonathan shrugged? "Bury Peter and Alice beside Papa and Mama on the hill, Ilene insisted! The three looked at Ilene and finally all offered a yes, one by one.

"The grave I dug for myself three years ago was never filled in, so it is probably still open, Ilene suggested? Jonathan took a deep breath, then suggested, "Let's say our good-byes and put them in Fathers wagon. Ilene grabbed the front of Jonathan's coat with both hands, "I can't say Good-bye! "I know, Jonathan replied! You and Mother just get up on the seat of the wagon. Father and I will carry the bodies out and put them in the back of the wagon.

Bo and Jonathan carried the bodies of Peter and Alice out of the store and placed them in the back of the wagon. Jonathan grabbed a couple of blankets from a shelf in the store and covered them up. He grabbed a couple of pickaxes and handed them to his father. Then he gathered up a couple of shovels and they went out to the wagon and placed them in an appropriated place. "I will put Sam in the coral, Jonathan suggested. "Is the ice think enough to cross with the wagon?

Bo asked? "Yes, I know where we can cross, Jonathan instructed, as they walked Sam back to the coral. Father, you ride my horse out to the hill and I will drive the wagon. "I can't believe what we are doing, Bo questioned? We all had such a good time just a couple of weeks ago. Christmas is next week and I can't even breathe right now! "I know, Jonathan offered in agreement! Everything I have done for the last fifteen years has been with Pete. It is going to take a long time for this to even sink in. The two began to walk back to the front of the store, when Bo suggested, "We should get after those two as soon as we can? "I know who they are and I think I know where they are at, Jonathan whispered. Don't say a word! You and I will tend to business tomorrow

95

morning after chores. I will stay with Ilene tonight and we will meet at the store tomorrow morning.

Moving along slowly the procession soon found the path and headed down it into the woods. The big oaks were asleep, but had left leaves still falling on the path. A light snow was falling, and the world seemed so perfect. Jonathan concentrated on keeping his precious load in good condition. The wagon was soon among the great pines, and they welcomed them with the wisps of wind moving through their branches. As they rounded the big boulders and saw the small valley open up with a greater amount of snow. The path seemed to get lost every once in a while, and Jonathan had to look out for deeper snow and reestablish his direction. The smell of wood smoke from the small shack was leading them onward as quickly as could be had.

It was over the creek in the shallow spot. The thin ice crushed beneath the weight of horses and wagon. Then it was following along the creek towards the small house. The wagon stopped, as Jonathan whispered, we need the ladder from the side of the house. The ladder was procured and carefully placed in the wagon. Then the small house was passed, it was a quick turn and up the long slope of the hill behind the house. Ilene offered some more tears of unbelief and shock as they climbed the hill towards Papa and Mama's graves.

Luckily the windswept snow on the hill was spares and so the travel continued on to the top. A bit of observation was necessary to locate the graves. Bo tied the horse off to the wagon, as the two gathered up the tools to identify the grave. Snow was scraped away to make the site more identifiable.

The ladder was placed into a grave, which Ilene had originally made for herself. Ilene stood there silently. She reached out her hands for a shovel from Jonathan without saying a word the two exchanged the shovel. Ilene climbed down into the grave and began to throw out the snow, which had drifted into the grave. Jonathan began to chop at the frozen earth that had departed from the grave some three years ago. It was not totally frozen, so it offered some sympathy to the group. The grave was cleared of its snow and it too offered some sympathy, as it had not crumbled in.Jonathan and Bo carried the bodies of their friends to the grave. Each one of the group laid their hands on the heads of their friends and offered short prayers. There were no tears held back at the heart breaking moment. Jonathan went down into the grave and received the two from Bo. He carefully placed them side by side in the snug position. Ilene handed the blankets they had been covered in, to Jonathan. "No dirt on their faces please, Ilene whispered! The ladder was removed and the dirt was slid down the edge of the grave. The frozen pieces were saved until last to fill the hole. Out of respect no one wanted to drop heavy pieces down on their friends.

"God speed my beloved, Ilene offered, as they stood at the now filled in grave! My heart shall be broken, until I see you again! Mother Alice, I shall be your daughter forever!

"Pete and Alice, you will always be my family, Jonathan insisted! May the grace of God be with you!

Patty and Bo stood hand in hand as they recited the 23rd Psalm:

Psalm 23: The Lord is my shepherd; I shall not want. He maketh me to lie down in green pastures: he leadeth me beside the still waters. He restoreth my soul: he leadeth me in the paths of righteousness for his name's sake.

Yea, though I walk through the valley of the shadow of death, I will fear no evil: for thou art with me; thy rod and thy staff they comfort me. Thou preparest a table before me in the presence of mine enemies: thou anointest my head with oil; my cup runneth over. Surely goodness and mercy shall follow me all the days of my life: and I will dwell in the house of the LORD forever.

Ilene found herself reflecting back to Papa and his favorite bible verse that he carried with him through the Civil War. At the end of the 23rd psalm, Ilene whispered the last bit: Surely goodness and mercy shall follow me all the days of my life: and I will dwell in the house of the LORD forever.

It was quite a long time standing by the graves. The thoughts and numbness were finally encouraged away by Bo and Patty. It was a hugging moment in the back of the wagon as the three sat in the end gate section, while Jonathan drove the team down the slope of the hill.

As the wagon came to a stop by the small house, as Jonathan proceeded to remove the ladder, everyone found themselves looking across the hill to the graves, they had just left. It was like a mental magnet. It takes everyone a different amount of time to clear the vast gorge of emotional loss, Jonathan imagined as he hung the ladder on the side of the small house. It was back up on the wagon and a slow continuation to the Trading store.

"I will saddle up Sam for you Ilene and you can ride him back home, Jonathan instructed, when they had almost reached the Trading Store. Jonathan deliberately pulled the wagon in a circle to end up covering the blood soaked snow where Pete had laid. "Meet me by the coral Ilene, Jonathan requested. Mother, after Ilene gets around the corner of the store, I want you to pull the wagon up to the store. I didn't want Ilene to see Pete's blood. I am going to take a shovel and cover it up after you move forward. Jonathan removed the tools from the wagon and leaned them against the wall near the store door. The wagon was pulled forward and Jonathan quickly covered the blood soaked snow with new bright snow.

"Father and I will start cleaning the blood from inside the store, Patty instructed Jonathan. "I am not going to let Ilene in or near the Trading store. I am going to stay with her in her house tonight. You and Father just get the stuff you intended to get this morning.

I will go saddle Sam and send Ilene home, and then I will come to help you.Jonathan could see Ilene putting the bridle on Sam as he rounded the back corner of the store. "Hey little sister, Jonathan offered softly, as he came close to Ilene. Ilene turned around and grabbed the front of Jonathan's coat with both fists. "I can't say Good-bye, I don't believe any of this, Ilene shouted! I don't understand any of this! I don't understand any of my life? I am going to lose my mind very soon! Jonathan stood there and pulled Ilene closer and closer at every word she spoke. After a burst of tears, Jonathan just held Ilene without a word. After all he thought, what words could there be? There had been lives so full of the future, now it looked like a black hole of a future.

Jonathan finished saddling up Sam and helped Ilene into the saddle. A slight tap on Sam's rump started the horse slowly on his way. "I will see you later little sister, Jonathan shouted out loudly, hope for the

98

words to be reassuring to Ilene. Jonathan retrieved his horse and put it into the coral. He left his horse saddled for later. He walked slowly to the back door of the store. It took deliberated motivation to get the door open. Not wanting to do something sometimes is like trying to get the mind to unlock a rusty door. "Get going Jonathan, Jonathan firmly instructed himself with a loud voice!

"Jonathan, we are done cleaning, Mother instructed! "Son, I wrote up a slip and put the money for the goods we are getting in the cash drawer, Father instructed the numb son. "Why, Jonathan questioned? "This is your business son, Father instructed! "I was so anxious to have this when Pete and Alice were here, Jonathan reflected. Now, now I can't breathe! I don't think I can run this or be here without them? Do you guys want to live here and run this? "No, Patty reflected quickly! "We can help until you decide, Bo offered! "Robbed and killed, Patty questioned? This place seemed so nice, but now it just scares me.

"We have to get home for chores now, Bo reminded the three. I will see you here in the morning after chores! How much money did you have in the register away?

"Forty dollars, Jonathan replied! All of this for forty dollars, Bo asked in a shocked voice?

"We always agreed that if we got robbed, we would just let them have whatever they wanted. I don't know what Alice did to get shot? She said she would just stand back with her hands in the air. The people that did this walk around on glass all the time. Always on edge, you know? "You know who did this, Patty questioned? "I do and Father will know tomorrow when he meets me here, Jonathan firmly instructed! You will know when we return tomorrow! "Don't be fools, let the Calvary take care of this, Mother Patty insisted! Take a day's ride and go to Eagle corners! We will discuss it tomorrow morning, Jonathan insisted, as he put his arms around his parents and ushered them out the door!

"I am going to get things done here and lock it up, Jonathan replied. Then I am going to go and help Ilene with her chores. I will stay with her tonight for moral support. She wasn't going to leave the valley before, so I know she will not budge at all now. I have to help her get through this somehow? I am not sure I can get through this? I guess tomorrow will be the tell tale! "Tomorrow, Mother Patty questioned? "Good night Mother, Jonathan offered! I love you both! Jonathan rode up to Ilene's small house and saw Sam tied outside the house with his saddle on yet. It was a decision to dismount and go into the house to see what needed to be done. It was not a surprise, as he had figured that Ilene wouldn't feel much like doing any work. It was a quick knock on the door and a call out by Jonathan, "Ilene? No answer as he went in. There was no one there as he made an observation of the fireplace. The fire was almost out, so he threw some logs on the fire and stoked it up. The saddles and bridles were removed and placed in the house. Jonathan led the two horses around the house to the coral. Still no Ilene! Jonathan took little Sam out of his stall, so he could run around in the coral for some exercise.

The harness was put on Sam to pull the wagon sled. An ax was found by the wood pile. The water barrel for water was loaded on the wagon sled. Then it was locating a bucket so he could be off to the lake to get water. Where was Ilene? Jonathan let his eyes search the hillside and the tree line in a hope for a glimpse of Ilene.

Still nothing! The water was retrieved and the chores were completed. The one nanny goat was milked and the nine eggs were added to Jonathan's pocket, as for a lack of something else to be had to carry them.Once Jonathan was back in the house he sat the milk on the table and began to take the eggs from his pocket and place them in a wire basket on the table. "I am getting a bit concerned, Jonathan whispered to himself. Where are you baby sister? It is starting to get dark. Jonathan grabbed up his saddle, blanket and bridle. It was a brisk walk to the coral, followed with a quick saddling of his horse. "Where to start looking, Jonathan asked himself? Like a magnet he let the new grave of Alice and Pete, pull him up the hill.

Nothing could be seen until he was right beside the grave. There, wrapped in a blanket was Ilene. "Ilene, Ilene, Jonathan requested? There was no movement; no sound from what Jonathan presumed was Ilene? Jonathan dismounted and walked over to the hidden blanket wrap. "Ilene, Jonathan spoke, as he patted the bundle. Jonathan pulled some of the blanket back to reveal the contents of the bundle. The hidden was not what he thought it would be. There was a Colt revolver pointed to the underside of the chin of Ilene. "Sweet Jesus, Jonathan proclaimed, as he quickly took the revolver away."I can't live and I can't die, Ilene chattered with cold chills! Jonathan tucked the revolver into his belt. With a clean scoop of the bundle, he walked to his horse. Not another word was said. The bundle was tossed over his shoulder as he mounted. The bundle was then pulled down in front of him. It was a quick ride down the hill to the small house. The bundle was placed in a soft chair in front of the fireplace. Jonathan quickly unsaddled his horse and placed the items in the house. Without words he left to return his horse to the coral. The crushing of the day appeared to not be over yet, he thought. He didn't know what to say to himself, yet to anyone else?

"I wished we had slept together in a marital way, so that I may have had a chance to have a baby in some sort of remembrance of Peter, Ilene unloaded an opinion, as Jonathan came back into the house.

We waited for that until we were married. Now I have less than nothing! My chance at a family is gone! Marriage gone! Nice home is gone! Happiness is gone! To have someone love is gone! Of all the things that have happened to me, there has been someone to cross my path and help me. Who will cross my path now and help me out of this pit? "I will tell you in a couple of days, Jonathan suggested, as he stood beside Ilene! "Say what in a couple of days, Ilene sounded out, as she threw the blanket back and jumped up! "You're a beautiful woman Ilene; Jonathan stated the obvious as he quickly hugged Ilene. I am not Pete, but you know I will help you. You're a temptation, but you need to heal. You have always been nothing but kindness to me, Ilene whispered.

"We haven't eaten all day, so I will make us something, Ilene stated. "I will pour the milk in the picture and wash out the bucket, Jonathan offered. I also have water left in the barrel, so I will fill the water pot on the fire and bring an extra bucket in the house. I will also get a little more fire wood in. "Hurry along, because what I am making will not take long, Ilene suggested.

That sounded like a better Ilene, Jonathan thought as he left the house. Jonathan soon returned with his bucket of water and an arm full of firewood. There were pancakes, eggs and milk on the table. The outer

101

clothes were soon off and a hand wash in the new water basin was appreciated. "Let's pray, so we can eat, Ilene suggested."Father in Heaven, have mercy on us! Forgive us of our sins and help us to overcome temptations. Thank you for blessing us with this food. Help us to overcome the pain that rails against us. Help us to bring justice to those that have been taken from us! To bring justice, Ilene offered loudly, as her fist hit the table top. We ask this in the name of our lord Jesus, who gives us hope. Let it be so, let it be so, Amen!

"It kind of gives me a chill, when you ask God for justice, Jonathan admitted! I never wanted to leave this valley,

because I fear all the ugliness that is beyond this valley, Ilene confessed.

I once thought this valley had protection, but now I see that it doesn't. When the mist comes in over the valley, it seems to hide itself from the world. I love the mist! I have always felt God in the mist. You know in the bible, when it says that God walked in the mist in the cool of the day? It's true that when hard things have happened to me, there was always someone sent by God to cross my path and help me. Like when Papa and Mama died.

"Peter showed up and peered into my grave. "Are you sick he asked? "No I replied! "Then rise up and live he commanded! During the night before I had seen the moon sitting on the edge of the earth. There was a great stag standing in front of the moon. I thought what a beautiful glory to God. Why are we even here?

"Then the herd of cattle belonging to the Smith ranch came to eat and knock down my hay field. Captain Bates showed up and made everything better than ok. I had hurled a stone at the man advancing at me. He dropped like a sack of flour. I thought I had committed murder?

"Then you and Peter helped me improve my income with a barn, horses and more goats with good sales. My thoughts were that God was giving me more than I deserve?

"Peter was greatly troubled and we had to rescue him from drowning. Jonathan you helped me secure love and a future. I fell in love with Peter!"The crazy Cougar attack where I surely would have lost my life.

I was helped by Peter and you. Peter made me feel like a beautiful young lady. I may never see or feel that way again? At the time I thought I was dead. I was very afraid! God have mercy, I requested!

"The feeling of being part of a family, when I felt so low, was removed by Mother Alice. She wanted the same and so did I. I felt a family connection I had not felt in years. God, thank you for sending love!

"Now the loss of Mother Alice and Peter leaves me in a state of blankness? I walked all the way up the hill, wrapped up in a blanket and pointed the revolver at my head. Father in Heaven,

Where are you now I prayed? Who cares if someone is sent to cross my path and help me, if the pain is so great? Revenge is hatred and now I will see hatred face to face!

"Do we go to the outpost at Eagle tomorrow, Ilene inquired? There needs to be justice for Peter and Mother Alice! "Perhaps, Jonathan offered, as he casually gazed at Ilene. Father and I are going to do some investigations tomorrow morning. Do you have any coffee? "Yes, I do, Ilene offered. I will make some. It sounds good. You seem very calm about all this, Ilene questioned? "It is just who I am, Jonathan replied. I am the opposite of Pete. Pete with his black hair and beard, well half beard anyway, Jonathan laughed. He is quick and fiery at everything that goes on. He is only five foot nine inches, but acts like a giant. He had a good heart to help others out. I love him like a brother, so yes there will be justice. I will protect you! So no you can't go along!

"I never asked yet, Ilene protested! I am moving around fairly well now. I have a Winchester and I can shoot it well. I have a Colt revolver and I can shoot that too! I am very good with my sling shot. "Nice, Jonathan offered casually! If Pete had been one step more cautious, he would be here with us. He should have stopped for one second at the corner of the store for protection. You are a lot like Pete, Ilene! Wonderful, but yet dangerous! "I am just, just scared for you Jonathan, Ilene confessed, as she dried the last dish!

"Thank you, I will keep that in mind, Jonathan offered, as he stood up. Let's try to get some sleep. I will sleep in the small bed, Jonathan suggested, as he pointed to Ilene's old bed. "Well, turn your head so I can jump into bed, because I don't have a night shirt, Ilene warned.

Don't be concerned if you hear me cry in the night. I go right to the point when I say something, but I also jump right into emotions if it compels me to do so. "I love you little sister, Jonathan assured Ilene. I want you to be well and safe! "Thanks Jonathan, Ilene replied! It is so good to have you here in this house with me. I love you right back! Good night Jonathan! Good night little sister, Jonathan offered back!

Compensation

Jonathan was up in the dark and had Ilene's chores done, before Ilene was even out of bed. The dropping of firewood, the milk bucket on the table, brought about a startled Ilene jumping out of bed. Jonathan quickly turned and began to remove the couple of eggs from his coat pocket. Ilene quickly began to get dressed behind Jonathan, but offered a few groans of trouble with the Levies. "I love to wear the Levi jeans and shirts you guys gave me, Ilene boasted. My leg is still a bit stiff though. I didn't hear you get up? "I couldn't sleep much, so I just got up and did the chores, Jonathan instructed. "All done, you spoil me, Ilene confessed! I will make a couple of biscuits and eggs quick. Ilene hurried about quickly to do the task, but to try to find the right words for what was on her mind.

"Let me go with you, Ilene requested as she rushed over to Jonathan? I can be helpful! I will follow your direction! "Ok, Jonathan offered with a mild tone! Gets our breakfast cooking and I will bring the horses around. Jonathan picked up the bridles and walked out the door. Ilene anxiously hurried with making the breakfast. "What have I asked to do, Ilene whispered to herself? I just don't want to be away from Jonathan, she answered herself. I am always alone she questioned herself? Now I am terrified to be alone, she answered herself loudly! The sound of that brought tears to her. I don't want to be filled with hatred, but I want justice!

"Breakfast in three minutes, Ilene instructed. Jonathan grabbed a blanket and saddle and went out. In a few he was back and grabbed the second set of equipment. Then the return was a direct setting at the table. Ilene quickly sat the items on the table with a hurried motion she sat down. Ilene's pray was a flurry of words."Father in Heaven, forgive us if we take life today! Guard us and protect our path! May justice be seen in your eyes and hands? Thank you for giving us the things we need in this day. Let it be so! Let it be so! Amen!

"Amen, Jonathan offered! The prayer gives me a chill. "There may be life taken in this day, Jonathan advised? You know you don't have to be a part of it. "Yes, I know, Ilene agreed! I just don't want to be away from you. It may sound silly, but to be away from you scares me. I am not scared at what may happen. I have been alone a lot, but now the idea terrifies me! Get your revolver and extra cartridges, Jonathan instructed. Get your Winchester and cartridges too, when we are done eating. "Always stay behind me and father, when we ride and whatever we are up to. Always be looking in every direction, not just ahead of us. Always, if you shoot, know what you are shooting at. Not me or father!

Ilene thought that the food was hard to swallow, finding herself drinking milk at every mouthful. She found herself eating in time with Jonathan, so as to finish at the same time. Just as soon as she was done, she hurried to the closet and retrieved the holster for her revolver. Then she carefully loaded it. The Winchester was loaded, with extra cartridges added to her pockets. How many cartridges did she need, her mind asked her? An extra box was added to a pocket for good measure. Ilene quickly located Papa's scabbard to be added to her saddle.

The two rode slowly in silence down along the creek, then over the creek at the shallow spot and up to the passage through the pines and big Oaks. There was only an occasional Blue Jay sounding, to wake up the morning. Once they were through the trees, they could see the trading store. The ride continued quietly up to the store. Jonathan dismounted, so Ilene followed suit.

The horses were tied as they waited for Jonathan's father. "We have to take of the horse in the coral, Jonathan advised. Fill the hay bunk, while I start the heater for the water. Ilene walked to the haystack and found a fork beside the stall barn. The bunk was easy to add hay. It was part of the coral and all you had to do was just pitch the hay right into it. Ilene could see Jonathan pumping water from a hand pump to fill the water trough as she walked back to his location. What nice features Ilene thought. "This is an easy way to get water into a trough, Ilene offered with appreciation. "As long as it doesn't freeze up, Jonathan responded.

The two began to walk towards the front of the store and met Bo walking towards them. "Good morning father, Jonathan sounded out. "Good morning son, father replied. "Good morning sir, Ilene reflected! "Greetings, Bo replied! I am surprised to see you coming along with us? "I wasn't going to let Ilene come along, but changed my mind and gave her instructions, Jonathan reflected. Stay behind us on horse and on foot. Always be looking in every direction. Don't shoot us! "I like that one, Bo laughed! Coming along and you have a fire arm too? Ilene opened the front of her coat and revealed the revolver. "My Winchester is on my horse. "So, I am guessing you know how to shoot, Bo smiled. "Yes, sir, very well too, Ilene offered soberly.

"Ok son, what are we up to, father requested? "I was right behind Pete when we came around this corner, Jonathan instructed as he pointed to the corner of the store they were standing by. There were two men. One had a mask pulled up, but the other had his mask down. That was the one that shot Pete. No mistake, it was Tim Reed! It's a guess right now, that the other was his brother. There are three Reed brothers, but there was only two here, that I saw. When Pete fell, I grabbed his revolver and emptied it at the two. I threw three shots at each one. I think I landed all the shots into them. They live two miles south, so I am guessing that they went for home? Their folk's live one mile further south from where they live. We will go check out their place first.

"Ok, son lets go check it out and see what happens from there, father offered in agreement.

Well Ilene, take a deep breath and saddle up! "Yes sir, Ilene agreed! The three saddled up and slowly went south on the wagon trail. Ilene followed directly behind her leaders. Bo was a tall six foot three inch man like his son. He was a veteran from the Civil war. He was a union captain, like Papa. You couldn't be in better company. Ilene felt pride being with these two, to the point of tears of pride finding the way to her cheeks. Ilene had never been out of the valley, let alone on this wagon trail. Well, except her birthday and Peter drowning. Ilene looked all around like a nervous chipmunk. It was very quiet riding in the snow. There were still a few sounds of Blue Jays and an occasional crow. Jonathan and Bo were going along slow and looking on the ground for something that she had no idea of what they were looking for.

A sudden stop caught her off guard and forced her to pull hard back on Sam. Bo came down off his horse and looked close at the ground. "Definitely blood, Bo sounded softly! It was quiet last night and no snow. These tracks are theirs and this blood is theirs. Bo saddled back up and the three continued on. "Tracks from the horses and now blood, Ilene whispered to herself.

Jonathan pointed to a house through the trees. "The horse tracks go up what is the lane to this farmyard, Jonathan quietly spoke. "It is too cold to not have a fire, Bo suggested. No smoke from the chimney. There are cattle in the barnyard coral. They are making a fuss like they have not been fed? Wounded and can't do the work? "Let's go part way up the lane to have a better look, Jonathan suggested?

Ilene suddenly felt a chill down her neck and it wasn't the weather either. It was the realization of the possibility of shooting at someone. Papa had always said you never point a gun at anyone unless you intend to shoot or even kill someone. Ilene felt her heart began to beat out of her chest. This was real as she followed the two men forward. It was a sudden realization that the Civil war was hell on earth. Now she knew the great penalties that Papa had paid.

Jonathan motioned for Ilene to come up closer between their two horses. "There is a horse still saddled standing over by those trees, Jonathan instructed, as he pointed to the location. "I see another horse standing around the corner of the house, Ilene added and pointed to the far corner of the house. "I just saw a piece of the saddle, Bo pointed out. I think these horses have been left saddled. It may even be since yesterday?

"I think I may have wounded both of the thieves yesterday, Jonathan reiterated his earlier instruction. They are both probably in the house? "The question is, Bo started to state with a hesitation? Is anyone else in the house? "Well, as I recall, Jonathan began. Tim and Terry live together and Tony still lives at home with their folks. Just to split the work up more evenly. "I am going to ride over to the horse by the trees and see if there is blood on the saddle, Bo instructed. It's easier to ride up to another horse, than walk. "Baby sister, you stay here, Jonathan instructed. If you see anything, shout out or fire your revolver. I am going to ride through the trees to go around the corner of the house and check the saddle for blood, like father.

"I will not be able to see you, so put your left arm across your chest, like this, Bo instructed, showing his left arm across his chest. Face Ilene so she can see you, then she can show it to me in the same way. If there is no blood, put your left arm straight down by your side. If you see a backdoor over there, raise your right arm straight into the air, like this. If there is a back door, that's where we are going in. If there is blood on both saddles, I am coming around through the trees to you Jonathan and we will go in quietly. No noise by anyone, until we have to. "Yes, Father, Jonathan agreed! "Yes sir, Ilene agreed! "Bo please, Bo offered with a smile.

Bo left in his direction and Jonathan left in the opposite. Ilene watched intently to both directions. "I guess the valley is better than out here, she whispered to herself. Bo was the first to reach his horse. He bent over and looked closely without dismounting.

A left arm came up and across his chest. Ilene repeated the left arm across her chest. Bo seemed to thump his arm a couple of times, so she repeated his gesture.

Ilene could see Jonathan on his horse looking closely to the horse that was around the corner of the house. Jonathan backed his horse up a step or two. He placed his left arm across his chest. Ilene repeated the gesture. She faced Bo and put her arm across her chest. She faced Jonathan and placed her arm across her chest and thumped it a couple of times. Jonathan raised his right arm straight into the air. Ilene raised her right arm straight into the air, facing Jonathan, and then she faced Bo and kept her right arm up. Bo began to move through the woods around the house towards Jonathan's location.Ilene pulled her Winchester out of its scabbard and levered a cartridge into the chamber. "Look in all directions, Ilene whispered to herself. It was totally quiet as she peered through the woods all around the area. An occasional head of cattle made a sound, from the coral. Bo and Jonathan had dismounted and tied their horses to branches at the edge of the woods.

The two disappeared out of sight. "Going through the side door, Ilene whispered to herself, as if she needed the instruction. It was followed by a quick look all around.

Then Bo and Jonathan reappeared at the corner of the house. They had their revolvers drawn, as they went slowly along the front of the house. Bo put his right arm up at a ninety degree angle. Then he stopped and tried to carefully peer into a window on the front of the house. He dropped down low and passed under the window, as if to not be seen. The two stood by the front door, just to the side. Bo unlatched the door and let it open on its own with just a slight nudge. After a split second he quickly stepped inside followed by Jonathan. The door was open and they both were in the house. Needing reassurance, Ilene whispered, "Now what?

Ilene began to do her looking around. Her breath was lost, when she saw two riders coming her way at a good distance. Jonathan and Bo were in the house and she was a long way away to try a shout. Ilene fired her

Winchester into the air. It startled the two riders, as their horses danced around a bit. "Hello, hello, Ilene shouted to the two riders! The riders had their revolvers out as they raced towards Ilene.

She had no idea as to who these people were. "Hello, hello, she shouted again! Ilene held her Winchester across her lap, so that no indication of aggression was shown towards the riders. "What is going on, one of the riders demanded as he came close. They kept their revolvers out. "Who are you and what's going on here, the first rider demanded again? "There are two men in the house that robbed the Trading store and killed two people yesterday, Ilene stated loudly!

"Nonsense the rider replied! "Truth, Ilene loudly stated! Jonathan saw one up close. "Jonathan, the second rider questioned? "Yes, Ilene answered! It was Tim Reed! His mask came off, but the other still had a mask on. He thinks the second one was his brother Terry. They killed Alice and Peter! "Killed Alice and Peter, the first rider questioned? The two riders went racing towards the house.

Ilene could see Jonathan just inside the edge of the door looking out. The two riders came to a sliding stop and leaped from their horses.

110

Jonathan fired his revolver into the air out of the doorway. "Drop your weapons, Jonathan shouted! Now, he shouted, as he fired again! The two riders dropped their revolvers and extended their hands into the air. Ilene slowly moved forward, until she had reached the edge of the trees. She kept the Winchester across her lap, but was prepared to shoot if she saw something ready to happen.

"My boys, the first rider shouted? "These two must be the other part of the family, Ilene whispered to herself? "Travis, I am sorry, but Tim and Terry are both dead, Bo informed the two men! "They were shot, trying to get away after the robbery and murdering of Alice Rock and Peter Rock, Jonathan informed the two. We followed them out here and found them both dead this morning. They bled to death!

"You two shot them, Travis Reed questioned? "No, Bo was not there, Jonathan instructed. I came around the corner of the store and fired. I saw Tim from a few feet away.

I guessed he would go home or go to your place. We just started here. "You knew who they were, but you didn't give them a chance, Travis Reed complained!

"Give them a chance, Jonathan shouted? Pete died in my arms! I want to know if you two knew anything about this. This was all for a crumby forty dollars, Jonathan shouted again in anger! "Tony and I were gone for a few days, as we took some cattle to the railhead, Travis declared! We just got home this morning. These two didn't need no forty dollars. "What a waste, Bo reflected! Let's go son, Bo offered, as they walked to their horses and let the two men into the house to do what needed to be done.

The three met up and started the slow ride back to where the morning had started. Bo motioned to Ilene to ride up between Jonathan and himself. "Hello, hello, Bo questioned with a small laugh? We heard you from inside the doorway of the house. "I didn't know who they were and I didn't want to appear like I was hostile towards them, Ilene explained. "No, that was probably a good move, Bo offered in assurance. "Will they be angry and come after us, Ilene questioned?

"Well, Jonathan stated? The three rode on quietly with the only sound being the crunching of the horse hoofs in the snow. The Blue Jays didn't even have anything to offer. "Let's hope not, Jonathan stated! "Loss and grief are very powerful, Bo stated the obvious! Jonathan or I have to make a trip to eagle corner and report this to the troop stationed there. They will probably come out here and investigate for their report. I will get ready to leave in the morning son, if you agree? "That will be fine, Jonathan offered. I will look after Ilene and chores around here. I will take care of the store and I still have a couple of horses stabled here.

"Do you guys need anything, Jonathan requested as they rode up to the front of the Trading store? We still owe you Ilene, so please help yourself to whatever you want. I can put some things in a crate and you can carry it in front of you as you ride home

. "Well, there are a few things I can think of, Ilene offered quietly. A couple of flour sacks tied together over the horse like saddle bags would be easier.

The three walked into the store following Jonathan's unlocking of it. Ilene picked up two flour sacks and then rolled up three blankets to put them tightly into one of the sacks. The triggering thought of the blankets she was replacing was because of the deaths and grave usage. She was frozen starring at the floor in an unaware thought pattern. "Ilene, Ilene, Jonathan requested? "Oh, sorry, Ilene came back to reality! I just can't believe I am never going to see Peter again or Alice. "I know, exactly what you are thinking, Jonathan suggested. I don't know if I can operate this store anymore? Jonathan put his arms around Ilene in a light embrace.

"See you son, Bo offered as he left the store. "See you father, Jonathan replied! "Do you want to stay here tonight, Jonathan asked? "No, I will be alright, Ilene replied! "Promise to not go sleep by the graves, Jonathan asked? "Promise, for today, Ilene pledged! "What else can I get for you to take home, Jonathan whispered? "My head can't think, Ilene offered. Let me see? Let me see? I need to replace three towels, two neck bells for the new Billie's and a sharpening stone. Do you have night clothes to sleep in? I don't want to sleep naked anymore. "Yes, in fact let's get you a robe too, slippers and night socks for the very cold days, Jonathan offered a list. "Are you really going to leave the Trading store, Ilene questioned in a whisper? "I don't really know right

112

now, Jonathan reflected. I can hardly breathe! Mother is afraid to stay with the store after what has happened. Father said he will help in any way I need. I need a partner, but Pete has been with me for many years. There is no one like Pete. May be you Ilene? You are the only one I can trust at this point. You are the only one I would even want to work with. "I don't know Ilene replied, as she put her hand on Jonathan's arm. Peter asked me after he had asked me to marry him. At the same breath he offered to live in the valley. The answer was easy, but now I feel frozen! Too many emotions of loss I guess?

"That's my feelings exactly, Jonathan whispered back. Pete killed the two robbers when we were returning from Minneapolis. Now I killed two of the Reed brothers. I sure know how Pete felt now! It is harder than I thought. It's hard even if you are trying to protect someone. Pete protected me, but I couldn't protect him. "I am so sorry Jonathan, Ilene offered, as she gave a hug of compassion. I hope I never have to take a human life. I know that God's grace is sufficient, but my mind is just not strong enough.

"The two Reed family members were really mad at us, Ilene questioned? Are we ok? "Well, you know how we feel, so to answer that, is difficult, Jonathan suggested. Father is going to Eagle corners tomorrow first thing. The Calvary will ride out here to investigate this mess. I don't think they were involved, so everything will probably just fall where it is. Just be careful and watch your back.

"Is there anything else we can stuff into these flour sacks, Jonathan questioned? "Some coffee, when you come to see me, Ilene requested with a smile? "Absolutely, Jonathan agreed! "Do you have garden seeds, Ilene asked? "Yes, but they are last years, Jonathan instructed! Spring is a long way off, Jonathan laughed! "I know, but even to start one plant of something, makes me happy, Ilene offered with a short laugh! Jonathan grabbed several boxes of matches as he passed them walking to the seeds. Seeds were stuffed into the flour sacks, until they could hold no more.

The bags were tied together with a short rope and loaded onto Sam. Jonathan gave Ilene a boost up for ease of mounting. "Love you little sister, Jonathan offered with a smile. Ilene sat on top of Sam with a gazing look at Jonathan. "Love you right back Jonathan, Ilene offered with a hope of joy! The two gave a short wave to each other as Ilene coaxed Sam to head towards home. "It's a crazy day Sam, Ilene whispered to the horse, as they went around the corner and into the trees.

The towering pines offered their words of wisdom to all that passed by. The breeze pushed on the branches and the words were interpreted to all.

The scent of pine filled the air and slowed the progress of horse and rider.

It was reviving, no matter how the day may have crushed. It was a place to ask and confess. Maybe, just maybe even a place for God to talk to your soul? If it was just a place for God to reveal his glory, that was ok too! The passage of the pines was lead into the passage of the great Oaks. The leaves may be gone, but the strength of their limbs offered strength. You just had to absorb it. Then it was the strength of the great boulders of granite. They were the twins that had stood for thousands of years. They were often touched and greeted in equal recognition. Ilene's recognition in passing was, "Joy and Peace be with me! Today the whisper, brought tears. Joy and peace didn't seem like the right names today. The tears lingered the rest of the way home.

Ilene entered the cold small house and brought her first attention to starting the fireplace. The sacks were toted into the small house for later unpacking. Then it was an unsaddling of Sam with replacement of the harness and collar. Off to the lake for water was next. The continuation of chores seemed to be a need for awakening from some mental freeze. It was even some starring at nothing in particular. A few shouts of Ilene to get to work, had difficulty in getting things done. Sitting in front of the fire in Mama's chair seemed to offer some peace and even some doziness too. It was some tap or rap outside from the wind that brought Ilene to a standing jump from the chair. A careful listen didn't bring about any identification either. When Ilene's heart rate came back to normal, it brought up the idea of wishing for a lock on the door, but there was nothing to complete the idea. However, there could be a loaded pistol. The holster was still being worn, so it was removed and the Colt was checked for cartridges. A bowl of ground oats was made for supper and then it was the trying on of the night clothes. It was the

114

night dress, the robe, sleeping socks and the slippers. Ilene found this better warmth, than regular clothes.

With a big sigh, the fire was stoked for the night.

The robe and slippers were placed by the bed over a chair. The chair was moved slightly to offer a straight view to the doorway. There had always been a clear view of the doorway, so why change it now, Ilene pondered the thought. "A first time for everything, Ilene whispered, as she placed the Colt under the blankets near her. "I hope I don't shoot myself in the night, Ilene whispered. The small house was dimly lit with the fireplace offering its warmth. There was a chill in the air and it wasn't from the cold outside. It was the thoughts of discomfort! She had never thought about nastiness coming in the night. It was unsettling. Tonight was different.

The night went by quickly as tiredness always wins. The robe and slippers went on quickly at first light scratched its way through the small window by the door. The fire was stoked up and the getting dressed for chores found its new schedule. The new night clothes were hard to remove, because of the coziness. "How many nice things do people have out beyond the valley to enjoy, Ilene asked herself the question? The Colt was placed back into its holster. The cartridges were placed on the table from yesterday. The sling with a few stones was placed in her side pouch, by habit. The door found its way open, with Ilene pausing for a gaze towards the ridge and the rising sun. The pause was for the trip that Bo had to make to Eagle corners. Well, she thought, it was for Jonathan out there somewhere in the sunrise. Bo had probably left hours ago. Jonathan had extra chores while his father was off on this trip. The chores went by quickly, so while Sam was still hitched up to the wagon sled, it was a good time to go to the woods and get a few loads of rounds for the fire. It was instilled in Ilene to get jobs done while the weather allowed for it. Deep snow would make a job like getting firewood in very difficult. Cold weather made getting firewood just unbearable. "Sam, we can just not have enough firewood, Ilene instructed the horse. Do you know how hard it is to get this wood without the help of a horse? Old Billie could pull a good load, but I had to help. I am sorry Sam, but I enjoyed talking to Peter, Alice and

115

Jonathan more than you. You are better talking to, than me just talking to myself.

Two loads was enough extra work for the day. Ilene was anxious to bake some bread, just in case Jonathan would come over tomorrow. Bo may even be back with the Calvary. Would the Calvary even be at Eagle corners and be able to come out here? "Sweet Jesus, please take care of Jonathan, Ilene whispered into the small room. Ilene picked a brown paper bag of baking soda from her one shelf. "The life of bread, Ilene boasted! Thank you Peter! It looks like we get to use a little extra goat's milk today. Ilene often skimmed the fat off the top of the goat's milk for the use of making bread and other fat purposes. A good portion added to the inside of here two baking pans was terrific for the browning of the bread, as well as its removal from the pans. The mixing was soon under way. It was a couple of harder fists going into the bread dough, at the thought that Jonathan may be in some kind of trouble. The people outside the valley may have more nice things, but they were living in a heap of nasty.

The dough was divided into two lumps and tossed into the buttered pans. Ilene leveled the fire in the fireplace so she could just sit her pans on the coals. "Now I get the hard part, Ilene instructed herself. I just have to sit in Mama's chair and make sure the coals under the pans are hot enough. A little extra wood was added to one side of the fireplace to burn down a bit, just in case. It didn't take long for the sweet aroma of the baking bread to fill the small room. The hardest part was to keep from falling asleep in front of the fire. She just couldn't mess this up, as the thought of what Jonathan had said at her birthday party. Baked bread was one of Jonathan's favorite foods. Alice had a real food cooking stove. "Alice, I am going to miss you so much, Ilene whispered into the fire, as she stared in disbelief. Thoughts started to bring tears. "Stop it. Stop it, Ilene yelled at herself!The bread pans were soon pulled forward out of the fire onto the hearth. They would be left to cool, while she went out to do the evening chores. There seemed to always be an accumulation of eggs and goat milk, so she knew what supper was after chores.

However tonight there was bread. "Tasty, Ilene assured herself! Maybe she could just have some creamy butterfat, on the bread and milk? A new tradition would start tonight with the changing into her new night dress, then the robe and slippers went on quickly. It seemed to make the reading of her bible verses more fun. Even the prayers were a little longer. It was a lot better than stripping all the work clothes off and jumping naked into a cold bed for sure.

Soon the rising sun was scratching its way through the small window by the door again. The fire was stoked up and the getting dressed for chores found a new and brighter joy. The new night clothes were hard to remove, because of the coziness, just as yesterday, but way more fun. The Colt was placed back into its holster. The sling with a few stones was placed in her side pouch, by habit. A chill came over Ilene, as she turned around and strapped on the holster. The door found its way open, but offered an unusual amount of wood smoke in the air. Ilene looked to the chimney on the small house for any particular reason, as to what the smell of smoke might be? The smoke curling from the chimney was the same as it always had performed. It was shrugged off and the chores found there requirements.

The bucket of goat milk and the bucket of eggs were in need of being brought into the house. Ilene hurried along with them, with the thought of more fresh bread. As she came around the corner of the house, her mouth fell open. The buckets were quickly placed on the ground. It was Tony Reed from two days ago at the Reed farm. "So you live out here, Tony smirked! Where is your counterpart, Jonathan? Hiding out around here? "No, you can just leave, Ilene shouted! "Leave, Tony smirked again! I think you and I are going to get acquainted in short order, Tony shouted, as he leaped from his horse quickly. Ilene quickly loaded a stone into her sling. Whir, whir, whir and snap. The stone found its mark and Tony made his last step going face down in a thud onto the frozen ground. Ilene stood starring at the man lying face down in the snow. She quickly ran to the front of the house and grabbed three short ropes, that she used for tying up Bucklings to turn them into wethers. Three extra ropes were stuffed into the sling pouch for no particular reason.

Ilene turned the man over onto his face to pull his arms behind his back. One arm elbow with the opposite wrist was tied and then the other. The third rope was used to tie the ankles. Ilene had learned the hard way by

117

only tying on pair of goat feet before, never again. After Tony Reed was tied up, Ilene turned him over on his back. "You are probably just knocked out or stunned, Ilene convinced herself. I didn't like the idea of what you were talking about. You are scary! What am I going to do with you?

Ilene walked slowly back to her buckets sitting on the ground. The buckets were quickly put in the house, but Ilene knew she needed to find Jonathan. A quick walk back to the stranger, but there was no movement. "He wouldn't freeze to death would he, Ilene questioned herself? It was another quick walk into the house and the fetching of two blankets was obtained. It was back out to the stranger and covering him up, so he wouldn't get too cold. Then it was a dash to get Sam back out of his stall for saddling. The blanket, saddle and bridle were put on Sam probably in record time.

Ilene made a quick ride to the front of the house with only a quick pause by the stranger, just to check for any movement. A quick ride down the creek, then across it carefully. Then it was a dash up the new fence line to the woods. There was no slow ride as usual through the trees. The ride was as fast as her heart was beating to get to the trading store. Ilene's mouth dropped open for the second time today as she came around the curve. The ride slowed to a turtles pace. The burning smell was now revealed. The store was totally burned to the ground. Ilene stopped in front of the burnt store. "Jonathan, Ilene whispered? Was Jonathan over to his parents place, doing chores or staying over here? Ilene rode around the burn site to the coral.

"Jonathan, Jonathan, Ilene shouted! Ilene tied Sam off on the coral. She went into the tackle room and then into the stall area of the barn. Jonathan's horse was there. The two stable horses were there. Out in the coral was Jonathan's wagon team. There was Papa's team she had sold to Peter and Jonathan. The two wagons were sitting by the far end of the coral. "Jonathan, Jonathan, Ilene screamed out?

Ilene stood starring at the burnt out store, then her head dropped and became buried into her hands. Tears began to flow for unknown reasons, perhaps just because she didn't know where her friend Jonathan was located. 'Jonathan, Jonathan, Ilene screamed into her hands again! It was a deep breath and a walk back into the stall barn."Think, think, Ilene instructed herself. There were three horses tied into their stalls. Jonathan always let the horses out into the coral, unless it was storming. There was no storm, so if they were tied in, he had planned to return shortly. "This is crazy, I am going to ride over to the Williams and see if Jonathan had stayed with his mother last night, Ilene specifically told herself. It was a quick dash from the stall barn to her Sam tied to the far end of the coral. Ilene froze in her tracks about half way to Sam. There was Mr. Reed on his horse at the end of the burnt out Trading store. Ilene slowed, but continued toward her horse."What's going on here, Travis Reed shouted? Ilene said nothing but walked towards her horse. "Where's my son Tony, Mr. Reed demanded? Tell me now, where is my son? Ilene didn't want to talk, so she reached for the reins to untie Sam. "You are not going to like it if I get off this horse and teach you some manners, Travis Reed shouted!

Travis Reed quickly came off his horse and started towards Ilene. Instinctively Ilene's hand went into her pouch and drew out the sling and a stone. "What are you going to do, chuck a stone at me, Travis Reed laughed? "Get away from me, Ilene shouted! Travis Reed laughed as he quickened his pace towards Ilene. Whir, whir, whir and snap a stone flew at Travis Reed. A dull thud and Travis Reed took no more steps and fell face down to the ground with a huge sigh of air releasing from his lungs.

Ilene starred at the motionless man lying on the ground. He had come quite close at maybe only fifteen feet away, Ilene pondered. "Quick, tie him up Ilene whispered to herself! She quickly pulled the ropes from her pouch and ran towards the still man lying face down on the ground. The arms were quickly pulled behind his back as before and pulled tight. Two ropes for added measure. Then it was a rope around the feet, like a tied up Buckling.Ilene stood back with a heavy breathing like she had run a great distance. "I need to find Jonathan, Ilene instructed herself! It was a run to Sam with a quick mounting. She raced along the coral, pasted the still man. Then it was around the burnt out store and down the wagon trail. A left at the fork and straight away a mile to the east, Ilene whispered to herself. Sam was pulled to a quick stop at the fork, as she came face to face with Bo and the Calvary a hundred yards away. Bo and the Calvary came to a stop right beside her. "Bo, Bo, I don't know where Jonathan is at, Ilene screamed! Bo came close on his

119

horse and gave Ilene a one arm hug. "We will find him, don't worry, Bo calmly suggested!

"The Trading store is burnt to the ground, Ilene loudly proclaimed! She turned Sam around and pointed towards the area where the store should be around the bended in the wagon trail. Bo and the troop quickly moved toward where the store uses to be. Ilene rode quickly with them. Everyone stopped and starred in disbelief at the sight. "How, Bo requested? "I was near being attacked and I needed to find Jonathan, so I would know what to do, Ilene informed Bo and Captain Bates. I came over here quickly an hour or so ago. I saw all of this and have not been able to find Jonathan. His horse is here!

"Who tried to attack you, Captain Bates requested? "It was Tony Reed over at my house, Ilene instructed. He threatened to cause me a nasty, so I thumped him and tied him up. He is lying on the ground in front of my house, but I did cover him up, so as not to get too cold. "Sergeant, go get the man, Captain Bates requested! The Sergeant quickly took two men and went on down the trail to Ilene's house. Do you know if Jonathan was in this fire? "No Sir, Ilene guessed! He stayed here the night before last, but I don't know about last night? "He was going to help his mother with chores, until I returned, so he could be at the house, Bo suggested unknowingly? "Men, search the burn out for human remains, Captain Bates ordered! Mr. Williams, you go to your house and check for Jonathan. Get back here as quick as you can. Ilene you inform me to everything that you know. Let's go tie up at the coral, Captain Bates instructed, as Bo raced away.

The troop, captain and Ilene rode to the back of the burnt out store to the coral. "Who is that, tied up there on the ground, Captain Bates requested in surprise? "That's Mr. Reed or Travis Reed, Ilene informed the Captain, as she dismounted. "He was going to teach me a lesson and sounded quite mean about it, Ilene offered. He got quite close before I gave him a warning and a stone. Captain Bates removed his glove and reached for the silent man's neck to check for a pulse. "Sir, shall we continue for human remains one of the Calvary troop requested? "He is alive, but he will probably have a bit of a head ache, Captain Bates instructed. He is not going anywhere, so continue on.

The four remaining solders quickly went into the burnt out store to search.

Ilene and the Captain walked up to the edge of the burn out and stood gazing over the remaining pile of ash and burnt items. "Should I help, Ilene asked? "No miss, Captain Bates instructed, as he put an arm around Ilene. I think you have had your hands full. Mr. Williams has instructed us of what happened with the robbery and the death of the two Reed boys. "Tim and Terry Reed, Ilene added. Alice Rock is gone! Peter Rock my fiancé is gone! Now my friend Jonathan, I fear is gone? "Don't go there, Captain Bates requested!

The Sergeant and the two Calvary soldiers quickly rode up with Tony Reed. The feet were not tied but the hands were still tied up. "That's one uncomfortable tying of the hands, Captain Bates offered. Definitely not going anywhere! "Hey Bitch, you are going to get yours, Tony Reed growled! "My name is Ilene, Ilene instructed sternly! Ilene had no idea why he thought her name was Bitch. Tony Reed toppled over as he was pulled from his horse. "Cut my arms loose, Tony insisted! "I think not, Captain Bates informed him! Let's search the burn out, Captain Bates instructed the rest.

The Sergeant and the other two soldiers quickly joined in the fire search, with the Captain watching from the edge. "Where is Jonathan, Ilene growled at Tony? "Don't know, dead I hope, Tony growled back! "You burnt this Trading store down in hope that Jonathan was here sleeping, didn't you, Ilene growled?

You left me with nothing! I am going to shoot you dead! You had better hope Jonathan shows up with his father. "You will get yours bitch, Tony growled! Before another word could be spoken, Ilene pulled her revolver and fired a shot right beside Tony's head.The Captain came running over to Ilene. "So I burnt the store, but I didn't kill Jonathan, Tony shouted in fear of his life. Captain Bates quickly removed the revolver from Ilene's hand. "I will hold onto this revolver for a bit, Captain Bates instructed, as he tucked it into his belt. I figured you set this Trading Post on fire. You had better hope that Jonathan was not sleeping here last night. You will hang before the end of the week! Captain Bates put his arm around Ilene and ushered her away with him.

121

"Sergeant, are you finding anything, Captain Bates called out? "No Sir, the Sergeant replied! "I see that Travis Reed is stirring a bit. Get a couple of men to bring him over by his son. "You two go get Travis Reed over here by his son, the Sergeant called out, as he pointed to two soldiers near the closer end of the burn out. Untie his feet, so he can walk over. The two soldiers quickly untied Travis's feet and helped him up. "Men, help Tony Reed stand up, Captain Bates requested.

Bo and Jonathan raced up quickly, as Captain Bates was chastising the two Reeds. "What has happened here Jonathan shouted, as he leaped from his horse? Sweet Jesus, how much, can a man endure? "Oh Jonathan, I thought you were in the fire, Ilene cried out! The two hugged each other as they starred at the burn out. Captain Bates called out for the men to stand clear of the search. "Sergeant, this is what is going to happen here! Travis Reed and Tony Reed you are going to rebuild this by instruction of Jonathan Williams. You will take wagons and haul in whatever is needed to rebuild this. "Captain, we don't have that kind of money, Travis Reed shouted! The Sergeant and this troop will help you sell everything you have to complete this project. You have six months to a year to do so. If not, you are going to prison! Do I make myself clear? "Yes, Sir, the two Reeds complained! Jonathan you make a list of what you can remember being inside the trading Post.

Missing

"I will help with the building, Jonathan offered. I am sure father will help when he can. It all depends on the attitude of these two! "Any issues what so ever and I will send these two to prison, Captain Bates firmly notified the Reeds! I don't want one smart mouth comment issued to either of these folks. Maybe this will help you two to get the stupid out of your heads! If your two sons could have gotten the stupid out of their heads, they would be alive now. It was all for forty dollars. I am sorry for your loss! I hope it's not too late for you two!

"Son, I have to get back to your mother, Bo instructed. It's been a long ride, Captain! I am a mile to the left at the fork, if you need anything. "So long Mr. Williams, Captain Bates offered! "Take care of yourself Ilene, Bo added, as he mounted up to leave.

"Let's go see what you own, Captain Bates requested as the Reeds were untied. Men, we may be herding cattle back to Eagle corners. Let's mount up Sergeant! "Men, let's mount up, the Sergeant instructed! The Reeds and the troop mounted up and headed towards the Reed farms.

 Jonathan stood by Ilene with his arm around her shoulders. "If this goes like I think it will, they will not have anything left to live on, Jonathan whispered. Let me show you something, Jonathan offered as he took Ilene by the hand.

The two walked to the back of the burn out. Jonathan pushed a partial frame over and began to toss some debris aside.

"This is a metal strongbox buried here, Jonathan explained as he began to pull something out of the ground. The box was brushed off and then Jonathan opened it up. This is our bank and hiding place for extra money. This was Pete's idea and a good one too. I guess I was a bit naive in thinking no one would rob us. There is also an insurance policy for the building and goods in here. "What does that do, Ilene asked? "Well little sister, Jonathan began quietly, I will take this in to the bank tomorrow and talk to an agent there and then they will look at this property. They will hopefully pay for our loss. If I leave early tomorrow, I should be back late tomorrow. It's all depending on weather of course.

"I would like to keep this strongbox at your house for now, if that is ok, Jonathan requested? "That's fine, Ilene quietly agreed! Do we need to hide it? "No, we will just slide it under the bed or something, Jonathan replied. I will take this insurance policy with me tomorrow. Can you come over tomorrow morning after you have done your chores and take care of these horses? "Sure, that is no problem, Ilene offered. "It is kind of a risk to keep these horses here, with no one really around; Jonathan spoke his thoughts out loud.

"Why, don't we take one wagon and team to my house, Ilene suggested. They were in the coral and small lean-to before. It will make any risks a bit less. We can also take Peter's horse and yours over there too. You can stay with me too, Ilene smiled hopefully. "Is that ok, Jonathan asked? "Of course it is, Big Brother, Ilene offered with another smile. "I knew I was crazy about you, Jonathan confessed! We will take your Papa's team and wagon and do just like you said. I am glad you are so smart and willing to help me out. What are the chances that you would go fifty-fifty partnership with me in the business? I will just give you half to work with me. It wouldn't cost you a thing? Just think about it, before you say!

The wagon was hitched up. The strong box loaded and various tools that were gathered from the fire. The remaining stock was cared for, with the two saddle horses were tied to the back of the wagon. The bridles, blankets and saddles were put into the wagon. The extra tackle and tools in the tack shed were also loaded. A slow trip began to take place as the two moved their belongings to the small house.

When you have a small house, it doesn't take too much to fill it right up. "Are you sure about this, Jonathan asked, as the small house began to fill up? "It's fun, Ilene laughed! I love you big brother! "Love me and big brother too, Jonathan laughed, as he pointed at his chest with his forefinger! "True, true, Ilene confessed! Peter and you were like two in one to me. I can't think about one of you without the other.

"Why does it smell like bread in here, Jonathan asked? Is this work just making me hungry? "No I baked some bread just for you, in hope you would stop by, Ilene instructed. It was supposed to be under different circumstances though. "Would you like some before we start chores, Ilene asked? "Would I, Jonathan was quick to give a reply at the thought! I love you right back, just for feeding me!

The evening after chores was very comfortable, as Ilene sat in Mama's chair and Jonathan sat in Papa's chair. It was a feeling of a real home Ilene thought. "I really want you to be my partner in the trading Store, Jonathan revealed again. You were going to marry Pete anyway, so why not? If I could think of a way to be more romantic, I would ask you to marry me. It has just been so close to when Pete died, I thought it was best to wait. Now it's the business that is upside down. It will right itself in a short time though. You have just been there for me and I want to be here for you anyway. I guess I just blurt things out? At least, at least, you will know how I feel, Jonathan stammered! Life seems so unpredictable and fragile? I know you want to live in this valley, but the Trading store is just to the top of the ridge anyway. It is just more efficient to have the living quarters above the store.

The two sat quiet after Jonathan poured out his thoughts. "Peter was always very quick to get things said and done, Ilene offered softly.

I always thought that you might be upset if I offered to marry Peter. Peter told me nonsense. I often thought you would be the one that would ask me to marry you? If you had asked me, I would have said yes to you. It is not the looks to me, or what you have or don't have. It's the goodness of a heart! There's a lot contained in that, but you and Peter both have that.

"If you ask me to marry you, I will say yes and do so as soon as the preacher can get here, Ilene confessed. Jonathan bolted out of his chair and landed on one knee in front of Ilene. "Ilene Rasmussen, will you marry me, Jonathan quickly requested? Ilene quickly took off her engagement ring from Peter. "Yes I will marry you Jonathan Williams,

Ilene replied just as quickly! Put this ring on my finger. "Is this ok, Jonathan asked? "It's more than ok and wonderful, Ilene agreed! "Can I kiss you, Jonathan requested? "Yes and you never have to ask to kiss me again, Ilene laughed! The two stood up and enjoyed some kisses and hugs. "I have never kissed a lady before, Jonathan confessed! It makes me weak in my knees. I love you Ilene and will cherish you forever! "I love you right back Jonathan, Ilene whispered!

The twenty mile trip was prepared to Eagle Corners early the next day. Ilene felt odd seeing Jonathan ride away. Some internal instinct wanted to make sure that Jonathan was never out of sight. "Silly woman, Ilene spouted to herself, as she began to take care of her chores. Smiles found their way to the surface as she cared for Papa's big team of horses. That was followed with tears as she cared for Peter's horse. "You are one emotional basket, Ilene scolded herself. For three years you have been here alone, now what? Jonathan had talked some more last night about joining him in the business. Are you going to do that? What am I doing asking the questions and then answering them? It was so generous! Could I do this and not be married to Jonathan? Peter has only been gone for barely a week.

Ilene took off on a wild idea she had as she completed her chores. Sam remained harnessed up to the wagon sled. The wheel barrow, shovels, hammers, rope and pry bars were added to the load. It was a trip to the burn out with her even getting in on the ride.

That was the fun part as she soon arrived. Jonathan's horses were cared for, and then Sam had some work to do with pulling a few heavy pieces from the fire. Ilene began to clear the burnt out store. With the bigger pieces pulled into a pile, it was Ilene's turn with the wheel barrow to scoop up a load, then another, then another. The floor of the Trading store was cleared of all burnt materials. Ilene scratched her head in a puzzled look several times to not find the floor burnt like the rest of the store. Jonathan would have to answer that?

There wasn't much left to clear as Ilene convinced herself to get home and do her chores. She had a smell of the fire on her after working at the burn out most of the day. It was a great hope that Jonathan would be proud and have lifted spirits from her great task. It would definitely be a bath time after the work of the day. A clothes washing too! It felt a bit strange that she wanted to look good and smell good too. It made her smile! The Lilac soap was one of the most wonderful gifts she had ever received. It filled the room of the small house and seemed to try to fill it with joy.

Ilene sat in Mama's chair waiting for Jonathan to return. It would be late, but she didn't know how late? She sat there in her new cozy slippers, night dress and robe. Sipping coffee, which she was beginning to like more than she thought she would. It was Jonathan's likening of coffee, which brought this about. There was almost a smile after every sip. The work of the day brought about a continual nodding of her head. Finally the fire had to be stoked and doziness was pulling her like a magnet to the bed. "I will just get up when Jonathan finally gets here, Ilene convinced herself.

The sun scratched and peaked into the window by the door. One eye opened and attempted to peer around the room. Then the thought of Jonathan not being seen anywhere, made her jump straight out of the bed. 'Not here, Ilene spoke, breaking the silence of the room! Another good look was made with the same futile results. "Jonathan couldn't get the duties done, so he had to stay longer, Ilene spoke out loud to convince her racing heart of the realities.

A stare at the almost gone out fire, didn't help. A slow walk over to get the fire convince in starting the day, still left doubts. "Get the chores done young lady, Ilene commanded! Then go over to the Trading Store and finish the cleaning of the burnt part. "Yes miss, happy to, Ilene instructed herself! You will be married in the very short future!

Feet and hands began to fly at the much expressive thought. Chores were done in short order. Water from the lake was done and Sam was left waiting to travel to the burn out. The ground oats in a pot was snatched from the fireplace and was quickly consumed. A broom was added to the tools of yesterday. "Hurry along Sam, there is work to be done, Ilene commanded with a joyful sound of happiness. Let's treat my husband to a great surprise! I may have enemies and nasty people around every corner, but we or I have a husband that loves me. We have a God that rules and loves us! Sam could enjoy the hay and company of the other horses in the coral, as he was unhitched from the wagon sled. He had enough lead rope to reach the water tank. "Well, as soon as the small tank stove thawed it out, Ilene laughed, as her thought s converted to words.

Tools in hand the young lady went to work at the continuations of removal of all things burnt. Sweeping of the wooden floor was even completed. Everything around the building was removed and scraped clean. "Everyone, get to building, Ilene echoed out loudly to herself!

"Ok, a voice behind her shouted out! Ilene had not seen the stranger on horseback behind her. "Hello, my name is Andy Thomas! I am an insurance agent of North American Insurance! "Hello, Ilene replied quietly! "Ilene Rasmussen, Andy added! "Yes, that is right, Ilene agreed in disbelief, that this stranger knew who she was. "Could I let my horse have some water and a bit of your good hay, Andy requested? "Yes, Sir, Ilene offered! Andy Thomas led his horse over to the water trough. Ilene gathered a fork full of hay with a delivery to the horse.

"Don't be surprised that I know who you are, Andy offered with a smile. Jonathan Williams did some business yesterday with me. I remember so vividly, because he had you added to the policy as a fifty-fifty partner.

I left early this morning so I could get here today and possible return home. Is Jonathan around? "I have not seen him today, Ilene replied? Did he not leave with you? "I saw Jonathan the afternoon of day before yesterday, Andy Thomas instructed! He told me he had a couple of other things to do, but wanted to get home that day. A banking thing, see the local preacher to arrange for your wedding was what he shared. Congratulations by the way, Andy offered with a smile and his out reached hand.

"I work out of the bank, so I happened to notice when he left the bank, Andy offered. I had to go over to the postal a few minutes later, so I happened to see Jonathan talking to two men, which I didn't know. I only noticed, because it was more of an argument, than just a talk. Just before I went into the postal, I looked back in that direction, because one of the men shouted something, which I didn't really hear what it was. He pushed Jonathan and Jonathan just put his hands in the air and stepped backwards. Andy Thomas began to look about and write down whatever he required. After a short time Andy began to explain what his papers were collecting for information. It was a blur to Ilene. The sounds seem to go right over her head. It was not able to get through the question of, where is Jonathan. Andy Thomas offered a pleasant greeting of good-bye. Ilene obliged him with an expressionless face. "What to do, Ilene asked herself? Jonathan would have to go by the store on his way to the house. "Jonathan, did you go over to your parents, Ilene asked out loud?

Ilene began to harness Sam up for the return trip home. A few stares at the nicely cleaned burn site, seemed to lose its pride of completion. "I can't control, what I can't control, Ilene instructed herself! It was a slow thoughtful return home, with no answers. A small bit of hope was still trapped inside until she arrived at the small house. "No Jonathan, Ilene whispered! It was a slow footed effort to get things done. It was the opposite of what had happened this morning. There seemed to be a chill in the air and it had nothing to do with the weather.

Fears seem to grip at Ilene like the icy lake. The three eggs in her pocket seem to scream out in a growing frustration.

Suddenly a bucket of milk was sat down and the three eggs went flying through the air towards the creek one after the other. "Where are you Jonathan, Ilene screamed! Where are you Jonathan? Where are you Jonathan? It was one loud scream with an egg throw after another. Ilene sank to the ground. "What's wrong with me, Ilene questioned? Jonathan come home, Ilene pleaded? You should be here by now. Ilene took some deep breaths and tried to convince herself that everything was just fine. There is so much going on, she offered as she walked to the house.

Ilene stoked up the fire as she stared into the coals as if they might have an answer. It was sitting down in Mama's chair and chewing on a hunk of crusty bread. A couple sips of milk and a dosing off. The hard day of work wanted sleep. You can't make answers out of something that is just not there her mind screamed. The restless mind searched for Jonathan. Maybe Jonathan was over to his mother and father's place. He was surely sharing the good news of the trip and the wedding plans perhaps. The warmth of the fire with the tiredness of the day finally won.The chores were done and wood needed to be split. The ax struck harder every time a tear started to find its way from the endless well within Ilene. It took several shouts of her name to find her way back to reality. "Ilene, Ilene, Ilene finally made the ax stop, Bo called out! Bo was standing by his horse at the corner of the small house. Ilene placed the ax into the large round, which she used for sitting the smaller ones on for splitting. Then it was a rush to Bo and into a sound hug. "Have you seen Jonathan, Bo requested, in a whisper, as they embraced? "No I have not seen him, Ilene replied, as she took a step backwards. "Let's go into your house, Bo suggested.

The two walked arm in arm into the house. "A coffee perhaps, Bo asked? "Yes, of course, Ilene offered, as she picked up the coffee pot. "I see you have been busy, at the burnt out store, Bo questioned? "Yes, that was me in my excitement, Ilene confessed. It was nice enough, so I thought I would get a start at the part I thought I could do. I wanted to surprise Jonathan.

The offer of marriage from him, made me quite happy, to say the least. 'Marriage, Bo questioned? "Yes the night before Jonathan left. He asked me if it was too soon to ask me to marry him. He laughed at Peter being so quick and getting ahead of him. That's probably why I am such a wreck, that he is not back yet. Then a man by the name of Andy, Andy, let me think? Sorry, Andy Thomas from American Insurance came by yesterday, when I was working over there. When I get emotional, my head doesn't want to think.

"Did he know where Jonathan was, Bo inquired? "Andy Thomas said he works out of the bank, Ilene began. He happened to notice Jonathan when he left the bank. He had to go over to the postal a few minutes later, so he remembered seeing Jonathan talking to two men, which he didn't know. He said he only noticed, because it was more of an argument, than just a talk. Just before he went into the postal, he looked back in that direction, because one of the men shouted something, which he didn't really hear what it was. Andy said he saw one of the men push Jonathan and Jonathan just put his hands in the air and stepped backwards.

"I signed some kind of papers, that I didn't have a clue as to their meaning, Ilene confessed. Apparently Jonathan had added me as a partner. After some approval, there will be a check at the bank in a few weeks. I mean at Andy's office in the bank in a few weeks. Jonathan told me it was Peter's instructions to have this insurance. Where is Jonathan?

"I see you have been over to care for the horses at the burn out already this morning, Bo offered. I went down to the Reed places first thing this morning. I went to the Tim and Terry Reed place first. Everything that was there the first time we went is gone. There are only the hay stacks. Then I went over to the home place where Travis Reed and young Tyler were living. There I found the young Smith from the big Smith ranch. He was there with some of the men from the ranch. He told me that his father purchased both of the farms from Travis Reed. They were just told that they were moving on because they couldn't make a go of it. It was a shock,

When I told them that they had responsibility in the burning of the Trading store. They didn't even know that the store had burnt down. He had plans to go to the store later today for supplies. Smith made an offer of helping rebuild the Trading store. It was nice of him to offer to help rebuild the store. They go to the Trading store all the time. When I told him that Captain Bates from the post had imposed a penalty of them paying and helping to rebuild the Trading store, he replied, "I don't think that will happen! I asked if they had seen Jonathan, but they hadn't.

"Ilene, I have a bad feeling about my son, Bo whispered! I was really hoping I would find him over here. Ilene quickly sat the cup of coffee down; she was carrying over for Bo. "I can't breathe, Ilene gasped! Bo stood up and embraced Ilene. "It's a bad feeling, Bo whispered! I would have loved to have you for a daughter in law. Jonathan talked to us about it, but when Peter asked Jonathan about what he thought of him marrying you, well Jonathan just stood aside.

"I really should get home, Bo confessed. Patty wants to know something about what I found out or didn't find out. She has already been crying about just not knowing and fearing the worse. Probably like you, I am sure. I am going to get home, then head out to Eagle Corners to talk to Captain Bates. I will be checking on you, when I can. If I find out anything I will let you know. "Thanks Bo, Ilene whispered, as Bo left the small house. Ilene went back and sank into Mama's old chair. The coffee became untouched. There were no thoughts of comfort to be found anywhere.

Little Sam

The weather started to change a bit, so it brought the mist from the lake down across the valley almost every day. It made work harder to do, but still Ilene welcomed it. The concealment and the idea of reflection back to the beginning of time intrigued her. It was when God came in the cool of the day to walk with Adam in the garden. It was just a bit of hope, rather than the idea that he would really show up. All the thoughts were not good, because when you have lived a very, very long time many things have happened. All thoughts of the past were not good. They were not all like the Great Stag standing in the moonlight gazing into a moon sitting on the ridge at the top of the hill. Ilene reminisced about the time Little Sam had raced across the hillside to offer her safety.

It had been one of those days when the mist had hugged onto the valley for most of the days. Taking the goats to graze the hillside was very difficult to do, when you wanted to watch over them closely. The sun had finally came through and shown itself in a very bright manner. After a long hot summer the grass was thin on the hill and it was the grass or whatever that grew in the trees and brush that made it more attractive to the goats. The difficulty of seeing the goats was a given.

Getting older brought about the idea of riding little Sam more appealing. Ilene would pack something to eat and fill canteen with water to keep her through the day. It was usually a ride to the woods and fine a spot for little Sam to have grass to eat. Sam had to have real grass to eat, where the goats could be happy with almost anything. It was easier to ride little Sam with a saddle, but Ilene felt a bit guilty with the saddle being on him all day. The grass of quality would be found, so the bridle would be removed and hung on the horn of the saddle.

Ilene would set at the edge of the woods and just stare at the goats or whatever. Sometimes if the ambition could be found she would cut wood for the winter fires. Old Sam had grown old with age, so he was traded for supplies. For a number of years Sam and Little Sam had taken turns pulling the wagon sled. Little Sam had many of the good traits of Sam. Ilene could be anywhere and if Little Sam could see her, hear her, with the ability to get to her he would just have to come a running.

Old Sam was always put into the coral, just to know where he was, but Little Sam was allowed to run about the valley at his own. Well, Little Sam was put into the coral when the weather was not good. The really cold weather was a sign to close the barn door. That was mostly for the chickens and the possibility of their eggs freezing.

When the mist came to the valley, Ilene found it fun to beckon Little Sam to come out of the mist to her. He wasn't always close to the small house, so you had to listen for him with great intrigue. Ilene would step out of the house quietly with even a soft closing of the door. "Little Sam, how are you this morning, Ilene would often speak? In the dryness of late summer you could hear the thumping of the hooves on the hard ground. It was usually a run. If Little Sam was close he could just suddenly appear out of the mist right into your face. That was the spooky appearance. If you heard his hooves thundering on the ground, you had better stand back close to the small house or you may well get run over. Sometimes, but not always Little Sam would give out a neigh.

Old Sam just didn't have that personality. The only thing Ilene could figure out, that it was just the attention Little Sam was given since he came to her as a colt. It was a great deal of fun to be out on the hill side and give a call to Little Sam and to see him racing across the hill towards her.

It was his thundering hoofs, his mane flying in the wind passing by his speed and sometimes his whinnying with excitement of her wanting to see him.

The mist of the day had finally lifted and the work of the day done to whatever the requirements had to be. The mist had started coming back after a short half day. The goats had been brought to the coral, but the

134

count came up one short. It was one Billy still missing. Ilene walked out a way from the coral to take in a view of the hillside, just to see if the Billy could be seen. Sure enough, there he was near the tree line. Ilene began to walk towards the Billy with a few hand claps, which would sometimes get the goats attention and bring him running towards her.

It just happened to be that the goat had more attention at doing whatever he was doing. As Ilene got closer to the Billy, she could see him eating on a Bull Thistle. Ilene laughed to herself as she continued to watch him on her walk to him. It had been a five foot tall Bull Thistle this morning and as tough, thorny menace anyone could come onto. It had, this morning hailed two large purple spiky balls to soon discharge its seeds from. When Billy had decided to start eating this was unknown to her. It now was only about a foot tall and as thick of stock as your wrist. Yet, Billy would bite off a three inch section and grind it up. Ilene felt a little bad as to bring him away from his conquest. She stood back and let him take one more bite, and then she would bring him back to the fold.

"Ok, Billy it is time to come home, Ilene spoke softly. Billy turned and gave up his prize. Just as Billy began to walk towards her a cougar sprang from the edge of the woods with a run towards the two. Billy bolted for the safety of the buildings, which brought the Cougar running towards her. Ilene couldn't breathe as her heart raced. Her Hickory walking stick from Papa suddenly became a means of defense for the first time in her life. "Get out of here, Ilene yelled! Get out of here! The lion slowed a bit, but continued at her. A quick hit across the face stopped the rush, but all the Cougar did was offer a sneeze of some kind.

Then it was followed with a snarl. Growling and snarling continued. Ilene began to take steps backwards, but the Cougar just kept low and crawled slowly towards her.

Ilene kept trying to reach her sling and a stone in her pouch, but each time the Cougar would rise up a bit and act as if it would spring at her.

"What to do, what to do, Ilene whispered to herself? "Little Sam, Little Sam, Ilene shouted as loud as she could? Ilene thought she could hear hoofs, between the growls. She didn't want to give up any concentration on watching the Cougar, but she was tempted to take a partial glance over her right shoulder. It was Little Sam racing like the Thunder towards her. Little Sam had never encountered or even known what a Cougar even was. The Cougar continued to crawl towards her as she tried to walk backwards.

Little Sam thundered past her with his ears laid back flat, a piercing squeal like Ilene had never heard before, by any horse. It was right on top of the Cougar without hesitation. The Cougar was definitely caught off guard at the aggressive horses attack. The thrashing hoofs caught the Cougar and sent it limping off towards the woods. Little Sam continued his aggression and the Cougar was soon whining away. "Little Sam, Little Sam, Ilene called out?

Little Sam came trotting back to Ilene with his ears still lying backwards. His ears soon relaxed as he came close. "Oh Little Sam, you saved my life, Ilene whispered as she hugged the horse like her life had depend on him. She could feel the horse heart beat in her hug. His breathing was as crazy as hers. It took s few minutes for the two to find their way back to normal. Ilene began to walk back to the barn with several deep breaths and a few shakes to try to calm down. It of course had several looks back towards the woods to keep checking for the Cougar.

The protection of her Heavenly father was definitely brought out in prayer that night after supper. She just knew that she wasn't going to be here if it wasn't for the help of Little Sam. Had God instilled these attributes into Little Sam, just for today? There had always been someone crossing her path, whenever she had a need or was in trouble. But could the hand of God train a horse like Little Sam? She just had to accept it as a yes!

Giving it All

The years ticked by as time knew no person or cared nothing for events. Ilene only knew her age if she made a math calculation. The day of the month mattered not, nor did the month of the year or even years themselves. Most of the time passing in the valley was untouched by anyone, except Ilene. Now a goat just looked like another goat. Sam was gone and little Sam was gone. The horse of time was Samuel, named after the prophet from the bible. Everything else looked the same.

Ilene's very rare visit to the Trading store for supplies had words of dislike tossed against it. It was 1929 and her fiftieth year of life. The work was just harder, but not yet unbearable. She had always hoped that someone else would be running the Trading store, besides Paul Smith. It was the never ending thoughts of when she had chucked a stone at him some thirty-five years ago. It knocked him out and she had thought she had killed someone. He had apologized so many times for his arrogant ways back them, but how do you erase your mind, even if you had forgiven him. What would her life be if he had caused her a mischief?

"Good morning Ilene, Paul Smith greeted. "Hello, Ilene replied, as she always did. There were never any extra words. Just get right to what she wanted. "I have a nanny and two wethers to trade, if that is ok?

"That's ok, Paul agreed.

The economy is not headed in a good direction. Nanny goats will still be good property, so you had better watch your goats, so no one tries to steal them.

The sound of steal them, gave Ilene a chill down her neck. That had never been a problem before. She heard the words but offered no reaction to them. "Two dozen candles, a gallon of kerosene, sack of flour, coffee, matches, sack of beans, sack of rice or corn meal for starters, Ilene announced. "You must have your wagon sled with you today, Paul suggested? "Iodine, salt for the goats and fifty feet of rope, Ilene continued. Is this an even trade for today, Ilene questioned? "You have over fourteen hundred dollars of credit here, so you sure don't need to be concerned about today's trade, Paul suggested. Pick a few more things for an even trade. "Just finish an even trade by adding some jars of food, Ilene suggested. "Ok, Paul agreed, as he grabbed a crate and began to fill it. Ilene began to carry the items out to her wagon, being pulled by Samuel. The items were quickly loaded.

It looks like the Bucklings were cut some time ago, Paul offered, as he looked at the goats. They look like they are big enough to be away from the nanny. I could use about ten Nannies, if you can give them up? I mean if you can remove them from their kids? "I have milked this nanny for about three days, so keep on milking her, Ilene suggested as she quickly turned Samuel to leave. I will bring you ten Nannies tomorrow morning.

Ilene knew it was the nannies that people wanted for their milk. A goat could eat anything anywhere and give you a lot of milk. They were way easier than a milk cow. The first baby kids were born in February and were well onto grass now. There were still over a hundred Bucklings and Doelings. There were sixty-three Doelings and that would be a very good start for a new herd. Perhaps tomorrow she would make herself ask Paul Smith if he wanted about thirty wethers? They would be just fattening up for someone's food. She had only kept twelve Bucklings this year. "I have so many goats to feed, Ilene whispered to herself.

It wasn't unusual for Ilene to stop at the Great Granite Boulders at the edge of the valley on the old wagon trail. "Hello, Peace and Joy, Ilene offered to the Great Boulders! You have been created to give praise to my Heavenly Father above. May I join you this day? The prayer was usually from the book of Acts. My breath is given to me from the same as he who has created you great boulders.

Acts 4:24-32 24 And when they heard that, they lifted up their voice to God with one accord, and said, Lord, thou art God, which hast made heaven, and earth, and the sea, and all that in them is:25 Who by the mouth of thy servant David hast said, Why did the heathen rage, and the people imagine vain things?26 The kings of the earth stood up, and the rulers were gathered together against the Lord, and against his Christ.27 For of a truth against thy holy child Jesus, whom thou hast anointed, both Herod, and Pontius Pilate, with the Gentiles, and the people of Israel, were gathered together,28 For to do whatsoever thy hand and thy counsel determined before to be done.29 And now, Lord, behold their threatening: and grant unto thy servants, that with all boldness they may speak thy word,30 By stretching forth thine hand to heal; and that signs and wonders may be done by the name of thy holy child Jesus.31 And when they had prayed, the place was shaken where they were assembled together; and they were all filled with the Holy Ghost, and they spake the word of God with boldness.32 And the multitude of them that believed were of one heart and of one soul: neither said any of them that ought of the things which he possessed was his own; but they had all things common.33 And with great power gave the apostles witness of the resurrection of the Lord Jesus: and great grace was upon them all.

The rustle of the Great Pines encouraged Ilene to move on home and take care of the work that was always there to be done. Today was to be an extra project. Ilene unloaded the supplies and retrieved ten extra bells to tag some nanny goats. There was plenty of grass and no need to feed any grain, but it was a clever way to identify which Nannies had the biggest kids and surely had no problem leaving them. A bucket of grain was placed into the narrow feed bunk. It brought goats running

139

from everywhere to get the grain. Then just close the coral gate. You only had to wait a short time for the goats to eat the grain. It triggered the babies to get their share through the milk. The nanny with the biggest kids got the tag of a bell around her neck.

"The Nannies are ready for delivery tomorrow, Ilene assured herself. Ilene made a quick count of the nannies, while opportunity prevailed. It took a second count as she only came up with fifty-one. She had fifty-three and sold only one this morning. Ilene went to the creek for a barrel of water, as she had not yet unharnessed Samuel. Then Samuel was saddled up for a look across the valley for a missing nanny. When you only have so many animals and they are so very important to you, you just know when one is not there. Riding along the creek and taking in the view was the easy part in the search. The ride thru the Aspens was also easy. Just to listen to the leaves of the Aspens was a relaxing moment. It was easy to stop, look and listen. The greatest fear Ilene was having, happen to be the thought of some wild animal snatching up the nanny. It was usually the kids that would possibly be snatched. Did one cross the creek this morning and follow her to the Trading store? The water was a bit deep to cross, except for one spot a hundred feet from the end of her valley. That in itself was only about fifteen feet, and then it was deep again after that point. Goats can swim, but they really don't like getting wet. The wagon trail through the Bluff was the only access to get out of the valley. She surely would have seen if a Nanny was going that way.

Ilene began to ride along the river. There was a river from the lake on the backside of the woods. It was a natural fence around the valley. The river was deep and wide, so there was no goat going into that river. It was the thought of another Cougar getting into the valley that gave Ilene a chill down her neck. The Cougar would have to swim across the river and it could. The idea of continuing her search in the woods was soon given up as darkness wanted to cover everything, especially in the trees. The early night shadows could give you a chill down your neck.

The preselected ten Nanny goats were added one by one to a long rope tether. It was a simple loop into each collar.

The end of the rope was looped onto the saddle horn for Samuel to lead the group to the Trading store. It started out very well, until the creek was reached. A slight tension on the rope by Samuel, gradually coaxed the string of ten goats across the creek. Samuel was way too strong for the ten goats to get away with anything. Once they were across the creek they fell into a line to follow each other. It was across the short part of the meadow and up through the wagon trail in the Great Pines, then the Big oaks. The goats really didn't have a choice, but were allowing themselves to be led in a trusting manner.Ilene was met in front of the Trading store by Brad, Paul Smiths son. He was a tall, good looking man, just a few years younger than Ilene. He was very shy and rarely spoke. Ilene often thought they were very much alike, but that is where it began and ended. "Good morning, Brad offered! "Hello, Ilene replied! "This is a clever way to bring these goats to the Trading store, Brad suggested. Could I take these goats a couple of miles like this, Brad asked? "Perhaps, Ilene offered! It was a common answer of hers, because there was no yes or no involved. I want my rope and collars, Ilene abruptly inserted!

"Let's tie these Nannies off and go take a look in the store for more collars, Brad offered. The two quickly tied the string of goats off on the hitching post and went into the store. Paul was at the counter in the back of the store. "Good morning Ilene, Paul offered! "Hello, Ilene replied. "There are ten collars here, but they have bells on them, brad offered with a display of the find. "That's fine, Ilene agreed. "Ok, I will grab a fifty foot rope too, Brad added to his find. "This is a replacement, Pa for what Ilene used to bring the Nannies to the Trading store, Brad instructed. Take a look out front and I will just take over to make the delivery.

Paul went to the door and had a quick look. "Nice job, Ilene, Paul commended! I see where it is easier to just trade, rather than mess around. How much do we owe you for the Nannies? "Eight dollars each, Ilene quickly stated! "Eight, Paul responded quickly! They are only worth about six and fifty!

"Go buy some for that, Ilene suggested! "No one else has any, Paul replied! Oh, very well, Paul grumbled! Brad, you just as well get going or you will be milking goats tonight. I need the price we talked about and maybe two dollars for the rope and collars. Brad quickly left with a salutation, "See you Ilene! "So now I owe you another eighty dollars,

Paul instructed Ilene. Don't you need something? "Ten sacks of oats, I guess, Ilene offered, as she glanced around the store. Deliver please! "Well that is thirty cents times ten, Paul quickly stated! You have less than ninety percent of the people out there, but yet you have more than ninety percent. You just spend less you smart lady. Paul scratched the figures down in his journal. I owe you over fourteen hundred dollars, Paul grumbled. "Two hundred pounds of potatoes, Ilene requested. "Now you are talking, Paul whispered with a smile. Eight fifty per hundred! "Two hundred pounds of carrots, Ilene added. "That's five fifty per hundred, Paul added with another smile. Garden not working this year, Paul laughed? "The garden is just fine, Ilene replied with a sobering glance. "Sorry, Paul apologized! "Two new Billies, Ilene requested. Not related to mine either. I will trade you Billie's from this year's crop and give you four wethers to your benefit. "That may take some doing, Paul replied with a scratching of his head. If I can find them, I will talk trade then. Brad can bring your supplies out tomorrow. Still over fourteen hundred, blast it any how! Thanks Ilene! "Yes sir, Ilene replied as she walked backwards towards the door. She wasn't sure what the blast it was? It must have something to do with the fourteen hundred dollars she had for credit. Ilene turned to open the door and smiled, as she thought the amount of credit was a very good thing.

"Samuel we have fourteen hundred dollars of credit, Ilene instructed the horse as they walked slowly towards home. Samuel, we have forty wethers that don't have much value. What should we do with them? I am not even sure we should have kept the twelve Bucklings? Samuel soon reached the Great Granite Boulders, so Ilene pulled the reins up for a stop. She dismounted and knelled beside one of the Boulders. Time for a prayer Samuel!

"Oh Great and Holy one of all that exists, the one who's hand has created all that I see. What do you want to do with these goats of yours? You bless me beyond what I can use! Perhaps, just perhaps, there is something I can do for you? Open my eyes and heart for your glory! I pray this in the holy name of thy child, Jesus Christ! My Lord, let it be so!"Well Samuel, you are my witness, Ilene whispered to the horse. For you, my friend, there shall be two extra handfuls of oats tonight. Samuel got his hug and extra oats that night. "Ok goats you are staying in the coral tonight, Ilene decreed! It's because one of you has come up missing. I am going to lie on the roof of the barn and watch over you.

Ilene lay on the roof of the small barn starring at the nightly stars. The Winchester lay across her chest, as she starred into the sky. The nightly mist for June was increasing. It hung up in the air with a gradual blocking out of the stars. It would be early morning before it would drop to the ground. It was mystical with the misty fog hanging over everything. To view under it for a great distance was no problem. Ilene kept looking across the hill side, then across the creek to the meadow on the other side. It was kind of a surprise when she first saw a lantern moving from the wagon trail down towards the creek. She was compelled to watch the goats for an understanding of her one goat disappearing. The only conclusion was that it had been stolen, but how.

The lantern moved along smoothly until she saw whomever wade into the creek. The stranger in the dark had no idea where to cross the creek. She could tell when the lantern went over the head of whomever. The water in the creek was very deep, except for one spot, that only a few knew about. The intruder went back to the far side and tried a spot much closer towards her upstream. It was still quite deep, but much better. The intruder again back out of the creek and sat on the far side bank of the creek. Possible wondering how they could steal a goat and get it back across the creek? After a short bit another attempt was made even closer to her upstream. This time the shadowy intruder had hit the spot that was premium for crossing, as it was only about eighteen inches deep this time of year.

The crossing was made, so now what was Ilene going to do with this attack of the night intruder?

Ilene didn't want to kill another human being, but had to protect what she had. "Father in Heaven, what shall I do, Ilene whispered? What? What? Suddenly the idea of shooting the lantern out popped into her head. I will shoot the lantern out and maybe the intruder will be frightened away? The intruder had made their way to the coral and was apparently searching for a gate. This must be someone different than who had stolen the first Nanny? The intruder stopped for thought. Crack the Winchester echoed. The lantern exploded in a flash. The intruder dove to the ground with a yelling of, "Don't shoot! Don't shoot! "State your business, Ilene called out in a calm voice? There was no immediate reply, but then the intruder offered, "I came to steal a Nanny goat from you!

That was honest at least Ilene thought. "I will sell you one, but I prefer the daytime, Ilene suggested. "I have no money and I need food for my children, the intruder called out. He seemed to be emotional about the statement, Ilene thought. "Do you know who stole my first Nanny that went missing, Ilene requested? Again there was silence for a short bit of time. "Yes, a sober reply came from the intruder. "You come back tomorrow in the daylight and I will give you a Nanny, Ilene offered! "Give me a Nanny, the Intruder questioned? 'Yes, I will give you a Nanny for your family, Ilene repeated. "Thank you, the intruder calmly sounded out! Bring the other thief with you, Ilene added the extra request! "I will try, the intruder replied!

It was silent for a period. "Are you sick, Ilene requested? "Maybe a little, but I am ok, the intruder quietly sounded back. "Rise up and live, Ilene called out! Ilene felt much better after that statement. "Why did I say that, Ilene questioned herself? A tear found its way down her cheek. Those words were first given to her forty years ago by Peter. Ilene saw the dark image of someone standing up and slowly walking back to the creek. The creek was crossed and the dark form moved across the meadow on the other side, until it disappeared up the wagon trail.

Ilene felt calm for whatever reason. Someone was coming to see her, but it didn't seem to matter.

"Two thieves are coming to see me, Ilene whispered to herself as she sat on a log round in front of her small house. It feels like the hand of God directing me to do whatever I am compelled to do. "I feel you oh Great Spirit of the Holy one, Ilene whispered! I have never felt this before. Let thy will be done for your glory!

In a short time Ilene heard splashing coming from the creek and two figures appeared through the mist. "Hello Miss, one called out? "Hello, Ilene replied! Come and sit down? Would you like some coffee, Ilene asked? The two looked at each other in surprise. "Yes, please the two chimed! Ilene went into the small house to get three cups and the coffee pot from the fire. The cups were filled and handed out. Ilene took her cup and returned to sitting on the log round.

"So, which of you stole the first Nanny, Ilene requested? The two men were probably in their late twenties. "My name is Rob and I am the one that has your goat, Rob confessed. "Why, Ilene asked? "I can't find game to hunt or work to be had, Rob continued. A milking goat would be so useful, so I stole your goat. I am sorry and I will try to pay for it or I will bring it back. It was so helpful for the family, I convinced my younger brother to come and steal one. This is Jack! My name is Ilene, Ilene introduce herself!

"I am going to forgive you Rob, but please don't do it again, Ilene stated. I am going to give Jack a Nanny and a wether. I am also going to give you Rob, a wether. I am also going to give each of you three potatoes and each three bunches of carrots. Follow me to the root cellar. The promised items were removed from the cellar and given to the two brothers. Then the two followed Ilene to the coral.

Ilene walked into the coral and laid a hold on the horn of a Nanny. The Nanny was gently led out of the coral. A kid followed the Nanny, which just happened to be a wether. A second tried to follow, but it was a doeling. Ilene pushed it back so it couldn't follow. Ilene walked back into the coral and just stood for a bit. A kid came up to her, which happened to be a wether. She scooped it up and carried it out of the coral. If you lead the Nanny slowly, the kids will just follow along. However, you should carry the kids, until you cross the creek.

"Thank you so much Ilene, the two sounded out together. "How can we repay you, Rob asked? "There is no charge, Ilene instructed! "You have so little and yet you give so much, Jack admitted. "In October or November you can bring the Nannies back to be mated to one of the Billies, Ilene suggested. They come in heat, but you can still keep milking the Nanny. You should stop milking when they are about sixty days prior to giving birth. "Thank you again, Ilene, Rob offered. I am so sorry for taking the Nanny. "Go in peace, Ilene offered, as she turned to walk away.

"Miss Ilene, Jack sounded out? If I may be so bold to make a request of you? "What is the request, Ilene asked, as she turned back towards the two. "There is a terrible great need for food out amongst where we live, Jack implored. Would you be able to give any other Nannies? I feel so bad even asking, but I am compelled to do so. Perhaps we can help you make your hay and firewood that you require? Ilene stood there looking at the two men. "I give freely to those that have a need, Ilene stated. Let it be so, until I am unable to do so! Go in peace, as I have said! Ilene turned away again and proceeded to her small house. It was a prayer of thanks giving, a cup of coffee and then a return to the coral to release the goats to the pasture. "Heavenly Father, if your hand lends to others to ask of me, then it is to your glory that I do so, Ilene offered boldly as she watched her goats spread out over the hillside.

There was a gradual, but steady flow of people coming across the meadow and then across the creek in the next month. Ilene pounded two stakes in the ground for the crossing point in the creek. Ilene placed one of the stakes to the north of the shallower water and one to the south. It looked like the thing to do, as the first people did the same as the thief. They would go to the closest point to the wagon trail rather than going north for a bit, then crossing the creek. Many came as couples or families. The question of why are you doing this, came up many times? The answer was always the same from Ilene. "By the grace of God, I am able to do so, Ilene would answer. Many would look around the yard and reply,

"It looks like maybe you should keep all your goats! Ilene would give no reply to the statement.

There were many that offered to return when they could and give back to her. "This I freely give, Ilene would answer. My Heavenly Father will care for me. A Nanny goat was selected by Ilene at each visit of those that declared a need. A wether was then picked out and also given. Three potatoes and three bunches of carrots were selected from the root cellar and added to the gift. There were seven Nannies and two Billies left,

when it appeared that the people stopped arriving. Of course there were the sixty-two doelings left, but no Billies for them to mate in the fall. There were only two of the Bucklings left, as ten of them were given away. Ilene had run out of the wethers, so she began to give a Buckling with a Nanny.One day without notice, two young men appeared in the

146

meadow across the creek and cut all the hay down. Then without a word they left, but a larger group appeared the next day and gathered all the hay up on flat racks. They forge the flat racks across the creek and stacked the hay by the small barn. The only words spoken were by a mid-aged man, which walked up the hill where Ilene was watching her goats. "Miss, where, would you like us to stack your hay, he asked? "You can make several stacks by the small barn, Ilene replied.

Ilene went down the hill to start doing her chores later in the day. There were maybe ten men putting the hay up in the stacks. Ilene had never had so much hay. Ilene recognized Rob as the first thief, as he came walking over to where she was placing a bucket of oats into the goat troughs. Of course the goats were running across the hill side to be sure that they didn't miss out on the lovely grain.

"Hello, Ilene, Rob greeted! "Hello, Ilene replied! Tomorrow we will be over here with firewood for you. "I have been cutting the dead wood from the top of the hill, Ilene instructed, as she pointed to the ridge. "No, no, Rob interrupted! We will bring the wood in the wagons. Many people have been cutting wood for you. The wood is cut and will be delivered to you. It is dry wood and ready to be used. Just show me where you would like to have it stacked?

Rob and Ilene walked over to where her wood pile was now and discussed the matter in about a minute. "Why, Ilene asked in a trembling voice? "You are the grace of God! Because you are a Queen to us, Rob replied, as he started to cry and quickly walked away.

The next day there were deliveries of cut, split and stacked wood placed at her required location.

There was many, many times more wood than Ilene had ever seen stacked by the small house. Ilene had always just dumped

the log rounds or pieces into a large pile.

This delivery was so neat and large, that she felt a little uncomfortable to start using the neat piles.

Even the rounds that she had were split and stacked. It was as if the grace of God was over flowing on her.On the third morning, Brad Smith, the son of Paul Smith showed up with two other men. They had

147

a wagon full of bleached white goats. "Hello, Ilene, Brad greeted! These goats are called Saanen breed of goats. "Hello, Ilene offered to the men! They don't have a single spot of any color on them. Ilene was in great surprise and fascinated by the bleach white color. Ilene felt like they were blemish free goats from heaven. She was lost in thought. "Ilene, Ilene, Brad sounded as he tried to get her attention away from her transfigured thoughts.

"Why so many, Ilene whispered? My Billies I asked for? "There are three Billies and ten doelings, Brad instructed. They are a gift from me! I went to the state of New York and brought them back for you. Brad swept Ilene into his arms with a jubilation of hugs. These goats give a lot of milk. They are the best goats in the world for that. The half grown goats were added to the coral, but you could pick them out, like corn kernels from a bowl of rice. "Why, Ilene whispered again?

"You gave away your herd and then some, Brad announced! That's like fifty nannies and fifty wethers, plus food with each one. I think you are the best person in the world! If I had not been so slow over the years; I would have asked you to marry me! Too shy! That's on me! I cried, when I heard about all that you were giving. I cried, because I love you so much. I am in my forties and you are in your fifties, so we will just have to be friends, if you can? "For sure, Ilene replied, with a hug and the feeling of a tear rolling down her cheek.

The Years Go By

The days trickled by, but no Jonathan, no sign of the Reeds. The Smith ranch hands came to rebuild the Trading store. Each morning Ilene went over to tend to the horses. The young Smith, who was the ranch Forman, was also the one who she had struck with a stone last summer. He pleaded his apology, but Ilene just didn't want to have a conversation with him. By spring the store was built and stocked with all manner of supplies. Bo and Patty didn't want to operate it and Ilene had no desire either. The owners of the two saddle horses finally showed up. They were more than happy to pay Ilene for their care. The two wagons and teams of horses were sold to Paul. Paul made the purchase, but growled at the thought of owing Ilene almost two thousand dollars.

It was the Smith ranch that paid for everything and the building of it. The insurance check was then given to the Smith's. Then the Smith's bought the store from Bo, Patty and Ilene. Ilene didn't want any of the money, so she let Bo and Patty have it all. There was an open invitation to help Ilene with anything she may need. There were seventy some little kids filling the pasture and coral. The Smith Trading store was more than willing to help her move the animals. There were purchases of goats for many, many years. All she had to do was ride Samuel to the Trading store and pick out whatever she might need. The items were very solemnly picked up in a very sparse requirement.

The years ticked by as Ilene sat with her goats in the valley. Jonathan never returned! The Reeds were never found! Bo and Patty Williams had their visits sparsely, and then passed on. A new owner by the name of Leonard took over the store. The metal chest under her bed never moved or got opened. Ilene's routine was the same each and every day, year after year.One day a young man or at least one ten years her youth

149

came walking up the creek bank. "Hello, the young man called out? Ilene sat on the bank with her goats spread out everywhere. She gave no responds. "Hello, the young man called out from across the creek from her position? May I fish in your creek, he requested? Ilene nodded her head in agreement and gave a small wave, but offered no words. "My name is Harold, the young man offered! Ilene continued to stare at the waters of the creek tumbling by, with no acknowledgement.

It was about an hour or so later, when the young man came by Ilene still sitting in the same spot. "Would you like two of the four fish I caught, the younger man offered? My name is Harold, in case you didn't hear me before. My wife is Dorothy and we live up on the bluff. If you look close, you can barely see our house from here. We just finished building our house, so now I may have time to fish. I love to fish. When I go fishing, I am more than happy to share with you. Harold prepared to leave and waved, so long! "My name is Ilene, Ilene finally offered!

A few weeks ticked by, when Ilene heard a knock on her small house door. Ilene opened the door and saw Harold standing there with a lady younger than her. They were carrying a basket with a blanket. "Hello, my name is Dorothy, the younger lady announced! Would you like to join us for a picnic lunch? The last picnic lunch Ilene had ever had was with Peter and Jonathan almost thirty years ago. Ilene stepped out of the small house without saying a word. Harold spread out the blanket by the creek in front of the small house. Dorothy held out her hand to take Ilene's hand. There was no return offer,

So Dorothy put her arm around Ilene and gently ushered her to the blanket. Harold and Dorothy sat down and Dorothy began to take food out of the basket, so Ilene sat down without a word.

After a two way conversation, Harold took his fishing rod and cast it the creek. Harold fished and ate whatever was offered to him. Dorothy kept smiling and offering food to Ilene and Harold. Dorothy talked about all manner of things, that didn't seem to land on Ilene's ears.

The words were as different as the food that she was offered. The strange items of fried chicken, potato salad, dill pickles cheese cake and lemonade? Dorothy was a cook? Harold delivered something called propane? Ilene said nothing and offered little shakes of the surprising tastes of the different foods.

Harold soon caught a fish and called it a Rock bass. He put it on something called a stringer and tied it to a stake so it could lay in the edge of the creek. Then there was something called a Pike, which was quite large. It seemed to be very exciting for Harold. Harold's excitement almost made Ilene smile. The two prepared to leave, as they picked up their picnic items. "So long Ilene, Dorothy offered! "You can have both of the fish, Harold suggested! Ilene reached for the smaller Rock Bass and left the larger Pike for Harold. This is the real prize, Harold laughed! Ilene had no idea as to what that meant, but she nodded her head in agreement. The two left offering their waves of so long.

A couple of weeks had passed by, before Harold came to do some fishing. Harold stopped and stared at the creek. Ilene was sitting on the bank a short distance away. Harold waved and smiled. He shrugged his shoulders and arms slightly, at the view he had of almost no water in the creek. Harold walked along the creek towards the lake. When he got close to the newly constructed over flow that was added to the road and accommodation of the water coming off the lake, he was puzzled. There was a small widening of the creek just at the over flow. He thought he saw some fish in the small bit of a pond, so he cast his lure into the pond.

It was in a very short minute and he had a fish. It was a Pike of good size and really should not have been in this small pond. Harold put the fish on his stringer and continued to fish. It was the quickest fishing and catching his limit that he had ever known. "This is a real problem to have this amount of fish in this small pond by this over flow, Harold instructed himself.

Harold took his fish and went down the creek a short distance, before crossing over. He walked towards Ilene sitting and watching her goats. Ilene stood up as Harold got closer. "Hello, Ilene, Harold offered with a smile. Harold didn't expect Ilene to respond.

"Hello, Ilene replied! "What happened to all the water in the creek, Harold questioned? "The building of that devise and road a year ago has taken my creek away in the summer time, Ilene whispered. I no longer have water to drink or even to take a bath. I cannot even wash up! I take my goats to the pond by the road. In the night time I go over the road and wash my clothes. I have taken a bath in the lake on the other side, but I am very afraid when I do so. My creek has a little water in the spring and after a good rain, but it doesn't last very long.

"The government wants what the government wants, Harold offered in disgust! The two began to walk towards the small house. I have a couple of fish for you. There seems to be a lot of fish in the small pond by the over flow. We are going to eat as many fish as we can, because of the government limit on how many you can have. Maybe you can help with that. I am going to try to catch as many fish out of the over flow pond, which I can. Otherwise they may just die! I don't have my horse anymore, so I haven't been able to put ice in my icehouse, Ilene informed Harold. "I will give you some to eat and keep some for you in our freezer. "Do you have a big icehouse, Ilene questioned? Harold suddenly realized that Ilene didn't know what electricity was or what a chest freezer was.

"Have you ever seen the chest freezer they have at the store, Harold asked? "Leonard helps me sell my goats, but I don't go into the store, Ilene confessed. If I want something, I just ask him. Maybe I need some garden seeds, kerosene, candles and some soap for washing my face.

"Well, we have a chest freezer, Harold tried to inform Ilene, and he tried to think of a quick way to describe the freezer. It is a large white metal box with a lid. It is an invention with other components to keep food frozen solid. The wires you see in the air carry electricity to run it and many other things as well. Harold pointed to the road by the over flow to indicate the wires in the air. Ilene had no comment, but seemed to grasp the idea.

"Let me see if I can help you with your water problem, Harold offered with a smile. In my spare time I do a lot of trading. I just happen to have six fifty-five gallon water barrels.

Three of them have a drilling for a water spout in the lower part of the bottom. We can put those three barrels right here in front of your house. I will use the other three in the back of my pickup to haul water to use for whatever you like. I will get right to it today! Ilene had no clue as to what was going on, but offered a, "Thank you, Harold! Harold quickly walked towards home with his fish.

Harold was a small framed man, but his heart was bigger than most. He had to be a scrapper to make a living, but he never gave it a second thought, when it came time to help someone. The fish were quickly cleaned and the barrels were loaded into the old pickup. A hose was formed from the hand pump in the yard and he began to pump, until the three transfer water barrels were filled. A small stand from unknown origin but, just right for the three barrels was loaded up behind the water barrels. A small twelve volt pump that was kept for no particular reason had a couple of long pieces of hose added to it. Harold smiled at his small invention. Then it was off to Ilene's small house.

It as a slow ride down the old wagon trail through the woods and not just for the smell either, it was a good and valuable load. Here was someone who had far less than himself. Harold knew all about such things and how difficult it was in the great depression. The pickup side window was rolled down, just to take in the fragrant smell of the great pines. The rustling of the big Oaks was just an added gift. The two big boulders at the end to the valley, just said we are the guardians.

"May I pass great guardians, Harold whispered, as he passed! He made this request, whether he walked by or drove passed. It was just the two giant boulders that had stood the test of time. It was just those two and no others to be seen. How and why, he didn't know?

Harold soon arrived at a narrow part of the creek, with actually had no water flowing. It was just a stone bed, which offered an easy passing over. It was then onto his destination of the small house. The stand was unloaded and then the barrels were placed appropriately. The small pump was set up to transfer the water to the barrels on the stand. The stand was just the right height to get a bucket under the spouts. The pump was clipped onto the pickup battery and the water transfer was under way.

In a very short time the three full barrels in the back of the pickup were off loaded into the three barrels on the stand by the house.

Ilene now understood what Harold had been trying to explain to her. She had not had this feeling of excitement in many, many years. She quickly hugged the short stature, bald, white haired man. Harold laughed with surprise and had to pull out a white hanky to wipe his eyes. This was a good day for sure. "Is this water good for drinking, Ilene asked? "Yes, it is from our hand pump and we drink it all the time, Harold offered with a laugh. "Perhaps for all these years I have taken my water for granite, Ilene confessed! Now, I am ever so appreciative of this water, you and the hand of God, for sending you across my path.

"God, Harold questioned? "Well, whenever something nasty, hard, sickness, injury or whatever happens, God sends someone to cross my path and help me, Ilene informed. It's just that, I believe, that's all. Sometimes I think I have nothing, when really I have more than most! Today I thought I was going to have to eat one of my goats, but you brought me fish to eat. It is a long way to cross the road to the lake and carry water to the house. I am ever so grateful to have this water here. You can see why I loved my creek for so many years.

"Last night was a full moon and it sat on the top of the ridge behind the house, Ilene reflected. In the full moon there was a great Stag standing and looking at the moon. I sat on the hillside,

Watching until I fell to sleep. I have seen the glory of the moon giving its all to our Heavenly Father many times.

It has only been seen by me twice with the great Stag standing and watching the moon. I watched, I prayed and I tried to add to the glory of God, well until I fell asleep. I am seventy years old and I was going to have to prepare one of my goats for food. I have done this many times and still can. However, I am just getting a bit tired. That sight last night was seen by me fifty-seven years ago. The first time I wished I could have stayed and watched longer.

I was too sad then! I know I watched last night for hours, but then I confess I fell asleep. My prayer last night was please; please take me from the face of this earth! If it is not your will Heavenly Father, then please send help!

The first time is when I buried my Mama beside my Papa. I lay in a grave awaiting my own fate. A young man came the next morning and asked me, "Are you sick? "No, I replied! "Then rise up and live he told me! Today, you gave me food, water and can I say friend? "Well, you need to stop or I may just cry, Harold instructed! I saw the full moon, but just agreed it was nice and left it at that! A friend, oh yes, just ask and I will help if I can. "Then thank you Harold and your wife Dorothy for now and future, Ilene offered.

Baby

VINTAGE BABY GIRL CLIPART

The young lady worked hard in her garden. It wasn't because she was in her in her late thirties and had the ambition to do so. It was more of the excitement in her heart and mind, which compelled her to do so. This year seemed more important than years gone by. The garden was quite large and contained almost everything you could imagine. As you approach well into your thirties you may consider that you are mid age, but here was a case of thinking you are still young. There would soon be many things that would need to be canned for the future winter months. The young lady would always can more than the two of them would need, but that was ok, because she would always find a need somewhere.

Working the garden was not the young ladies only ordeal, as she worked a full time job on an elderly home as a cook. Her stocky composition didn't look as if she had an unlimited working ability. This year had more ambition in it than last year. There was always time to visit her close neighbor, Ilene. It was a regular visit to see the old woman. Well, old as in respect to the young ladies age. She was thirty years older than what she was, which should have brought about the idea of retirement. Ilene would never retire as she had lived alone all her life in the little valley down from the ridge that the young lady lived on.

It was a rare day off from work, so it would be a perfect time to visit Ilene. The usual picnic basket was filled to the brim. It was always an unusual picnic fill. Today it would contain just two sandwiches and a quart of lemonade. The remainder of the basket would contain washing soap, a new shirt, under clothes, some current newspapers and canned foods. The various assortments of canned foods were in her jars from last year. It varied from week to week or so, but always had the canned foods. Full jars were delivered on time and the basket would return the empty from visits in the past.

The sunny day seemed to bring the best out of the birds in the area, as they all added to the collection of song. It may have been the sunny day, spring nesting or maybe just because the young lady felt so good about the day. The filled basket was snatched up and the journey began. With the garden all planted and still a strong waft of turned up soil as she passed by, it gave her an extra smile. The great Oaks rustled their leaves as she began down the old path, that use to be a wagon trail down through the woods towards the valley below. Her short cheerful husband would take his riding mower and run down the path and out into the valley towards the creek, just to give her a better walking path.

Oaks quickly put on their leaves and shaded the path completely already. It had gone from a sunny warm day, to a cool shady day. The brisk walk would shake it off and the heavy basket offered its own exertion. Half way down the Oaks gave way to the great pines, so the natural sound changes so, that even a blind person could tell where they were on the path. At the break of the great pines into the valley offered the two centuries of granite boulders. The young lady had her own thoughts about these two. Guardians to the valley she would often reflect. It was time to sit the heavy basket down and to take a rest break.

The young lady offered a few pats of her open hand on the granite guardians. A look out across the valley to see what might be revealed. On the far side of the creek she could see the herd of goats. There were a few here and a few more there, as they were spread out on the hill side. It appeared to be so peaceful? Her friend Ilene may be in the small house, cutting wood in the tree line or perhaps just sitting and watching her goats.

The view was not reflecting where her location was today. There was a post in the ground on either side of the creek at some distance from her location. The poles were to let her and others that were aware as to the shallowest place to cross over to the other side. An invigorating strength returned from the rest time. The basket was returned to its carrying position. It was on down the path to the two post location for crossing over. The young lady always used her oldest pair of shoes for the journey, as the water crossing had to be navigated. The crossing point suddenly revealed the location of Ilene. She was a little further down washing some clothing or such. It was a very careful crossing, as the spring waters were still somewhat apparent. It was well above the knees yet. Cold enough to give you a chill too! There was no dawdling crossing over.

The young lady saw the greeting from the distance of an arm wave. It was returned to Ilene as an equal greeting, as she continued on down the opposite side of the creek. The basket was sat down and a hug was offered to each other. "That was a tiring tote, the young lady offered! "You bring down such a heavy load, Ilene relied. The two sat down on the bank of the creek. "I can believe that the water is very cold washing today, the young lady remarked. "Yes, very cold, but it has to be done, Ilene agreed. I am still washing winter things. This is far better than snow, Ilene laughed, the young lady joining in with the laugh.

"How, are things going for you, Ilene asked? "Very well, the young lady quickly informed. The garden is all planted, so that's a big job done. Two more months for the bun in the oven! "I think I am as excited as you probably are, Ilene suggested. I have always wanted a family up until about thirty years ago. Now you are just starting when I gave up. I guess I should have been more prayerful of having a husband first. I gave up on that idea when I was twenty!

I didn't think I would ever get married either, the young lady announced. Strange! I have my youngest sister married at less than sixteen.

We both have a bun in the oven and may even have children of the same age, the young lady laughed! We are having fun writing back and forth every week. I guess we are both headed for August?

"Your baby goats sure have grown, the young lady offered with a smile, as she handed a sandwich to her friend. A surprise this week! It is a sandwich which I know you have never had.

It is one of my husband's favorite sandwiches. Take a bite and tell me what you think? Ilene took a bite and carefully examined the taste in her mouth. "It has a little spicy flavor with a hit of meat perhaps, Ilene offered? It has your mayo with some chopped up cucumber mixed in? "Very good, the young lady replied. The spicy meat is called Braunschweiger! "I like it very much, Ilene offered! The lemonade was poured, as the two sat gazing into the babbling creek. The creek is very hypnotizing, the young lady suggested. "I have set watching this and listening many, many times and I never get tired of it, Ilene informed the young lady.

"Let's tote this basket up to your house and get any empties you have, the young lady suggested. I am going to need all the empties I can gather together for canning this summer. The two each latched a hold on the basket to begin the walk to the house. "It sure is a lot easier when two carry this basket. The young lady offered with a smile.

The basket was unloaded onto the small table. Ilene began to gather up the empties she had for the basket to be returned. "I love the smell of this soap, Ilene offered, as she took in a deep breath of one of the bars. I need a bath, but the idea of the cold water gives me a chill and I am not even touching the water, she laughed. "You know that you are always welcome to come up to the house, the young lady offered! The offer had stood for a long time, but Ilene never came up to the house.

The two offered hugs of departure. Ilene always wished the young lady wishes of health and happiness for her and the coming baby. "Do you need anything, the young lady would always request? "I always have more than I need, Ilene would reply! The young lady would never suggest bringing anything. What she would bring would be a last minute of just whatever.

If what she saw in Ilene's procession was all she needed, then she thought she had a hundred times more than she needed. "Hope to see you soon, the young lady offered as she departed the small house! "Thanks so much for everything, Ilene replied! Especially just for you!

With empty jars in the basket, the trip to home was considerable easier. There was no need for a rest stop at the guardians.

The two giant boulders were passed, but not ignored. "Good day to you granite guardians of history, the young lady saluted, as she passed! The birds still had plenty of joy in them as she walked up the path. The songs of spring still passed her by as she went up the inclined path towards the garden at the top of the ridge. It was a slow walk by the garden with anticipation of new rows popping up through the soil. The sun seemed to pull the young growth right up out of the rich smelling soil. It was an exciting time for new life. The young lady smiled to herself as she entered here small, beautiful little home.

Not every day was set up for a visit with her friend Ilene, but she was never forgotten. There was an opening in the ridge where you could see the valley from one end to the other. There was always time to go to the opening and sit on an old stump. In most morning, especially in the spring and fall you could gaze out into the valley and see the mist or fog, which ever you prefer calling it. Sometimes you could just see the top of the mist blanket and others you could look under it. The young lady preferred looking in under the mist, because then sometimes, just sometimes she could locate Ilene and her goats. The goats were always the easiest to locate. Ilene was only a rare sometimes. A few lucky times she had seen Ilene located on top of the blanket. It had been times when the mist had settled into the valley and Ilene had been up on the ridge cutting firewood. Cutting firewood in the clouds the young lady had imagined.

The young lady and Ilene made a time of engagement. This was the first time they had actual set a date to get together. They would meet at the sentinel granite boulders a week before the young lady would have her baby. The young lady thought that it may be a spell before she may be able to return.

It was at the bottom of the trail, just before the meadow. It was a safe location for Ilene. It wasn't too far for the young lady to travel. The young lady would pull her red wagon that she used around her garden.

A typical basket was assembled with canned foods, two sandwiches, lemonade and some current newspapers. Two new sheets and pillow cases were the added surprise. The young lady felt very well as she began the short journey.

It was an average summer August day, with only a slight chance of rain. The birds were semi quite as she walked down the trail to the meadow. She thought this was because of the cloudy condition of possible rain. Nesting was done and baby birds were well grown. Baby squirrels were jumping out in the trail, trying to learn squirrel things. There were a few chipmunks looking for the nuts from the big Oaks, but they were only finding what was left from last year. Soon there would be abundance.

Ilene was already at the desired location and was offering her usual wave. The young lady returned a wave and a smile, that they had made the rendezvous. "Oh, your little red wagon, which you have spoken of, Ilene, offered surprised. I was concerned that you may carry your basket and it may be a bit heavy too, carry? "This wagon may just the trick to use all the time, the young lady suggested. I have my sitting board in the bottom of the wagon too. I thought I might sit in my wagon today. I just lay the board across the wagon frame, like this. The young lady demonstrated the position. Then I can sit when I do garden things. Easier getting up, you know?

"I brought Billy and my cart up here to haul a possible basket back with me, Ilene instructed. I don't have a horse anymore, so Billy does the hauling. His load is usually firewood and always downhill. Of course he has to pull the empty cart up the hill behind the house to the tree line. I am so glad we could meet at the edge of the meadow. "Of course, the young lady replied with grace. "The older I get, the more of a panic I have about leaving the valley. It's more of a fear of meeting others and not being able to defend myself. It has been a great blessing for me to have your husband, Harold to take my goats out of the valley to sell for me. He has fetched so many things back to me too! It has made an old lady lazy!

"Oh, jumping jiminy, the young lady announced out of the blue! There was a pain and it took my breath away! "Contraction, Ilene questioned? "I don't know, the young lady whispered back with a blank stare. Oh, there is another one! That was painful, the young lady stated! I had better get back. Can you help me Ilene? Ilene turned as white as a Leghorn chicken.

The young lady tried to stand up, but found it very difficult, as Ilene reached for her to assist.

"I won't be able to walk back up the trail, the young lady announced, as tears began to flow down her cheeks. Ilene grabbed Billy by a horn

161

and pulled the cart close to the young lady. "Sit on the front of the cart and I will get you up to your house, Ilene offered as she assisted. Just as soon as a comfort sitting position was obtained, Ilene began to tug Billy by the horn. It didn't take much to get Billy started. Ilene then went behind the cart and offered some assistance by pushing at the back of the cart. Ilene began to vomit as she pushed on the back of the cart. Her legs were weakening. Her fears began to mount, the further she left the valley. Billy leaned into his harness to pull the cart with great effort. Ilene tried to push with all she had, but the addition of tears seems to weaken her.

The top was reached, so Ilene quickly went to Billy and tugged at his horn to direct him towards the small house. "Take me to my car, the young lady requested! Just as soon as the car was reached, Ilene went to assist the young lady to a standing position. "Can you get my purse from the table inside the door and my case from just inside the door, the young lady requested? Ilene didn't answer the request, but went straight to the house. Ilene was swimming in her head. "Purse, case, she didn't know what they were, she whispered? The storm door was pulled open, but the inside door would not pull or push. "Turn the knob, the young lady instructed! "Turn, Ilene instructed herself! The turn easily released the door.

There was a small case on the floor and a smaller case sitting on a table. Ilene grabbed the two items and hurried out the door, back to the car. The young lady was already sitting in the car. The large case was handed to the young lady. It was quickly transferred to the seat beside her.

Then the smaller case called a purse was handed on. "Thanks Ilene, the young lady quickly offered. I have about twenty miles to go, so I will hurry onward.

"Take care and be brave, Ilene announced, as the car quickly left the dooryard.

Ilene fell down on her hands and knees and proceeded to dry heave. She felt so dizzy and weak. After several minutes she stood up and turned Billy around. Ilene sat down on the front of the cart. "Go Billy, Ilene requested! Billy began to walk back to where he had first arrived.

162

The top of the trail was reached and Billy instinctively turned to head down the incline. Billy went slowly down the trail and continued on to the creek. It was a full stop at that point, so Ilene had to take a horn and walk before Billy over the creek. Ilene sat back on the front of the cart. "Billy, let's go, Ilene requested? Billy went all the way to his usual spot of getting harnessed beside the small house. Ilene unharnessed Billy and stored the harness in its storage box on the side of the small barn. Then she just fell to the ground from the nervous strain she had just endured. It was a matter of just trying to breath.

It Billy breathing in her ear, that startled her back to an awake state. Ilene lay there with her head spinning still. Her breathing was returned to a normal resting breath. The world wouldn't stop spinning. She had to close her eyes again, just to feel like there was some control on her part. "What is happening, she questioned herself? She continued to lay there. "Have mercy Heavenly Father, she whispered! Her prayer continued, until she fell back off to sleep. It was the rain drops falling on her face, that made her arouse. She sat up, and then stood up. A smile crossed her face at the feeling of being ok.

The days clicked by and turned into weeks. Then it was a month. Ilene kept wondering about the young lady and the new baby? It was near two months, when Ilene saw Harold's old pickup coming across the meadow. It drove to the shallow spot in the creek and crossed over. Ilene walked down the hill from where she had been sitting with the goats. Harold had parked and gotten out of the pickup, by the time Ilene had arrived at the front of the small house. "Hello Harold, Ilene greeted! "Hello, Harold whispered! Harold usually greeted in a more rambunctious manner.

Harold stood there starring at the ground. "I don't have the words, Harold offered in a half cry! Our baby is gone! Ilene took a deep breath and stepped backwards with a quick fall into a sitting position. She too, had no words. Harold quickly turned around and picked a box of items out of the back of the pickup box. A shuffled walk brought the items to the front of the small house and sat them down.

Ilene was still sitting on the ground, so Harold offered her his two hands to rise back up. The old woman received a well placed hug from Harold. The only words Ilene offered were, "I have your basket! Ilene

163

retrieved the picnic basket with empty jars in it. The basket was handed to Harold from the tear filled face of the old woman. "So sorry, so sorry, Ilene managed a whisper! Harold patted Ilene on the shoulder, trying to hold back tears of his own, as he quickly got into his old pickup and left.

Mission of Mercy

There was always a mission of mercy from Harold or Dorothy, usually on weekly bases. Food from the cooking job with a bit of required items that Dorothy thought might be needed. If Dorothy couldn't do her delivery, Harold would complete the mission.

Harold was able to get a summer job of mowing the ditches for preventive snow blockage on the roads. So for a quick hour job each summer he would go down to the meadow and mow some hay for Ilene's goats. As Harold was able to buy, sell or trade almost anything he felt was worthwhile, he would end up with farm equipment too. Several years he was able to pull a small hay rake behind his pickup and throw the hay into a windrow. It could then quickly be tossed into the back of the pickup and hauled across the waterless creek and stacked into a pile by the shack of a barn.

In Harold's travels he would stop by the little town dump grounds. Each town in the Midwest would have one. The greatest excitement would be finding something he could sell for scrap metal. He had a mental list of all the various things that people he knew would be looking for. Ilene was always on the list, even if her items would be only a gift. When a pile of wood scrap found its way to the dump ground, it was a triumphal thing. The long pieces of wood were added to his building pile for a future shed. The smaller pieces were an easy find for firewood.

They were for his use and the building of a pile for Ilene in the winter.

When the local saw mill found themselves in an over supple of slabs from the logs they milled, Harold offered to take all they wanted to haul to his little place on the bluff above Ilene's valley. With his chain saw cutting the slabs was like eating cake. A pickup load could quickly be delivered to Ilene's winter pile. When Harold saw the face that rarely smiled, brought to smiling, he knew life for Ilene was good. What was good for Ilene was good for Harold's heart.

The finding of a box of dishes one day at the dump grounds was a smile to Harold as a great find. The box was delivered the very day. "Ilene, I have something today, that I think you will like, Harold instructed as he moved the box out of the back of the pickup. "Is it better than a load of firewood, Ilene questioned? Ilene's need was a very, very short list of, water, food, firewood and her goats. Harold sat the box on the tailgate of the pickup. Ilene made her way over to the pickup with the help of the walking stick made of Hickory, which her Papa had made for her over fifty years ago. "Dishes, Ilene spoke quietly! "Well, they are a pretty fancy bunch, I assure you, Harold offered with a smile and his usual laugh. A while back when you offered me a cup of coffee, you poured yours into a bowl and mine into a cup. "Yes, Ilene agreed! The cup, the bowl and the two spoons I have are from my Mama's set of dishes. They were her Mama's, so they are over a hundred years old. These dishes look very happy. With all the flowers, they look like you shouldn't even put food on them. "A full set of eight, Harold laughed! "Eight, Ilene replied! I have never had more than three people in this house. Now I am a woman of excess! Very nice Harold! Bring them into the house and set them on the table.

Harold brought the box into the small house with a feeling of great pride. Ilene reached into the box to grasp a handful of silverware. An unusual item came out with the grasp. The silverware was laid on the table, but the odd item remained grasped. "What is this, Ilene asked? "It is a can opener, Harold instructed! "Well opener describes what is going to happen, but what is a can, Ilene questioned? "You know like a can of fruit, vegetables or perhaps soup,

Harold explained. It is a small metal container that food is stored in. Have you ever canned food into a jar? "No, I put my vegetables into the root cellar. I use to put my meat and milk into the icehouse, but I haven't had ice for years. "The next time I come over, I will bring you some cans of food, Harold offered excitedly! It is a great way to have some food stored and ready to use whenever you like.

It was but a short week later Harold brought a large box of canned foods of all kinds to Ilene. The pickup delivery was either water or firewood. Today there was a box sitting on the seat with a pleasant surprise. The wood was unloaded and the pickup was backed up to the door of the small house. Harold, with great pride and joy fetched the box off the seat and placed it on the tailgate of the pickup. Ilene came slowly out of the house, followed by a small goat. "Here we have canned food, Harold boasted! Ilene clasped a can in her hands. There was great awe and wonder without any words. The words and the picture tell you what is in the can. "Good thing for the picture, Ilene claimed. I can't read anything that small anymore. "See the small kernels of corn in the picture, Harold pointed out? "I have never had corn out of my garden, Ilene confessed. I have had ground corn many times, so I will take you at your word that these are kernels of corn.

"The smaller cans are soup, Harold instructed. Make a bunch of soup and put it into a can for later. It stays stored in the cans until you want to use it. "What kind of soup, Ilene asked? "This one is vegetable and this one says vegetable beef, Harold read the labels. "Vegetable Beef, Ilene repeated! I had beef once. Peter and Jonathan were my friends for a short time, when I was younger, Ilene instructed. They brought me some beef to put in my icehouse. "There is mixed fruit, peaches, pears, peas, yams and green beans, Harold picked up each can slowly and called out its contents. My favorite is pork and beans right out of the can, Harold laughed!

"Let's take this box in the house and we will see if you can open the cans, Harold suggested. The box was delivered to the table and Ilene retrieved the odd tool called the can opener.

Harold thought he would start with the pork and beans, encase he had to eat them himself. See this small triangle and this wheel on here?

"Yes, Ilene replied! When the picture and words are in the upright position, you place this point on the edge of the can and squeeze these two handles together. You keep them in your grasp as you turn this small knob. The small triangle will cut the top of the can open. You continue all the way around. Now the lid of the cans can be very sharp, so be careful with the lids. Use a knife or a spoon to lift the lid out of the way, just as a precaution. Ilene placed the opener on the edge of the can and gripped the two handles together, then began to turn the knob on the tool. The can turned and the lid was soon cut loose. A table knife went down into the edge of the can and up came the lid. Ilene was so happy she placed her head next to Harold's chest and replied, "What a wonderful thing! "Yes it is, Harold replied with a smile!

"Now, the best part, Harold suggested. Take a spoon and have a bite. "I don't need to warm or cook the stuff in the cans, Ilene questioned? "You can go either way, Harold laughed. Sometimes we warm things up and sometimes we don't. If I am in a hurry, I open a can of beans and just eat them. I like warm soup, so the soup we are always warming up. Most things I like warmed up. The Pork and Beans are the ones I usually eat cold. "Thank you for such a wonderful thing, Ilene offered!

Greetings

During the summer, I had been introduced to Ilene. It had been by accident as my dad, uncle, and older brother went for a walk. We went down a steep path toward a river that lay in a small secluded valley below the tree line. The trees started out as hardwoods and rustled their leaves in the breeze, with an inviting "come in here for an adventure." They soon faded away as the aroma of the pines beckoned to have their way with us. The path was narrow, but showed signs of travel. My uncle often went down to the river to fish. The branches often brushed against you; with a wishful "Let's play." The sound of the squirrels chatting and the cry of the blue jays added to fragrant air. The bright sun was partially blocked out by the enormous pines. With their hundred years of age, they towered to the sky and expressed their strength and majesty. I was told that I dawdled a bit too much, but I just couldn't help it. It was just too wonderful. "Don't let us get too far ahead, so you get lost, Uncle Harold advised.

I hurried along, but was anxious that I would miss out on seeing something. Then I came to the two large boulders that caused a quick bend in the path, which threw us into a sunny open valley. They were as large as a small house. I had to touch them and hug them. Wonderful!

In the short distance, you could see a small building. A small dark object bobbed up and down a short distance from the building. We questioned my uncle as to what the object was in the distance.

"It's not an object, but an old woman, the name of Ilene, Uncle Harold instructed us. She is cutting meadow grass for her goats for winter feed.

We will just walk by and just say hello. She likes to be left alone, so I will do the talking. "Ilene has lived here all her life, Uncle Harold

169

instructed. I visit her when I come down to the river to fish. She was born in 1879, after the Civil war. Her parents died from influenza when she was thirteen. We will just let her be!

As we got closer to the dark object, it was still hard to tell if she was standing or sitting. I saw eight or ten goats grazing and another three or four small ones lying in the tall grasses. My uncle said hello and expressed we were just going for a walk today. She nodded and said nothing. I walked a little closer for a better look. I gazed into her hooded old face to see two piercing blue eyes. She looked 150 to me. I was six and everyone seemed old to me. Everyone started to move on, but I couldn't resist saying, "Hi! I reached out my hand as if it needed to come into contact, just because I had uttered a word. "I like your little house, I spoke. Ilene said nothing, but stared back at me as I stared at her. One of the little goats came over to her, and I stretched my hand toward the goat. The little goat made a small nibble on my fingers. "I like your goats, I said quietly. Just then, my uncle called out from a distance to come on along. I said, "Good-bye, and Ilene responded with "Stop by sometime.

I hurried to catch up with the small group and expressed how Ilene wanted me to stop by sometime. My uncle again expressed how she liked to be left alone and she didn't like going into town. She only went to the small store for certain things. She had lived in the small shack her whole life and never said more than a few words whenever he stopped by to say hello or give her something.

We often went to a favorite aunt and uncles for Christmas or New Year's. We traded back and forth for every other year. This was the year to go to their home for Christmas. Oh, we usually went for a visit at least once per month, and it was something I always enjoyed. They lived on the edge of a small town in Northern Minnesota.

They had heavily wooded area surrounding the home, which brought about many exciting adventures.

Summer passed, fall passed, and soon, it was Christmas. We found ourselves at my aunt and uncle's celebrating and having a good time. The grand meal was done, the kitchen cleaned, and everyone spread out doing the admiration of the small gifts received. My aunt asked my brother and I if we would like to take a Christmas meal to Ilene. I was all for it, but my brother didn't care to. Aunt Dorothy prepared containers with all sorts of good things that could feed a family for days. Another bag contained a dark blue coat, scarf, and mittens. There were large candles, matches, and two pans. She asked me if I could carry all of the items. I assured her that I could carry more, and I felt I had the strength of Santa Claus. When I was dressed, she gave me an envelope and informed me that it contained money and to shove it deep into my pocket. She helped me out the door with my load and informed me to not be a bother and wish Ilene a Merry Christmas.

I soon found the path and headed down it into the woods. The big oaks were asleep, but had left leaves on the path. A light snow was falling, and the world seemed so perfect. I concentrated on keeping my load in good condition. I was soon among the great pines, and they welcomed me with the wisps of wind moving through their branches. I rounded the big boulders and saw the small valley open up with a greater amount of snow. The path seemed to get lost every once in a while, and I had to back out of some deeper snow and reestablish my direction. The smell of wood smoke from the small shack was leading me onward as quickly as could be had. I soon reached the door of the shack, and because my hands were full, I tapped on the door with my foot. There was no answer, so I tapped a little harder with my foot. Still nothing, so I sat one of my loads down and tried to open the door. The door slowly opened, and I stepped in with cargo I carried.

The room was dark except for two small candles flickering. I sounded out a Merry Christmas and a small goat came over to me. It had walked out of the darkness of the far edge of the room. It startled me slightly, as I had not expected to see a goat in a house.

I pushed the door closed with my back. Proceeding to the table, where I placed my cargo of packages down on the table with the two candles. Another small sound rustled from the corner of the room, and a small bundle moved toward me. "Please sit, a small voice requested. I did so as I peeled back some of my clothing. I then began to explain what I had in the packages and the wishes of my aunt and uncle. I produced the envelope and handed it to Ilene. "It is money to do with as you need, but I didn't know the amount, I continued. Ilene continued to say nothing, and it left me uncomfortable. I wasn't sure how long I should stay and not be a bother. "If I am a bother, just ask me to go, I blurted out. A small hand crept across the table and touched mine, as my arm rested on the table. Still no sound, but I guessed that the hand was saying "stay a bit longer.

"Would you like me to light one of your new Christmas candles, I requested? I guess I was at an awkward position, as what to say or do, so I just pushed forward with whatever popped into my head. With no one saying no, I took the green one with the scent of pine and lit it off one of the other candles. The scent of pine filled the little room and increased the amount of light substantially. I now could see the little wrinkled face and long grey hair. The eyes were still very blue as I had remembered from the summer.

I blurted out, "Your eyes are very blue. When you are not sure of what to say, things seem to just jump out. Do you celebrate Christmas? Do you visit anyone? I asked two questions, and it made me feel I was probable being a bother. Maybe I should go, I suggested. The little hand came back across the table, but this time, the little voice said, "Please stay! No one, but your uncle and aunt come to visit me. I see people when I go into town, but no one acknowledges me. I have never felt loved all my life. I am just some kind of outcast and now I am an old outcast! Even as I have gotten older, it seems people want to avoid you. My parents are the only ones to say they loved me. They have been gone since my teen years. A lot of this is my fault, no one else's. I have just been too shy.

"As for Christmas, I have believed and even hoped for a small Christmas celebration, Irene stated. I used to read the Bible and the Christmas story, but I haven't been able to see well enough for years to do so. I use to bring in pine boughs for the fragrance. The candle is wonderful. Ilene began to recite the Christmas story. The only I love you have been by me reading from the bible. To know that Jesus loves me has been enough. She would pause for a moment and then continue.

And it came to pass in those days, that there went out a decree from Caesar Augustus, that all the world should be taxed.(And this taxing was first made when Cyrenius was governor of Syria.)And

172

all went to be taxed, every one into his own city. And Joseph also went up from Galilee, out of the city of Nazareth, into Judaea, unto the city of David, which is called Bethlehem; (because he was of the house and lineage of David:)To be taxed with Mary his espoused wife, being great with child. And so it was, that, while they were there, the days were accomplished that she should be delivered. And she brought forth her firstborn son, and wrapped him in swaddling clothes, and laid him in a manger; because there was no room for them in the inn. And there were in the same country shepherds abiding in the field, keeping watch over their flock by night. And, lo, the angel of the Lord came upon them, and the glory of the Lord shone round about them: and they were sore afraid. And the angel said unto them, Fear not: for, behold, I bring you good tidings of great joy, which shall be to all people. For unto you is born this day in the city of David a Saviour, which is Christ the Lord. And this **shall be** *a sign unto you; Ye shall find the babe wrapped in swaddling clothes, lying in a manger. And suddenly there was with the angel a multitude of the heavenly host praising God, and saying, Glory to God in the highest, and on earth peace, good will toward men. And it came to pass, as the angels were gone away from them into heaven, the shepherds said one to another, Let us now go even unto Bethlehem, and see this thing which is come to pass, which the Lord hath made known unto us. And they came with haste, and found Mary, and Joseph, and the babe lying in a manger. And when they had seen* it, *they made known abroad the saying which was told them concerning this child. And the shepherds returned, glorifying and praising God for all the things that they had heard and seen, as it was told unto them. And when eight days were*

173

accomplished for the circumcising of the child, his name was called JESUS, which was so named of the angel before he was conceived in the womb. And when the days of her purification according to the law of Moses were accomplished, they brought him to Jerusalem, to present him to the Lord; (As it is written in the law of the Lord, Every male that openeth the womb shall be called holy to the Lord;) And to offer a sacrifice according to that which is said in the law of the Lord, A pair of turtledoves, or two young pigeons. And, behold, there was a man in Jerusalem, whose name was Simeon; and the same man was just and devout, waiting for the consolation of Israel: and the Holy Ghost was upon him. And it was revealed unto him by the Holy Ghost, that he should not see death, before he had seen the Lord's Christ. And he came by the Spirit into the temple: and when the parents brought in the child Jesus, to do for him after the custom of the law, Then took he him up in his arms, and blessed God, and said, Lord, now lettest thou thy servant depart in peace, according to thy word: For mine eyes have seen thy salvation, Which thou hast prepared before the face of all people; A light to lighten the Gentiles, and the glory of thy people Israel. And Joseph and his mother marvelled at those things which were spoken of him. And Simeon blessed them, and said unto Mary his mother, Behold, this child is set for the fall and rising again of many in Israel; and for a sign which shall be spoken against; (Yea, a sword shall pierce through thy own soul also,) that the thoughts of many hearts may be revealed. And there was one Anna, a prophetess, the daughter of Phanuel, of the tribe of Aser: she was of a great age, and had lived with an husband seven years from her virginity; And she was a widow of about fourscore and four years, which departed not from the temple, but served God with fastings and prayers night and day. And she coming in that instant gave thanks likewise unto the Lord, and spake of him to all them that looked for redemption in Jerusalem. And when they had performed all things according to the law of the Lord, they returned into Galilee, to their own city Nazareth. And the child grew, and waxed strong in spirit, filled with wisdom: and the grace of God was upon him.

Now his parents went to Jerusalem every year at the feast of the passover. And when he was twelve years old, they went up to Jerusalem after the custom of the feast. And when they had fulfilled the days, as they returned, the child Jesus tarried behind in Jerusalem; and Joseph and his mother knew not of it. But they, supposing him to have been in the company, went a day's journey; and they sought him among their kinsfolk and acquaintance. And when they found him not, they turned back again to Jerusalem, seeking him. And it came to pass, that after three days they found him in the temple, sitting in the midst of the doctors, both hearing them, and asking them questions. And all that heard him were astonished at his understanding and answers. And when they saw him, they were amazed: and his mother said unto him, Son, why hast thou thus dealt with us? Behold, thy father and I have sought thee sorrowing. And he said unto them, how is it that ye sought me? wist ye not that I must be about my Father's business? And they understood not the saying which he spake unto them. And he went down with them, and came to Nazareth, and was subject unto them: but his mother kept all these sayings in her heart. And Jesus increased in

*wisdom and stature, and in favor with God and
man. (Luke 2:1-51)*

I was very impressed at the old woman reciting the huge length of bible passage. This year had been the first year I had been to church and heard the Christmas story. I explained how I had come to go to church and how Pastor Petersen came out and picked me up to go to church. My parents had never gone, so it was all new to me.

I stood up and went over to the other side of the table and knelt down by Ilene. "I love you with all my heart, Ilene," as I gave her a gentle hug. No one saying they loved the old woman seemed a hard bit to swallow. An odd felling came over me as I felt tears rolling down my cheeks. I wish I would have known you a long time ago. I will be your friend, I whispered, as a lump came into my throat. "You will make an old woman cry," she tried to say, as she cleared her throat. I have nothing to give you, but what I know. Well maybe the old bible on the mantle, Ilene mentioned and pointed to the area.

Believe always in the son of God, in the Christ child, and the Spirit of God will come upon you and comfort you always. The Spirit of God has always brought me comfort.

Ilene stopped and stayed silent for a short time. I was impressed, so I needed to say so. "Wow Ilene, you know so much, I offered. There was no response, so I thought she didn't hear me. How do you memorize so much? "This is just a small part of what is stuck in my head. When you just have God to talk to and maybe a few goats, it's not so hard. I use to read the bible every day, but when my eyesight became very lacking, I was glad I had bible verses in my head.

"So you have been alone since you were little, I asked? There was no response. Oh, I am sorry for making such a big ask. "No, not at all, Ilene offered! I have nothing in my life worth mentioning. I just have never been asked about anything nor had anyone ever care about how I am doing or what has happened to me. The little old lady seemed to be crying. It was an odd little sound. It made me almost cry for the sadness I had for her. I stood up and walked around to her side of the table again. I began to hug the small bundle of cloth and the hidden life source from within. "Ilene, I am going to remember you forever. It will

176

be a remembrance of great love and admiration. "That is kind of you, but it may prove to be easier said, than done, Irene suggested!

Rather than go to the other side of the table, I sat down by Ilene. As I sat by the old woman I put my arm around her as if I could wish into her all the love, which she had missed out on. It was silent for a period of time, when suddenly Ilene began to speak. "Thank you for the hug! It was like my parents came close! Your aunt and uncle come by a every now and then. They just drop off something and say a handful of words. You are filled with something different and it moves me. I wish I could have known you seventy-five plus years ago.

There was no comment made by me, but my head was trying to imagine what it would have been like that many years ago and living in some kind of small house like this. Suddenly as she had stopped, Ilene continued, "I was thirteen or so when my parents died. Papa got the flu first, so Mama tried to keep me away by making a small tent away from the house for me to stay in.

Then Mama got sick, so I began to take care of them both. It wasn't long and Papa died, so I buried him behind the house on the hill, at Mama's request. I didn't know what to do and really became quit terrified. I had no problem digging the grave, but I couldn't put the dirt back on top of Papa. Mama instructed me to put a blanket over him and it would be alright to then put the dirt on him. I got it done, but I cried all the time.

"It was just a couple of days when I awoke one morning and tried to wake Mama. I couldn't wake her and I was so sure she would get better. After a day or so she started to get cold. Mama told me that this may happen and that I must bury her by Papa. I dug the grave again! There was just no putting the dirt on Mama, even after I had covered her with a blanket. I took a blanket and wrapped myself with it and tried to pull the dirt in on both of us, but it was just impossible!

There were tears running down my face, but I just kept taking deep breaths, as to not interrupt Ilene. "I kept hearing rise up and live, but there was no one around me. I stood in the grave and looked out across the meadow, but there was just no one around. As I climbed up out of the grave and began to shout, "I can't do this! I can't do this! The next thing I knew, I was running across the meadow towards the woods. I froze stiff in my tracks, when I saw a black bear stand up in the edge of the woods. There was contemplation between running straight towards the bear or quickly returning to cover up my Mama, before the bear came to find her.

"The bear took off into the woods, so I just turned around and walked back to do what had to be done. It was a one shovel, then thoughts, one shovel and thoughts. It was very late into the night with the moon shinning over head. The moonlight completely revealed the two mounds of dirt. So many thoughts went through my head, but it wasn't about anything in the future, it was mostly about when I would get sick and how would I bury myself? There was enough room between Mama and Papa, I thought. Finally I went into the house and retrieved a blanket and lay down between the two graves. I ended up digging a grave for me; because I was sure I would be sick and die too.

A strange moonlight came in the night and when I looked, I saw a Great Stag standing and starring at it. It was a great glory to God and I felt good about it. A couple of the goats came over and lay down beside me and there I fell asleep.

"The next morning a young man came by the name of Peter, he asked if I was sick? "No, I answered! "Rise up and live then, he suggested! The next day I made a couple of crosses for Mama and Papa. The goats came by and begged to be milked, so I did so. This distraction and that came by, so I was busy. I went and found some wild flowers and planted them on each of the graves. I seemed to cry at every movement.

"After about a week I stopped sleeping between the graves. I never got sick so there was no grave for me to dig. It was a busy time of planning, that if I started to get sick, I would have a grave for me, but it just never happened. Oh, many, many times over the years I would sit by the graves and read the bible. I would have huge prayers filled with hope of the angels coming and taking me away. I memorized many bible verses, so, I could recite them when I was working away at something.

"When I walked up to the little store, I never would say a word to anyone. There were several owners over the years. Peter and Jonathan who I came close to marrying, but tragedy took that away. The Smith family after the fire set by the Reeds. Leonard, who is the now the owner would ask me this or that but I would usually just shake my head or shrug my shoulders. He helped me for many years selling my extra goats. It was the only money I ever received. There was no clue in my head as to how to sell my goats. Papa just said if I ever needed help, I could go ask at the store. I never told a soul that Mama and Papa had died. My tongue didn't want to lie or to tell the truth. It was just a shrug or something.

"My purchases were very much the same all the time. Garden seeds, blankets, clothes, candles, matches or tools. All of the owners would try to add other things to my purchase, but I would just push then aside and give my usual shrug or nod. It was mainly that way, because I didn't know how to really deal with the obligation or gesture. I think a lot of people just thought I couldn't talk. I tried to go to the store

when there was no one else around. Many times I would hide in the woods watching to see if there were any people around, so I could go to the store quick and leave so no one could see me. It was always keeping a good set of clothes just for going to the store. Wash up, brush my hair and good cloths and then off to the store.

"Selling the goats was always a challenge, because I insisted on leading them up to the store and tying them up and going back to get more. It was always the insisted offering of going to help me. I couldn't let anyone see where and how I lived! It seemed to crush in on me somehow and made me un-easy to the attention.

"I do have something to give you, Ilene blurted out after a short silence. I have never had anything to ever give to someone, earthly I mean. I think you are the one, Ilene offered in a little louder voice. I want to give you my blessing! "What does, that mean, I asked, in a puzzled manner? "Well, I believe that God blesses those who love him and they can pass it onto whom they are compelled, while they are alive. I am sure that I will not be alive that much longer. The sound of that made me take a couple of deep breaths. "Is this something from God, through you, I asked? "Yes, that is what I believe, Ilene added!Ilene put her hand on my head and began to speak in a language, which I didn't know. I just thought she knew some language other than just English.

179

After a couple of minutes she spoke in English. "All that you have given me Great and Holy, let these things pass onto the one who sits here with me and speaks words of comfort and love to me. That which seeks to take his life, send your guardianship of angels to protect and speak life to him. May thy hand bless him a hundred fold and many times more? May thy wisdom be imparted unto him! Ilene fell silent, so I felt like I should say something. "I think Ilene, that what you give me is worth more than any other gifts or treasures, I offered what seemed to jump into my head.

You should go back to your uncles, before dark," she added. As I left, I wished Ilene to be well and I would come back to visit, when I returned to my aunt and uncle's. "I will not forget you. You are my friend! Merry Christmas,"

I said proudly. It may be awhile before I get back to see you. I felt a rush of strength and emotions come upon me. Ilene had given me something, which was hard to describe.

I knelt on one knee, "Thank you Ilene for giving me of your heart. I may not totally understand what it is, but it felt very, very important. Today my aunt asked me to do something and I was compelled to honor her wish. I am so very glad I came to see you. As I stood up, I gave Ilene another hug, "so long, until we meet again, I offered!

I left the little room and closed the door behind me. My head was full of thoughts of what her blessing would really mean. There was no knowledge in my head of what any of this was. It seemed like something powerful. It seemed like Ilene had a built treasure from God and had given me all this treasure from the years she had accumulated from God. I felt so privileged, so honored. She was the oldest person I knew. She was the poorest person I knew or was she? I couldn't wait to see her again. Surely she wasn't going to pass away. It gave me a shutter and it wasn't from the cold either.

My mind was so busy on the way back to my aunt and uncle's, I hardly saw the trees and squirrels. This was the second greatest day of my life. Almost the first! Who would have known? The music over the woods and a voice from messenger was the greatest! What was my life going to be! I promised to never forget Ilene! I just had to always remember her. Just had to! She had said it was good in words, but may prove to be harder in deeds. She had just read scraps of what ever came her way, but she seemed so smart. That smart just reading the bible?

Picnic

There were a few quick stops over the next couple of months, but no time for me to see Ilene. I asked my uncle how Ilene was doing, but it was just an ok, I guess. Haven't seen her! My thoughts tried to be kind, but it just seemed that no one cared. Was she even alive? "Please God make it possible for me to see Ilene again, I whispered, when we stopped by in late May.

A few weeks later a letter arrived from my aunt. Would Fred be interested in staying with my Aunt Dorothy for a week in June, while Uncle Harold was gone? She didn't want to be alone. Would he be interested in making some pocket money doing painting? My response was, "Just making it happen and can't wait! Was this an answer to a prayer? I said," Thank you Holy God above!

The second week of June soon arrived, so my aunt and uncle came down to pick me up. Wow! A whole week to stay with my aunt would be just grand, but yet I had no clue as to how it might go. It didn't matter, because it would be grand. In the back of my mind I was sure that Aunt Dorothy would let me go and see Ilene. We talked about the things they wanted me to do for the pocket money. Mowing their big lawn? No problem! Painting the outhouse? No problem! Painting the picnic table? No problem! Help clean out the laundry shed? No problem! Helping with the garden?

No problem! Painting the outhouse, no problem!

The first day I had the outhouse painted inside and out. The small store in town was still open so my Aunt Dorothy sent me down with a list and on the bottom of the list was a note of picking out whatever I would like. It didn't take my brain long to pick my items, as they would be a bottle of strawberry soda and a small bag of M & M''s. When I returned Aunt Dorothy made a remark,"Oh are these your favorites? "Kind of, I replied! "You are not sure, she laughed! "Well, if there is time, I would like to take these items to Ilene! "Really, Aunt Dorothy questioned? "When I saw her at Christmas, I promised to try to see her as soon as I was able to and that has been six months, I offered an explanation of the items. "Well, then you should go tomorrow, Aunt Dorothy insisted! "I will paint the picnic table in the morning and then go, I replied.

When I had finished the picnic table, I found that my Aunt Dorothy had made a picnic basket, complete with a red and white checker cloth to sit on. There were Peanut butter and jelly sandwiches, M & M's, strawberry soda with two tin cups, apples and oatmeal cookies. Nice I thought! So I was off on my visit to Ilene.

The path out behind my aunt and uncle's place was dry and green. It was the opposite of the winter travel I had made. The trees looked bigger when they were in the green leaf state. The big Oaks were full of sound and rustling in their glory. A few squirrels were searching the path for a lost acorn, I guessed. I tried to take in as much as I could, but my mind was wondering how I would see Ilene, It had been six months and that seemed like a long time. It was through the Oaks and then the big pines with their competition. They tested the air with their own sound and of course pouring out their scent. The pines win I thought, only because I was partial to them. The arrival at the huge granite boulders, then it was the view of the meadow. It was pausing at the view only for a moment and that was to see if I could see Ilene anywhere. Nothing!

I hurried along the path as if time was more important than it usually was. Soon I found myself on the front stoop and tapping on the door. Nothing! I opened the door and shouted out, "Ilene! Ilene! Nothing!

I heard a small goat, bleat. It came from behind the little house,

So I proceeded to walk around to the back side of the shelter. It was a sudden stop at the corner, as I saw Ilene sitting in the grass and slowly cutting out a small area around some wild flowers. I was looking for Ilene, but yet I felt surprised to see her. "Ilene, Ilene I called out! The small figure turned in surprise. I walked over to where she sat. It was a quick sitting down with my basket. A rush of tears came to me, so I was forced to take a few deep breaths. "Hello, Ilene! I am so happy to see you! Ilene made no sound, as I placed a hug on her. I sat back a bit to have a look at the hooded face. Ilene pushed back her hood, revealing the ancient, but showing the crystal blue of her eyes. I had never seen Ilene in the light and beauty of the outside daylight. Her long silver hair seemed to have a brilliance and life of its own in the light.

'How are you today Ilene, I inquired? No verbal response, but a slight nod of being ok. "I don't see well, but I recognize your voice Fred, the whispered voice, from Ilene sounded. Ilene went quiet again and starred into nothingness. I am a bit afraid today, came her next whisper! I slid over a little closer to Ilene and put my arm around her. The small bundle felt more like a clump of clothing than a person. "Then by the hand of God through me, I will strengthen you today. My heart and soul send you love, Ilene! May all your fears be removed! What a beautiful day God has made! A power of emotion seemed to come over me and I needed a few deep breaths to keep the tears from bursting forward. I heard Ilene make a small sound, which seemed to be some kind of a cry.

"Today I am sitting with you Ilene in a beautiful meadow, your meadow, I offered in a slightly raised voice, as to try to offer some joy to the moment. I have never been in a more perfect place with a more perfect person or perfect time. The whispering little cry seemed to increase. I had to think quickly. What Heavenly Father am I to do, I thought? Your Holy Spirit is taking away your fear Ilene, I expressed with joy! It's hard to cry and be afraid at the same time. A weak hand soon lay upon my hand on my knee. I was grateful to know that my care was being felt.

"Look at what I have brought, I expressed with a bit of excitement. It's a picnic basket with a cloth to sit on and everything. I quickly spread out the red and white cloth, right where we were sitting. Then I placed the basket on one side. "I have never had a picnic, Ilene admitted, as she gazed at what I was doing.

I read a small piece, in old magazine years ago. I remember a family sitting around just sort of a cloth of red and white squares. There was a basket with the lunch like you have brought. "My aunt and uncle brought my brother and me on a picnic two years ago and that was my first picnic, I admitted! So that was the only one I have ever been on. But this one will be my best picnic ever, because this is for you and me.

"It seems odd, Ilene expressed! "How so, I asked? I didn't know why she had said such a thing. "I am eighty-seven and you are about ten for starters. In the middle of a meadow! Sitting by my parent's grave! This old, black shack of a house! "You could think of a hundred reasons, because you are just that smart, I protested! This is a beautiful place! What God has created, push it not aside! I have so much compassion and respect for you, that there is no room for anything else. "Now, who is the one with wisdom, Ilene protested in return! "We have no fears within us today, I boasted with a small laugh! "I do have to admit that I had a picnic when I was about sixteen, Ilene offered. Peter, Jonathan and I went fishing by the lake.

Reaching into the basket, I retrieved the small container of the Peanut butter and jelly sandwiches. "Peanut butter and jelly sandwiches, my favorite, I expressed! "Yes, I have had these a few times, Ilene offered. Your uncle had given me some of those, made by your aunt. Oh, when he has gone fishing in the river, he would drop off some, among other things. I then produced the two metal cups and the bottle of Strawberry soda. "Have you ever had Strawberry soda, I asked? "No, was the whisper from Ilene! What is it? "Soda is a sweet, fizzy drink, I offered for a description! I poured a bit into one of the cups and handed it to Ilene. A very cautious sip was taken, and then a moment of silence as if it was the most important sips ever taken. "It's the taste of the strawberry jam with a sensation of tickling your nose, Irene described. "Nice, I laughed! "Well, I have three things

I brought, which are probably not the best for you, I confessed. The third is candy, which are called M & M's. Have you ever had these? "No, but I have seen them in the little store, Ilene instructed. The owner, Leonard, tried to give me some a few different times, but I could not accept them. I opened the bag

and held Ilene's hand to pour one out into the cupped portion of her hand. A green candy dropped into her hand. "They are green, Ilene questioned? "Maybe, I laughed, as I had the knowledge that there were different colors, and Ilene was caught in a time of surprise.It seemed to be a great mystery to Ilene. She studied the small candy in her hand. "It seems to have a hard and green surface, Ilene whispered? The small candy bit went into her mouth. "It's sweet, but not like the soda or jelly, confessed Ilene! "It's chocolate, I admitted to her! "So chocolate is sweet and green, Ilene questioned? "Not exactly, I laughed! I took Ilene's hand and tipped out another candy. The candy bit that came out was orange. "Its orange, a surprised voice expressed! I wondered why there were different colors on the outside of the bag. I handed the bag to Ilene for her to examine. I was thrilled to see the total amazement in front of me. It was something in which I had taken for granted. One small hand joined the other. One hand offered the other a small dispensing of a brown, red and blue candy bit from the concealment of the candy wrapper.

"After working yesterday I went to the store for my aunt, I offered into the silence of the lady sitting before me. She told me I could pick out something for a treat if I liked, so I choose these things to share with you. "This was to be your gift, Ilene questioned? "Yes, it was a reward or gift, I suppose! "Your aunt and uncle have given me a few things over the years, but not as much fun as this, Ilene expressed. Are all people like this, Ilene asked? My head went, wow. How do I answer this?

"No, sadly to say, I finally offered! I see people as wanting for themselves, more than giving or helping. Maybe one out of ten will give or help without expecting a return. "Your aunt and uncle helped me get something called social security a number of years ago,

Ilene offered up out of nowhere. It was because the government wanted taxes paid on my valley. My parents did something called homesteading on this land, so it was theirs. Yet, for some reason they seem to want it back. I am very grateful for their help to keep this and stay here. I don't have any need for the money.

The government gave me money for this hand and want it back from this hand, Ilene explained, as she showed her left hand, then the right hand.

"Where did you come from Ilene, I questioned? Silence, seem to take up a long time. It actually made me a little uncomfortable. Perhaps I

186

had asked something, which I should not have asked. "Well, right here, Ilene offered! It seems like a hard question, in which I wish I had more of an answer to. I have read a few scrapes of some pages about different places and the bible which tells about different places. There have been some newspapers from your aunt. In the woods, across the meadow and to the little store, I guess is my limits. I was born right here in this house. "So your parents homesteaded this land, I offered. Did they ever say where they came from? "My Papa's folks came from Europe, he was Danish. My Mama came from out east. Papa brought the goats from out eastern United States. He was in a war called the Civil war. After the war he homesteaded here. He was in an army called the union, which wanted to free people from slavery. He never wanted to talk about it. He said it was hell on earth and didn't want that stuff in my head.

I remembered how happy Mama and Papa were about this home, so I just couldn't leave. I say I couldn't leave this place, but it was more of Mama and Papa buried here and not wanting to leave them. We had everything right here. Papa would hunt in the woods and fish the lake. We would store up what we got from this area. There was a garden for years by the house, but not in the last few years. I am dried up and there is nothing left of me. Every day I pray for the angels of heaven to come and escort me from here. "The day you leave, my heart will be sad, I blurted out! I will never forget you. I will hold you in my memories with great love and purpose. "You probably will, but never let it be your burden to carry, Ilene insisted!

"The blessing you gave me at Christmas was a big thing to me, I confessed with great hope. Did your folks give you a blessing? "No, they were sick and passed away, with no opportunity. Papa believed deeply and read from the bible every night. Mama and I would sit with great anticipation in the candle light.

Papa always read with great enthusiasm. We would have many questions, but Papa seemed to always have the right answers. Sometimes he would look up a scripture to get the best answers. He would teach Mama and me on schooling matters every night too. There were two such different worlds, but so much fun. If I hadn't had what they taught me, I wouldn't be here. "Was some of the blessing you gave me, in a different language, I asked? "Sometimes when I pray or even think about Jesus our lord or our Heavenly Father, it stirs a fire within me. It's the Holy Spirit bringing my love and praise to the heavenly throne. I have sat in the moonlight in this meadow and praised our lord for hours. It is one of the most wonderful things of my life. I have read about different sins in the bible and don't have a clue as to what they are. I am very glad I don't have the exposure to them. However, I know I am still of a sinful nature and ask for forgiveness of my lord. I have even gone into the river and baptized myself as John the Baptist did in the wilderness. "I wish you could baptize me in the river, I invited! "I am so old I can't even stand here on dry ground, Ilene offered!

Ilene sat quiet for a bit and turned the palms of her hands upward, as they rested on her knees. Ilene began to speak about the Holy Spirit, "When the Holy Spirit gives you utterance, and you can just feel the love between you and God. Just sit and give yourself and time to your Heavenly Father. Praise him and the Holy Spirit will come upon you. The little things are just as important as the big things. If I think I am having a bad day, I still give God the praise! Today is one of the best days of my life. I thank you and I praise God for all this. For some reason I felt a chill, the way she said thank you and praise to God in the same sentence. Ilene began to speak in a language I didn't understand, so I remained very quiet and just watched her. Ilene looked very old and dried up, but still there were tears running down her face. It was nicely warm and a fluttering breeze.

The breeze fluttered at her silver hair. I knew she was praising God in her loving way. I was caught in the moment with just the whisper of, "Jesus over and over on my lips. Tears began to run down my face for no explanation.

I wanted to remember this moment in time all my life.

After maybe fifteen or twenty minutes it was all quiet. "One day we will be in a better place, Ilene sounded after the silence. Do not turn away strangers, for they may not be of this earth. Do not reject that which comes your way, for the hand of God will keep you. Do that which gives your Heavenly Father glory! I heard what Ilene was saying, but I didn't understand it in that moment. Ilene just sat with her eyes closed and said nothing.I began to pick up the picnic items and put them

188

in the basket. "Ilene, I whispered, I should get back to my aunt, so she has no worries or concerns. Can I help you with anything, before I go? "Help me up, Ilene requested? As I helped Ilene stand, she wrapped her arms around me; it felt like a bundle of cloth hugging me. I was slender fellow and her height was the same as mine, but I think I may have weighed twice as much as her. As she stood there, she whispered, "Thank you for this moment. "Oh, but thank you, because I think I have received the greater portion. The hug was mutual and lasted for a few minutes. I had kept the few M & M's and a part of a sandwich out of the basket and placed them in Ilene's hands. "I will try to come back and see you while I am here with my aunt this week. I don't know the rest of the work I have to do or when my uncle may return to take me home. I walked away and turned for a moment to wave. Ilene met the wave of her own with a half lifted arm.

When I returned, I thanked my aunt for helping me make this a great day. The request of the moment was, "Would you be interested in starting the painting of the house, Aunt Dorothy asked? It wasn't going to be done until my uncle came back home. "Sure, it's only a two day job, I replied! Aunt Dorothy laughed," two weeks maybe! "I can help, if you point me in the right direction, Aunt Dorothy offered with a smile. You see Aunt Dorothy was almost completely blind. However, I couldn't say anything, but sounds great!

So it went like this early the next day. I would hang a string with a bolt on the end of it for weight. It was a small nail with the string hanging down. Aunt Dorothy did very well. I would just check on her each time I moved on down the side of the house.

I worked from the step ladder and she worked on the ground. Every once in a while I would see her tap her finger lightly to test where she had painted. By the end of the second day, the light blue mist house was painted. The white trim was a great accent. My aunt had little misty blue paint spots on her arms and face. We both laughed at what it looked like and she confessed the bugs made her do it. It was the tapping of her finger to test where she had painted, and then at some point a fly would be a pest.

The painting project brought about a great confession from my aunt that evening. "I love you Aunt Dorothy and so does Jesus Christ the son of God, I shouted out after finishing the dishes! "Oh, I don't know about that, Aunt Dorothy replied! I mean about Jesus! "How can you say that, I questioned? The silence fell like heavy snow. I waited for her to respond, as I helped her find her chair to sit. "Well, you will be eleven in two months, she stated! In one week less than that it will be eleven years since God took my daughter away. I stopped breathing, when I heard that. I had to find a couple of deep breaths, before tears would start. It was a lot of excitement between your mother and I being pregnant at the same time. There were letters every week between us, because of no phones you know. Laura was still born, luckily you were ok. I guess I didn't believe in God before, so why believe after. For not believing I sure blamed him for the loss. You know that there were no children, as you can see the house is empty!

"I have shared this when I visited Ilene, Aunt Dorothy confessed. She told me of great sadness in not being married and not having a family, so we had some of this in common. Peter was going to marry her and got shot. Jonathan was going to marry her and he mysteriously disappeared. Jonathan had shot two brothers robbing their store, when Peter was shot. The rest of the Reed family may have been responsible for Jonathan disappearance.

After a moment of silence I began to tell Aunt Dorothy about Ilene. How she had been thirteen and lost her parents. How she lived her life and how especially she read the bible. She memorizes all she could. She was really smart without even going to school. How she never had anyone,

but she knew that God was with her every moment. How she had praised God in some unknown language to me. Aunt Dorothy began to cry, but I was compelled to continue on with how Ilene felt about God. I even added what she had blessed me with last Christmas, when I had delivered the Christmas food and gifts. I put my hand on Aunt Dorothy's hand and insisted that God loved her no matter what she felt. Bring Jesus into your heart I finally added! I handed a couple of tissues from a box on the table to Aunt Dorothy. I kissed Aunt Dorothy on the cheek and again told her that I loved her. If you know that I am real, than surely the one that gave you life is also real. "All you need to do is ask Jesus to forgive you of your sins and come into your heart, I informed Aunt Dorothy! Aunt Dorothy said, "Jesus, forgive me, help me to believe? I sat on the floor by her in her rocking chair for a long moment of silence. It felt good. I would not have been able to say any of what I did, if it hadn't been for my connection with Ilene. Life, God is mysterious! The invisible paths, that crosses in life.

It struck me suddenly about the three things Ilene had told me. I thought it best to write them down, before I may forget them.

1. Do not turn away strangers, for they may not be of this earth.
2. Do not reject that which comes your way, for the hand of God will keep you.
3. Do that which gives your Heavenly Father glory!

That's interesting, I thought. They seemed to be things to "DO'! Are there beings that are not from this earth? That's a little nervy I thought. The things that God gives you do not reject or throw them away. Why would I want to? Give god the glory? Sure why not, he gave me life, through my parents. I don't really know what this is, but I will try to do these!

The next day I had to return back home, as Uncle Harold came back. He was so surprised to see how much work had been done. He thought he would end up painting the house, when he returned. He gave me twenty dollars! The most money that I could ever remember having was about three dollars.

I wanted to give ten percent to my church, so he made the bills come out just right so I could give two dollars. Uncle Harold thought it was silly, but Aunt Dorothy thought it was grand. She said she understood and couldn't be more proud.

It was about two months before we got back around this way to seeing my aunt and uncle. My Dad needed some welding done for a piece of farm equipment. During a lunch preparation I asked my aunt if I could have a sandwich for Ilene. I was given a sandwich for Ilene and myself, plus a cookie for each of us. Two metal cups and a quart of lemonade. Nice! I hurried on to Ilene's new home, right by my aunt and uncles.

My hands were full as usual, so I tapped on the door with my foot. After tapping a second time and still hearing no sound, I sat the lemonade down and opened the door. "Hello, I sounded out! Hello! I reached down and retrieved the lemonade, then pushed the door closed with my foot. I saw Ilene stirring up from her bed. While placing the items on the table, I continued my conversation," How are you? It's been about two months, since I saw you. I brought some lunch and wanted to talk with you for a short bit. There was still silence, but as I reached Ilene, she gave me an unexpected hug. I return the gesture, with an, "It's good to see you my friend! We walked back to the center of the room and sat by her old table and benches. Ilene sat on the end of the bench, while I sat down in a side saddle approach. I presented the sandwiches and poured the lemonade in the two metal cups. "Courtesy of my aunt, I offered! "It's so nice to see you again, Ilene whispered! I gave the little bundle a second hug.

House in the Misty Valley

It was a late spring stop at my favorite aunt and uncles. My dad needed a piece of farm machinery welded. When you have no phone, you just go and hope for the best. Trips like this are usually planned around another need of something on a trip usually to town. In this case some chicken wire was needed to expand a pen at home. The product had to be gotten in an adjacent town. It would be passing right by our relatives. I was extremely pleased at the idea, which my older brother and I wouldn't have to stay home and work on a project.

The spring of sixty-six was a spring of a lot of flooding. It was always a curious issue to keep looking for the most flooded area. Everyone had some water problem s of their own, but in most cases you just offered your, "I am so sorry or can I help in some way? Most folks just took care of their own problems in the best way they could. Aunt and Uncle lived high up on a ridge, so we knew they wouldn't have any issues as we arrived.

Uncle was busy pounding nails as we pulled into the dooryard. Off the corner of the dooryard he was building a small structure, that would overlook the ridge and into the valley. Interesting I thought, as we climbed out of the vehicle and greeted uncle. "What are you up to uncle, my older brother and I quickly quizzed uncle?

"Ilene lost her house in the flood, Uncle informed us. It all happened very quickly. I was suspicious of that happening, so I had been looking through the tree line gap on the ridge, about right here, uncle offered as he pointed to his current location. About two weeks ago I took a look out in the valley below and saw Ilene sitting with her goat's way up on the side of the hill behind her once was house. Her small creek had grown about ten fold. The small house, small barn and all the pens were just gone.

"There was no way to get over to where she was located, as far as crossing the creek, Uncle Harold soberly informed? I shoved my flat bottom boat that I use for gathering wild rice into the pickup. I drove down the old wagon trail into the meadow and turned around. I backed the pickup as close to the creek as I darned to venture. I launched the boat and crossed the creek. That was work, because of the current that was being created. It was a good hike up the hill after that. Needless to say, I was very happy that Ilene only has six goats right now. She was ok! She lost everything she had! She even lost her coat in the water.

"It took a great deal of time to get her and the goats over to this side, Uncle continued. She insisted on holding onto one goat at a time as we crossed over. It was probably for the best, but at the time I was a bit frustrated. Load one goat and she would hold onto it as I oared across the creek. Six times we went across. The goats were very stable as she hugged them in the crossing. The goats on one side waited together and the goats brought across waited together on the other side. We didn't have to chase after any goats at all. We tied the goats in the edge of the trees. There is a good supply of grass for them. We still have our guest bed in the wash house, so Ilene is staying in there while I work on this small house. She is not feeling well at all, to say the least. Try not to bother her, Uncle directed at me and older brother.

"Let's help you build, Dad offered! Extra tools were found to help Uncle. By sundown the little building was complete. It had a flat roof, just because it was the easiest to build. The green rolled roofing was on the roof as well as on the outside walls for siding. The cost had to be kept down for obvious reasons.

There was one small window beside the door for light. Brother and I finished nailing the green rolled roofing in place, while Dad and uncle installed a small wood stove, a sink and some electrical.

We all worked on moving the bed, table and chair out of the wash house into the new small house. I walked with Ilene to the new small house holding her hand. I didn't really know what to say to her. I got a couple of I love you Ilene out, but she had no response of her own. Uncle sent brother and I to the house to ask aunt if she had any pans or dishes for Ilene. There were items of food, dishes, soap, towels, cloths, bucket and many other things. Aunt just took one cardboard box after another and filled them with anything she could think of. She wasn't looking for anything of extra. She took some of everything she had as she opened each cupboard in the kitchen and bathroom. It was actually mother removing items from cupboards, because aunt was blind to the point she couldn't see what was in a cupboard. She put things away and just used a memory of feel for what she wanted. We just carried the boxes over and placed them on the little table that we had carried over from the wash house.

It was on to uncle's wood pile by the shop with his wheel barrow to haul wood to stack by the door. Some of the wood we had to split as per Uncles instruction to be sure it would fit easily into the little wood stove. Uncle called the small wood stove a Franklin. He had taken the small stove to heat his shop right out and installed it into the small green house. The little house looked nice to me, but Ilene had absolutely no reaction to it at all.

The description of Ilene's reaction as being nothing was described to my aunt by me. "Ilene has had her life so turned upside down, it has made her sick, Aunt Dorothy explained to me. It makes her extremely sick just to come up out of her valley. She is very uncertain of her future. She is afraid of losing her goats. Harold is going to build some kind of pen and shelter for her on the back side of the little house. It will be room for just a couple of them though. She is eighty-eight years old, so she can't really do much?

Uncle and Dad walked and talked slowly following the new trench dug by a machine and covered back up. It was a trench for a water line from my aunt and uncle's basement and it was very deep. Like over six feet! Then there was an electrical wire buried at about two feet. These water and electrical lines came up under the floor of the little green house.

"Ilene's house was not much of a house at all, Uncle informed us. It wasn't much, but I guess when you have lived in whatever for so long, it doesn't matter. It's yours and you own it! It's when your entire life is ripped away from you in a matter of hours. It's painful, maybe just a huge disbelief of what has happened? If she doesn't start eating pretty soon, nothing will matter? When I heard that, it gave me a chill down my neck. Even I knew what that meant.

"Uncle, can I move the goats around to a better grass place for each one, I asked? "Make sure you clip the chains back in place so they can't get away, Uncle requested. Check their buckets for water too. Each goat had a collar and a light chain clipped onto it. The chain was clipped around a tree of piece of equipment. I found a better place for each of the six goats. The buckets were filled with water. I gave each one a good petting and apologized for the big change in their lives. Wondering free to being chained up had to be a big thing for them I thought.

We left, but there wasn't a day for many days that I didn't think about Ilene and her goats. I prayed for them all! It was my conversations with Grandma Hanna that helped. It was my unsaid words that heaped up in my head. What would I do if Ilene died or worse yet, what would happen if Grandma Hanna died? I had many chills about every thought I had along that line.

It was about a month later when we were instructed to stop by Aunt Dorothy's and Uncle Harold's. The garden didn't grow much anymore, as it just wasn't planted. There was a large strawberry patch however. We were going to pick strawberries and share the pick.

A story of chilling proportion was revealed to us, when we arrived. Uncle had been the one taking food for meals over to Ilene. Uncle had to do a road trip, which would take him away most of the day. There were stakes in the ground from the house over to the small green house where Ilene lived. A sisal rope was from stake to stake, except where it crossed over the drive lane. It looked fairly fool proof? Most people would question this as, "What in the world is this? Aunt Dorothy had already used this several times.

Some food was made and the trip over to Ilene's was set out. It was along the rope with one hand on the rope, the other held the food container.

The rope came to an end by the drive lane. With no thought of concern the food container was shifted to the other hand. It was a slow shuffle across the gravel lane. Aunt specifically felt for the gravel under her feet, so that she would know when she had crossed the lane. The gravel could no longer be felt, so she felt around for the rope. The rope couldn't be found?

A chill of fear suddenly grabbed a hold of her. She shuffled a little to the right and then to the left, but the rope couldn't be found. It was quickly becoming very upsetting. Aunt Dorothy just sat down and let the tears of fear flow. The thought of just walking to the left and then to the right a bit further would surely reveal where the rope was at. The only problem was that she was going right and left, but she was turned around and moving parallel with the rope. When this proved to be all in vain, she thought she could just turn around and get back on the lane. Now she was walking away from everything towards the tree line.

Suddenly she was getting poked with tree limbs. If you went a short distance through the tree line, there was a steep bank that headed down towards the ridge and a drop off. The fear was overwhelming. Again Aunt Dorothy was crying in a fear she had not felt before. Soon a small goat began to nibble on her fingers. She hugged the small goat with such relief. She knew the goat couldn't really help her of did it? The company of the small goat took away all the crying and fear she had built up inside of her.

Then a small voice sounded out. "Dorothy, Dorothy! Are you ok? It was Ilene's voice. "I was bringing some lunch over to you and now I am lost, Dorothy replied. I am so glad to hear your voice! "Good thing you found my goats, Ilene whispered. "Well, they actually found me, Dorothy confessed. "Let's eat your lunch and then we will get you back to the house, Ilene suggested. The two sat right there and ate the sandwiches and had the lemonade. "Good thing you didn't go in the other direction, Ilene instructed. There are no trees before the steep embankment, just a big tumble!

Ilene helped a very, very grateful Dorothy back to her house. Arm in arm they moved slowly through the dark for one and aged for the other. "Don't be concerned about bringing food over, Ilene protested. I am an old woman, short for this world. "Don't say that, Dorothy quickly protested! I just realized that we both need each other. "If the people in this world could truly see and believe that, the world would be so nice,

Ilene stated! The arm connection ended and each returned to their separate worlds.

On a Dusty Road

"I have a story for you, that happened just a few weeks before I turned eight, I offered! Could I tell you, I inquired? "Please do, the whisper requested! So when I was here before you told me to be aware of strangers and to treat them with respect. I asked Pastor Petersen about what was in the bible about such a thing and he gave me a verse. It goes like this:

Be not forgetful to entertain strangers: for thereby some have entertained angels unawares. (Hebrews 13:2)

"Yes, I know that one, Ilene offered!

"Well it happens like this. It was a week before school, and I had no particular chore to do. In my indifference, I asked my mother if there was anything she needed doing. "Would you be interested in walking over to Matt and Helen Polio's for some eggs, she asked? "Sure I would, I offered. It was a little over two and a half miles in one direction, so a five-mile walk for two dozen eggs was a good distance. I have always needed to be doing something, so I thought nothing of it. To please my parents was all good. She gave me the fifty cents for the two dozen eggs, and I set off. "Lady, do you want to go for a walk with me, I requested? She never objected to anything I said. I started walking, so she started walking with me.

The sun was bold, but the air offered the freshness of fall. I love fall, so the walk down the lane through the wooded area was offering the brilliance of new start of colors. In northern Minnesota, fall gets started the last of August. A few squirrels jumping in the leaves made me stop to watch their activity. Lady would stop every time I stopped. Just to enjoy the moment I believed. Their disappearance below the leaves in search of an acorn, then their reappearance with a bulging mouth was a laugh. I think I could watch them for hours, but there was a journey to continue on. The scolding of the Blue jays and the cawing of the crows echoed through the woods as I walked down the lane was music to my ears. The thoughts of the coming school year also echoed in my head. Hardly a day passed without having thoughts of the loss of a dear friend of mine last April. Someone being killed in front of you leaves a visual impression that will last a lifetime. I truly feel for the young at heart who go through this. The more you know someone the sharper the pain. It's called Love! The entire world should get to know each other a little more.

Upon reaching the end of the lane, I made the left-hand turn with a watchful eye up and down the road for any traffic. There wasn't a soul in sight. When I paused, Lady would pause! I rarely ever saw anyone. It was almost another mile before I would reach the lane of Matt and Helen Polio. It was also a mile in the other direction to reach a neighbor's lane. In a short distance, the land started to open up to a hayfield on one side. The other side had poplar trees as far as one could see. The hayfield looked promising for a third cutting. That didn't always happen in this part of the country. It more often didn't happen. It was a beautiful field of clover, so I quickly walked down through the ditch and picked a handful. It caught Lady off guard, because I went down into the ditch so quick. Just as soon as she realized I had left the road, she came bounding over to where I was in the clover field. She just reached me and I ran back up onto the road.

As I walked on my way, I had a couple of sniffs and a taste. I played with the blossoms and gave them a close examination. The small sphere of purple gave of its fragrance, thus the name sweet clover. In very little time, we reached the lane of our neighbors.

 It was about a half a mile in length, but you could see the farmstead in the distance. I loved this lane because it had towering pines on the south side. They were monsters! Even in the brightness of the day, they offered a dark seclusion in their interior. The aroma was intoxicating as I walked beside them. They talked to you in the lightest of breezes. These trees were a favorite of Matt and Helen, as they would often take a walk down the lane, just for the enjoyment of them. I came across a large pinecone on the lane, so it became a game of it as I tapped it along ahead of me with my foot. When I came closer to the door yard, I gave the big cone an extra kick to send it on its way.

There didn't seem to be anyone in the door yard. The garage was closed, so the car or pickup wasn't available for a clue, as to if anyone was home. We didn't have a phone, so there was no calling ahead. I looked around for the big Collie dog, but he wasn't to be seen. I walked up to the house door and knocked, then waited for a sound of evidence, as if anyone was home. I soon heard someone in the kitchen. Helen appeared at the door with a smile from her round happy face. "Oh, good afternoon, Helen burst out with happiness. "I have a visitor. You're Freddy, right? "Yes, I returned. I came over with this basket to get two dozen eggs.

The kitchen smelled of baked goods. It probably explained the appearance of Matt and Helen and their jolly disposition. They were hard workers and had a beautiful little farm. There were a lot of cows to milk, maybe thirty or so. "Please come in and sit down and have a little something, Helen invited, in her quick short phrase manner? "That's awfully nice of you, Mrs. Polio, I replied with appreciation. "Oh, please just call me Helen, she responded!

"Where is Buster, I asked Helen? "Oh, he is with Matt in the pickup, gone to town. If Matt is in the pickup, going somewhere, there's Buster. That's right; Buster is your collie, Ladies brother. Our last collie was also a related to their mother. Small world! We love these Collies! Maybe someday your Lady will have pups? If she does, don't forget us!

Helen quickly snatched a plate and glass from the cupboard. She poured a glass of milk and sat it before me. There was a large window in the kitchen, which looked out at the stoop and dooryard. I saw Lady just sitting on the stoop and waiting for me.

Helen then cut a large piece of a caramel coffee cake. She then cut a large slice of fresh bread and smeared on the butter. She seemed so quick, as she placed it before me. The sweet warm scent already had me. "You can adopt me if you like, I suggested, with a smile! She laughed and brushed her hand over my head. "I will get your eggs while you eat, Helen promised. So you brought your friend with you today, Helen implied, with a smile? She quickly opened the refrigerator and placed a basket on the counter. She wiped each egg with a damp cloth as she placed the eggs in my basket. "I am going to give you two and a half dozen in your basket because it fits so well. "You are the best, I complimented! "You have a big family over there, Helen replied. There is just enough room for me to add another piece of coffee cake to your basket. Helen cut another large piece and wrapped it in a paper towel. "You are so generous, I offered with another smile. "Thank you! Thank you! I don't often get young people around here, so the pleasure is all mine, Helen chimed. "Thanks again, I offered, as I took a hold of my cargo to start the return trip home. "Bye, bye, Helen offered with a smile. Safe trip, she added as we stepped out the door. See you next time Lady!

Every so often, I switched hands so that one arm would not become too tired. I thought I would wait awhile before I ate the piece of coffee cake, which had been added to the load. You know, that even though you are getting full, you could still eat something that is so tasty. In no time at all, I reached the end of Matt and Helen's lane. Big trees crowded to the end of the lane with a small patch of brush, which obstructed the view of the road. I started the turn onto the road as I looked over my shoulder for any traffic.

Lady had already stopped and appeared as though she was starring through the brush clump. I quickly froze as I saw an elderly gentleman walking toward me.

I am sure my mouth was open, as I checked myself and wondered what to say. "Hello, I spoke, as he quickly approached. "Hello, the stranger returned. No one lived for maybe three or four miles in the direction the stranger came from. "Lady, let's go I instructed! I turned and began to walk with the stranger, as he caught up to me. What else am I to do? I thought. He seemed to slow his pace to match mine. I searched for some words as we walked but a short distance.

"Where are you headed, if you don't mind my asking? I didn't want to be rude, but I thought I should say something. "Down a dusty road, he replied! "What is your name, I asked? "I am but the one who walks a dusty road!I kept looking at Lady and her unusual expression. She would tilt her head this way and than that, looking at the stranger. "I am walking about a short mile to our lane, to fetch these eggs for my mother, I returned the favor. "That's quite a journey with a basket of eggs, the stranger spoke. "I am off to school next week, I blurted out, as I tried to think of something else to say. "Is that good, the stranger asked? "I am not feeling like it is, I replied. "Are you ill, the stranger asked? "I am not sick sir, I assured him. The stranger seemed to always look straight ahead, as I turned to him each time I spoke. "Are you troubled, the stranger asked? He stopped and looked at me, so I stopped.

Lady was trying to get a sniff of the stranger. She then turned her head this way and that. A strange question and I felt like I was on the spot. "I don't wish to be a bother, sir, I insisted. I couldn't see an expression in the bearded face. It did seem he waited for a reply. "I lost a dear friend a few months ago, I admitted, as I sat my basket of eggs down. I felt uncomfortable standing there. That was the only thing I could think of, that bothered me. No one seemed to care, and that bothered me also. I didn't understand her death—and right in front of me at that. My friend Pastor Petersen says it's the sin and pain of the world that allows things like that to happen. He says there is a season to live and to die. He says prayer will bring the answer. I am not good at praying, but I have asked the Big Voice if he had an answer.

We walked for a moment and said nothing. "So what do you think, the stranger asked? "I believe God allows different seasons. I first believed in God,

when I heard the messenger talk to me, I answered in the best way I could. No one in our house believes in God, but I believe I can talk to my Father in heaven at any time. He sends messengers from time to time. I don't want to believe anything else. I believe all things are possible with God. Pastor Petersen told me that it says so in the Bible.

"Life is a dusty road, but always believe, the stranger responded, as he stopped and placed a hand on my shoulder. As he said something, I didn't understand.

My mind was on the life is a dusty road and this guy's name being a dusty road. Lady lowered her head between her front paws as she seems to be stretching or something. The old man said something I didn't understand, but I didn't ask him to repeat what he said. It caught me by surprise. I felt like the tall stranger liked me. I didn't know this stranger. "Would you like my piece of coffee cake, I asked the stranger? He seemed like a nice man, and I wanted to give him my cake. As he seemed to have given me something in his words, I thought. I picked the wrapped-up roll off the top of the eggs with my free hand and offered it to the stranger. He hesitated, so I sat the eggs down and offered it with two hands. "Thank you, the stranger replied! Let it be so! I never have known if that meant something. "You are certainly welcome, was my reply! You are a fine fellow, and I could talk with you every day, if it was possible. May all your days and time be blessed, I offered!

In a short distance more, we reached my lane to home. "Have a good day, I offered with a wave. "This is my way home! He raised his hand up as if to wave and said something, which I again didn't understand. Lady stopped at the intersection to our lane. I walked but thirty feet up the lane when I sat the basket down. I quickly ran back to the road to ask the stranger his name and was he a neighbor, because surely his name was not Dusty Road. "Hello, I shouted out! Then as I looked around, not seeing him, I whispered, Hello! Lady stood there looking up slightly. I looked down the road, expecting to see him, but there was no one in sight. I started to run down the road a few steps and looked back and forth on the road. I looked toward the trees, in the marsh, and across the clover field. Nothing! How could someone walk so fast? I thought. The road was flat in all directions. Lady just stood in the intersection and looked off into space.

I went over and knelt down beside her and looked in the direction she was starring.

"Come silly Lady, I coaxed! You are just starring off into space. I went back to my basket and continued home. Oh well, I thought, he must be Swedish, because of what he had said.

For some reason I felt so light and fast. I went out after supper and just ran as fast as I could up and down the lane. I had never done that before nor did that after."What do you think about the stranger, Ilene, I asked? "I felt it was to be so, Ilene whispered! The stranger spoke something like what you spoke, when I last saw you. "It was probable a language of heaven. It was healing from the throne of heaven. We couldn't look upon the angels of heaven, so they visit us in what we could understand. "How, did you know the stranger would come to me, I asked? "I didn't know, Ilene answered! When you were here I simply prayed for you to have compassion and protection on that path which you walk. "Will something else happen to me, I asked? "I have no; prophesy, for you, Ilene seemed to reply sternly!

I sat quietly and slowly eating the lunch. There was a feeling of me being an idiot. Not knowing hope to continue, my eyes scanned the little room. The little hand pump by the sink seemed to be a great addition to Ilene's life. Plywood walls painted white. Plywood ceiling painted white. There was a wood box near the new little wood stove. The wood stove had sheet metal behind it and to the sides. There was a large metal collar around the pipe going through the ceiling. There was a small shelf by the bed with a few pieces of clothing on it. The shelf was maybe three feet off the floor. A second shelf was by the sink at the same height. There was a bed and the table with its benches. That was it! The top half of the door had glass for light or window I guessed.

The silence broke with Ilene stating a bible verse:

"To everything there is a season, and a time to
every purpose under the heaven. (Ecclesiastes 3:1)

I felt better, when Ilene broke the silence. "Thank you, I replied quietly! I never expounded on why

I was saying thank you. Ilene probably thought it was for the bible verse. "For those who follow the Lord with their hearts, their seasons will be according to his purpose, Ilene stated! It seemed very profound somehow, I thought. It gave me a chill, even if it was warm in the little house. "Is your life, what you thought, it would be, I inquired? "Not at all, Ilene confessed! Do you see trial or trouble with the way I have lived my life? There was another chill down my back. It was the stupid feeling again. "Not at all, I responded! For some reason I wish I could have been here seventy-five years ago, to offer a kind voice and lending hand. To have the knowledge of the bible, as you do, makes me, well makes me very proud of you!

It was silent, well almost. There was a tiny sound coming from a bent over head of Ilene. Now I made her cry, I contemplated. I straighten out on the bench and put my arm around her. I brought my head a little closer and whispered, "I am sorry if I may have made you cry! "I am an old woman and near death, Ilene sounded out! There is that chill again down my back. No one in my life has ever said that they were proud of me! If my parents had been around longer, they may have been able to say so. I know my parents told me they loved me, but it has been so long, it's like a mystery. You came across my path and my head, my heart and my soul are tortured with emotion. Not a bad thing, mind you, but a wishing of it would never end. Seventy-five years ago? Yes, I too wish you had been there! For two months I have sat on the bench in the sunlight and moonlight and dreamed dreams of your endless company. You just never know when someone will cross your path and give you just what you need. It may not be like some of the great injuries or losses I have had in life, but just like you in this moment of compassion. Just to take away some fears!

Just then I heard my name being called out. Be of great happiness and I will try to see you as soon as I can. Now I must go! I hurriedly collected all the items I had brought. As I started for the door, I stopped, turned around and walked over to kiss Ilene on the top of her head. "Love you friend, I offered! Quickly leaving, but anticipating the time I may visit again.

In the Cradle of Gods Arms for Six Days

It was the middle of January, 1967 and I was being picked up from the hospital. I had no clue as to what had been going on for the last week. Life had gone on, except for me. For six days my feet had not walked upon the face of the earth. It seemed odd as we traveled down the snow piled roads towards my aunt and uncles place. Because a trip had to be made to get me, we just as well stop and see my aunt and uncle on the way home. My body was lying in a hospital bed, but I wasn't there!

When I was eleven years old, I became very sick. It was a terrible snowstorm that had already lasted for a week. An uncle that we had rarely seen had come to visit and got stuck with us. We lived deep in the northern woods of Minnesota and at least three miles to the main road, just a mile and a half to get down our lane. With our old B John Deere, my dad tried to push the snow on the lane, but it was useless. "I was in too much pain to even care when I heard my dad tell my mom it was no use. My uncle said he was willing to drive as fast as he could just to try and get through the lane. They decide to try something as I was bundled up, and we set out. First I heard thirty miles per hour then forty miles per hour, and then each large drift we went through it was a speed decline. 'We need to go a lot faster,' my dad told my uncle. Then it was fifty miles per hour when we hit a big drift, and I passed out.

The next thing I knew, I was floating around in a hospital room. I had never been in one before, so it was all new. I watched myself lying in bed and a nurse I didn't know sitting beside the bed. I was actually very amazed at seeing myself lying there. How could this be? It was very

207

quiet in the room when suddenly I heard a voice. 'Come forth,' the voice requested. It seemed to come from outside the window. I went over by the window and looked out and saw snow and that I was at a very great height. 'Come forth,' the voice sounded again. I reached out to the window, but it had no touch or resistance. I went through to the outside and didn't fall or feel the cold. I was amazed! There was a small thick cloud with a voice that said, 'Come forth.' I went into the small cloud, and instantly I was in a bright wooded meadow. "'What is this place, I asked? 'It's a place of rest and waiting, the voice instructed! I went over to a large tree with a lower limb and touched it. I deliberately wanted to touch it, and I could. Then I said, 'I will pass through you, and did. I was confused and then some. I gave a thought of 'I shall sit upon you limb and did. I just sat there for a long time. 'Great Voice, why am I waiting here, I asked? 'For time to pass and protect your soul, the voice instructed! That didn't seem to resolve anything. The voice seemed to know what I didn't know. 'Big Voice, do you have a name, I asked? 'I do, but it can't be revealed to you, the voice replied. 'You may call me Messenger, the voice added. "Suddenly, I was hit with a thought. 'Are you the messenger from three years ago, I asked with excitement? 'I am that messenger, the voice replied! 'You are the one that helped Pastor Peterson find me and be my guide,' I replied with great excitement. 'Then you are connected to my Father in heaven? 'I am a servant of the Ancient One and the King of Light, Messenger instructed. 'Perhaps I shouldn't be here, Great One,' I insisted. 'You are at risk, and we are here to protect you from that which is evil, Messenger instructed. 'We, you are many, I asked in surprise? 'Always two but sometimes more, Messenger instructed. 'Ask of me what you will, Messenger instructed! 'So I will go back to my life then, I stated in a question? 'Yes, Messenger answered!

I hopped off the branch and went exploring. I saw no animals or bugs. I saw no dead trees or grasses. Most everything

I asked was answered with 'they are not in this place because there is no death here.' I wanted to ask something that I could take with me, but what? I saw a brilliance of light far away. 'Can I go to that light, I asked? 'No, it is not for you, Messenger instructed! I went to another tree and hopped up on a low branch. I sat there thinking and watching.

'Can I take something back with me that I can give to others, I asked, not even knowing what I was asking?

There was no response! 'Messenger, are you there, I asked? 'I am here, Messenger replied! 'Observe what I show you! Suddenly, there was a tall jug-looking item. It was clear, and you could look right through it. 'Your soul is like a vessel, Messenger instructed. Then a small amount of colored material appeared above the vessel. It clouded the vessel, and then some more was continually added. Soon it became black. 'The colored material represents sin, Messenger instructed! Then light as bright as the morning sun burst into the vessel. It was clear and shown of a great brilliance. "Only the King of Light, the eternal son of the Ancient One, may wash away all sin.

It was at that point I heard the music I had heard three years ago. I was compelled to fall to the ground and did so. In a burst of light, I was lying in the hospital bed. The nurse that was sitting beside the bed jumped up and hugged me. She was crying an extreme cry as my face was getting wet. Soon there was a roomful of people praising God. It was the seventh day since I had arrived at the hospital. My ruptured appendix had poisoned my body. There was nothing left to be done for me. Soon my mother was brought back into the room. She had been at a counselor's office to deal with her emotions. I had never seen my mother cry before. My face was wet again!

After all that had happened, I felt an excitement to visit with Ilene again. That was all that was in my head. I suppose it should have been more to see my family, but I couldn't control what was going on. The excitement only grew, when my Dad said he would have to stop by Uncle Harold's and have some welding done on a farming part.

As we drove down the wintery roads piled high with snow, it reminded me of all that I had missed being off the face of the planet.

I knew no one in my family would give any thought to what had happened, but Ilene would surely have a reflection and knowledge to give me. Nice!

We pulled into the driveway of my aunt and uncle's. I looked at the small green shack, as soon as it could be viewed. I expected a small curling stream of smoke from the little wood stove. Nothing! Then I

209

thought I would see an area cleared free of snow to the Ilene house. Nothing! It was buried almost! I could barely see the front door. My heart leap from my chest and I lost my breath. I couldn't reveal my panic, but I knew I had to hurry and ask about Ilene. My stiffness didn't slow me, as I hurried to the small newly painted house of my aunt and uncle. It was my handiwork and looked good! "Hello, hello, I sounded, as I threw open the front door. It was a hand shake to my uncle and a hug for my Aunt Dorothy. They both sounded out, "It is so good to see you! How are you? "I am fine and dandy, I replied! Never better! After a greeting between my folks and aunt and uncle, dad went straight for the help request for a small bit of welding.

"Aunt Dorothy, it looks like I should go over to Ilene's little house and start scooping a bit of snow, I questioned? "No, Ilene is no longer with us, she informed me! She placed a hand on each shoulder and continued. Ilene died the day you went into the hospital. The sound hurt my ears, my head and my heart. I gritted my teeth as hard as I could to keep the tears back. Then I held my breath, as long as I could, as I stepped away from my aunt. I went to a frosted window and gazed at the small bit of green house, which still showed above the depth of the snowy winter. Winter was harsh and I don't mean the cold and snow!

www.ingramcontent.com/pod-product-compliance
Lightning Source LLC
Chambersburg PA
CBHW071729120626
46550CB00002B/450